THE IRISH SCISSOR SISTERS

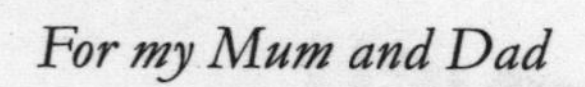

For my Mum and Dad

THE IRISH SCISSOR SISTERS

MICK McCAFFREY

This edition published in 2011 by
Y Books
Lucan, Co. Dublin, Ireland
Tel/fax: +353 1 6217992
publishing@ybooks.ie
www.ybooks.ie

Paperback	ISBN: 978-1-908023-33-9
Ebook – Mobi format	ISBN: 978-1-908023-34-6
Ebook – epub format	ISBN: 978-1-908023-35-3

A CIP catalogue record for this book is available from the British Library.
10 9 8 7 6 5 4 3 2 1

Typeset by Y Books
Cover design by Graham Thew Design
Cover images: Front left courtesy of Courtpix
Back image courtesy of *Evening Herald*
Printed and bound by CPI Group (UK) Ltd, Croydon, CR0 4YY

Contents

Author biography

Mick McCaffrey is an investigative journalist with the *Sunday World*. He has previously worked as News Editor of the *Sunday Tribune* and Security Editor at both the *Sunday Tribune* and the *Evening Herald*. He has specialised in crime journalism for the last nine years. *The Irish Scissor Sisters* was Mick's first book and spent several weeks as a No.1 bestseller in 2007. Mick is also the author of the No.1 bestseller *Cocaine Wars: Fat Freddie Thompson and the Crumlin/Drimnagh Feud*, which was adapted for television by TV3 in 2010.

Praise for *The Irish Scissor Sisters*

'This is a unique insight into the underbelly of a "new" Ireland. Riveting.'
Joe Duffy, RTÉ

Praise for *Cocaine Wars*

'Well-researched and authoritative account of a vicious gang war.'
Irish Independent

'An Intimate knowledge of the engagement and a commendable level of research render this account indispensable for interested parties.'
Sunday Business Post

'An in-depth exposé.'
Irish Daily Mirror

'Explosive.'
Sunday World

Acknowledgements

THANKS TO ALL the members of An Garda Síochána and the legal profession for helping me with the research for this book. I really appreciate all they did for me.

Also thanks to Chenile Keogh and Robert Doran at Y Books, as well as Kieran 'Consig' Kelly for his legal advice.

Mick McCaffrey, October 2011

'It was the most grotesque case of killing that has occurred in my professional lifetime.'

JUSTICE PAUL CARNEY

Introduction

The murder of Farah Swaleh Noor on 20 March 2005 was one of the most brutal crimes that Ireland has ever experienced. The fact that the thirty-nine-year-old Kenyan was stabbed over twenty times and beaten over the head with a hammer was shocking enough, but it was what happened to his body that horrified the nation. It sickened even the most experienced murder detectives. Farah Noor was chopped into eight pieces in the bathroom of an inconspicuous flat, close to the centre of Dublin. His body was then transported to the nearby Royal Canal and dumped in a watery grave.

The fact that two seemingly ordinary young Dublin women were responsible for the murder and subsequent dismemberment, meant that the case would capture the public's imagination and live long in their memory.

Irish people in the twenty-first century are well used to violent crime. While the Irish economy grew, organised crime equally prospered and threatened to spiral out of control. In 2005 the country was awash with money. Never had we known such prosperity. It was this boom that led tens of thousands of people from across the world to make Ireland their new home. One of these people was Farah Swaleh Noor. People arriving from abroad, however, would find the extent of the seedy underworld bubbling just beneath the surface hard to believe.

Linda and Charlotte Mulhall, however, were not brought up expecting to be criminals. Although their lives were far from perfect, there was nothing to suggest that they would become two of the most infamous killers in Irish history.

They came from a relatively stable background and had the support of a loving extended family. Somewhere along the way, however, things went tragically wrong for these women from a respectable estate in Tallaght, South Dublin. What drove these women to kill a man – especially as he was involved in a long-term relationship with their mother?

Thirty-year-old Linda was a doting mother-of-four, yet she had problems. Bad relationships and domestic abuse were part and parcel of her everyday life. She was also involved in a relationship with a vicious man who beat and abused her children, which led to the authorities taking them into care. These troubles led Linda to turn to drugs and alcohol to get her through each day. At the time of the murder, however, she was trying to get her life back together. She had won custody of her children and had returned to live at the family home in Kilclare Gardens. She was attempting to get some stability back into her children's young lives but then it all went wrong.

Linda's twenty-two-year-old sister, Charlotte, led more of a nomadic existence. She often spent weeks living in Kilclare Gardens but would then disappear for months at a time without telling anybody. She worked as a prostitute on the streets of Dublin, dabbled in drugs and drank too much. Charlotte wasn't the only member of her family selling her body. Her mother also worked as a prostitute and the two women often spent nights working alongside each other.

When Linda and Charlotte left Tallaght to go on a drinking session in town on the day of the murder, they were armed with ten ecstasy tablets. Linda had easily bought them on the street and neither woman ever had any difficulty in purchasing hash or heroin from a network of dealers across the city. Gardaí believe that the use of E tablets was a big factor in Farah Noor's death. The drugs made the women hallucinate and could have been what drove them to kill. E tablets are freely available throughout Ireland for less than €10 a tablet.

In the middle of what is universally regarded as an epidemic of serious crime, the murder of Farah Swaleh Noor still managed to stand out, horrifying and fascinating the general public in equal measure and putting pressure on the government to act to reduce the spiralling murder rate. The trial of Linda and Charlotte Mulhall was one of the most widely reported court cases in living memory. The courtroom was packed each day, with dozens of journalists from all the main newspapers, TV and radio stations eager to satisfy the public's hunger for every gruesome detail of the shocking murder. Barely a day went by when the trial of the Irish Scissor Sisters didn't make the front pages. Even now, over six years after the horrible killing, the Mulhall women are still front-page news and will probably always command headlines no matter what they do.

Charlotte and Linda Mulhall are currently in Mountjoy women's prison. Linda is serving a fifteen-year jail term for the manslaughter of Noor, while Charlotte is serving a life sentence for his murder. As Charlotte told detectives when she finally confessed to killing Farah Noor: 'I'll be locked up for a long time, I suppose.'

Mick McCaffrey
2011

The Day of the Murder

NOBODY KNOWS HOW long it took Farah Noor to die but he had long since left this world by the time Charlotte Mulhall had plunged the knife into his body for the twenty-second time. The dead man had injuries to most of his vital organs. His heart was repeatedly pierced; his liver was badly damaged, while his stomach and bladder also had a substantial number of knife wounds. He had also been stabbed twice in the back. There was no evidence of Farah having put up a struggle and his hands showed no defensive wounds. Linda Mulhall, Charlotte's sister, probably brought the hammer down on Farah's head at least ten times and the attack is thought to have lasted anywhere from three to five minutes. Their mother, Kathleen, Farah's girlfriend, was in the sitting room while her two daughters committed the savage murder on 20 March 2005.

That morning had started out like many others for Linda and Charlotte Mulhall. The two sisters got up and were bored.

The younger of the two, Charlotte, was restless and was eager to do something. She asked her older sister what they could do but much to her annoyance, Linda reminded

Charlotte that she had her son with her for the day and couldn't get up to much.

Not one to be easily put off, Charlotte, or Charlie as her family called her, went to the back room and came back with a bottle of vodka.

It was just after eleven in the morning and Linda thought it was too early to be drinking.

Giving her sister a filthy look and reminding her that there was never anything to do, and that today would be no different, Charlotte poured out two large vodka and cokes.

It didn't take much to persuade Linda to have one, and soon the two sisters were on the couch, enjoying what was to be the first of many drinks that day, while Linda's eleven-year-old son was amusing himself around the house.

It was a scene that had been played out in No. 31 Kilclare Gardens in Tallaght many times before. It was one that would never be repeated again.

Not long after the sisters began drinking, twenty-one-year-old Charlotte's mobile rang. It was Kathleen, the girls' mother.

Kathleen was in the city centre, drinking with her boyfriend, an African called Farah Swaleh Noor, and she wanted her daughters to come into town and join them.

Charlotte was delighted with the invitation and immediately said yes, but Linda was less keen. Charlotte begged Linda to change her mind but her older sister remained firm. Her son was in the house and she was reluctant to leave him on his own. She didn't particularly want to see her mother or Farah anyway. She resisted but Charlotte knew that she could always change her thirty-year-old sister's mind, so she kept at her until Linda finally agreed.

When Linda suggested bringing her son into town with

them, Charlie went mad. How could you get a decent day's drinking done with a kid in tow?

Eventually, Charlotte won out and Linda agreed to leave her son with her brother Andrew and to join the group in the city centre. Charlie was delighted. She told her mam that they'd get the bus in and see them around O'Connell Street.

Charlotte had another reason for wanting to go out that day. The year before, she had spent her twenty-first birthday in Kilclare Gardens, having a few drinks and had ended up depressed. She vowed that there was no way that she was going to let that happen again and she was determined to keep the promise she'd made to herself. This year her birthday would be different. It would be one to enjoy, one that she'd remember. After all she was going to be twenty-two the next day, 21 March 2005.

It was to be a birthday that would haunt her for the rest of her life.

Once Linda had given in and decided to go out for the day, she poured another two vodkas and began to loosen up a little. Things hadn't been easy for the mother-of-four recently. Her ex-boyfriend, Wayne Kinsella, a vicious thug, had been jailed for seven years, nine months previously, for physically abusing three of her children. At the time the social services had taken all four children away from her and placed them into care. Linda had taken it badly but she had struggled through. She had been delighted to get the children back, but in the time without them she had been using heroin and drinking heavily. She had moved back into her father, John Mulhall's, house with her children to try and get her life back on track.

The sisters went upstairs to Andrew's room in the three-bedroom semi-detached council house they'd lived in all their lives and started to get ready. Charlotte spent her time living between the house in Tallaght and a flat in Summerhill. The twenty-one-year-old began by putting on her heavy eyeliner. Both the girls wore a lot of make-up and Charlotte was rarely seen without her trademark Cleopatra eyes. She spent ten minutes in front of the mirror making sure that she looked perfect. Charlotte felt inferior to her older sister, who, with her long blonde hair and slim figure, was easily the better looking of the two. Charlotte thought that her frizzy curls and round figure were nothing beside Linda but it never stopped her getting attention. She always had a boyfriend on the go and every weekend she would work as a prostitute on the canal at Baggot Street for extra cash. She was popular amongst the men down there who were more than happy to part with their cash in return for sex with Charlotte. Linda was applying her heavy foundation but was concerned about her new lip piercing. It was swollen and the bar was hurting her but thankfully the vodka was starting to numb the pain.

Enjoying themselves now, and having a really girly morning, the sisters tried on a number of outfits before deciding what to wear. Then they headed back downstairs for one last drink before they went into town.

Linda kissed her son goodbye and said she wouldn't be long and was just going to meet his granny in town. The child barely looked up. He was used to being without his mam and well able to look after himself. He'd already been through more than most eleven-year-olds. As the girls left the house Linda called back to say that his Uncle Andrew was in the house and would get him anything he needed. With that the door slammed shut and the sisters were gone.

They walked to the end of the cul-de-sac and down the

main road to the bus stop and waited about ten minutes for the 77 bus to bring them into town. The sisters had a smoke while they waited for the bus and looked up at the sky. It was a sunny day but dark clouds were moving in and it looked like there could be rain on the way. They sat upstairs on the 77 and lit up two cigarettes and chatted during the forty-five-minute journey into town.

The bus eventually got into town at about 1.15 p.m. and the girls got off on the quays. Charlotte used Linda's mobile to ring Kathleen and find out where they could meet-up.

Kathleen was hanging around O'Connell Street with her Somalian boyfriend, Farah. The girls walked up Dublin's main street, looking out for their mother. They finally saw her with Farah at McDonalds, at the lower end of the street. The pair of them were drinking cans of beer and looked like they'd already had a few. The girls greeted Kathleen and Farah with hugs and kisses and the group walked back up O'Connell Street towards the Spire.

As soon as Kathleen saw her eldest daughter she noticed her lip. Concerned, she asked Linda if she was okay. Farah had a look too and it was decided that they should do something about it. By now the lip was very swollen.

Farah said that he knew a good place that sold cheap rings around Henry Street so they walked up O'Connell Street and turned left onto Henry Street. Kathleen and Farah were holding hands but the thirty-nine-year-old Somalian looked pretty tipsy and was unsteady on his feet.

He couldn't remember where the shop was and they walked up and down Henry Street a couple of times while he tried to figure it out. Sick of wandering the streets looking for a new lip ring, they eventually gave up.

Instead they headed to Dunnes Stores on North Earl Street. Farah bought a large bottle of vodka from the off-licence and Kathleen went into a newsagent and got four bottles of coke and gave each of them a bottle. They poured half of each bottle of coke onto the road and Farah passed around the vodka bottle as they all mixed the spirit with their remaining cokes. They strolled around, drinking and chatting, with Farah and Kathleen in great form, laughing away.

Farah finally remembered where the lip-ring shop was and they went back to Henry Street, into the GPO Arcade and Linda looked at the rings. She saw a small silver one she liked and paid €7 for it and put it in straight away, slipping the bar into her pocket.

They spent some more time walking around the city centre trying to decide where to go. None of them had much cash so they couldn't afford to go drinking in a pub. They were all on the dole and the money they got from the Social Welfare didn't stretch far enough to pay €5 for a pint in a pub in town. Charlotte finally suggested that they should go down to the Liffey Boardwalk and sit on one of the benches there and continue drinking. The Boardwalk had been built to be a walkway that would allow tourists and workers to enjoy a pleasant stroll along Dublin's River Liffey, but it had been virtually taken over by drug dealers and addicts. They came from the various methadone clinics around the city to do deals there. Most ordinary decent people had been driven away from the Boardwalk but the Mulhalls fitted right in and were comfortable amongst the junkies and alcoholics. They found a free bench and continued to polish off the litre bottle of vodka.

After they'd been there a while, Linda whispered to her

sister that she had a load of ecstasy tablets in her pocket and asked Charlie if she wanted one. Charlotte was a heavy drug user and happily dropped an E tablet, or 'butterfly', as did her sister. They clinked their bottles and said cheers, as they washed the pills down with vodka and coke.

Kathleen had been watching her daughters and demanded to know what they were up to. Linda confessed about the drugs in her pocket and Kathleen took one, as she didn't want to be left out. She didn't want the girls to have all the fun, but as Farah was already very drunk they didn't give him one. The Somalian had started drinking cans back in their flat at 17 Richmond Cottages, in nearby Ballybough, as soon as he got up that morning. He'd been on a bender for the previous three days, celebrating St Patrick's Day with Kathleen. He'd got into a fight in a pub on Paddy's night and the guards had spoken to him but he was still in good form, even though he hadn't been sober for a while now. Farah had a reputation as a bad drunk and everyone who spent any time with him knew how alcohol could change the man. He became loud and aggressive with booze and wasn't a nice person to be around. He was in good spirits now though, even if he was a bit drunk. The last thing he needed, however, was drugs, so the women didn't offer him an E tablet. As Linda gave her mother the pill, they sat back and relaxed, exchanging banter and gently slagging Farah.

Linda had ten E tablets in the little see-through bag in her jacket pocket and over the next few hours the three women took two more pills each, as they sat there drinking. Linda listened to the radio on her mobile phone and Charlotte chatted to Kathleen.

Linda and her mam had a strained relationship and were

not that close. Forty-nine-year-old Kathleen had walked out on her husband and six kids three and a half years earlier to be with Farah Noor. This, understandably, had caused war within the family and Linda hadn't really forgiven her mother, but she kept the peace for the sake of the day out. She didn't think too much of her mam's new boyfriend though and couldn't understand much that came out of his mouth, especially with all he'd had to drink. She barely said two words to him for the whole afternoon.

Charlotte was more easy-going and felt that if her mother wasn't happy with John Mulhall, then she was right to leave. Kathleen and her ex-husband despised each other. He was furious that she had given up on twenty-nine years of marriage to run off with a black man and he had threatened Farah Noor. The Somalian believed him and had gone to Cork with his new girlfriend to make a fresh start. Unlike her father, Charlotte thought Farah was sound and had been down to visit them in Cork a lot when they lived there for a year or two. Kathleen had hardly spoken to John Mulhall in over three years and they were both happy with that set-up. She missed her children, though, and her two youngest, Marie and Andrew, lived with their father in Kilclare Gardens and she rarely saw them. The couple had decided to leave Cork for good and came back to Dublin in September 2004. They told people that Farah had fallen foul of an IRA man. They had got a flat together a few months before, up in Ballybough.

A few hours had passed by on the Boardwalk, with them happily drinking and relaxing, but the sun that had made the day so pleasant had long since disappeared and it had started to drizzle. The winds were very strong, especially beside the exposed River Liffey and Farah did not have a jacket. He was wearing only his beloved long-sleeved Ireland-away jersey. People rarely saw him without it. The weather wasn't the only problem though. The three or four days of drinking were finally catching up with Farah. He crossed the thin line between him being a pleasant person and a monster. He started picking fights with Kathleen and getting aggressive. Kathleen's daughters couldn't understand what he was saying as he switched between bad English and his native African language. Linda shook her head and turned her radio up higher and Charlotte paid him no attention. Kathleen was obviously well used to Farah's outbursts and started shouting back, giving out to him for ruining the day. After about half an hour of rowing, Kathleen got fed up and told her daughters to get up, that it was time to leave.

The sisters didn't even have time to ask their mam where they were going. Kathleen had already pulled Farah by the arm and was leading him up the Boardwalk, to O'Connell Street. As they walked up past the Spire, the fighting continued. The couple shouted and screamed at each other, with little worry for who heard or saw them.

Linda was well pissed off at this point and stormed ahead of the group, listening to her earphones. She'd left her kids to come in to listen to her mam fighting with a drunken refugee. She was not one bit happy.

Even the happy-go-lucky Charlotte was annoyed and left the pair to it. She walked on ahead of them but Linda was still about sixty feet ahead. She was practically galloping up O'Connell Street. Charlie ran after her older sister and put her arm around her shoulders. They stopped walking for a minute and Linda asked Charlotte if they were still fighting each other, but she didn't have to wait for an answer – she could hear the two of them shouting behind her.

When Farah and Kathleen were only a few feet behind them again, Linda and Charlie linked arms and continued up O'Connell Street towards Ballybough, which is about a ten-minute walk away. They were between Burger King and the Carlton cinema when Farah saw a little Chinese boy, who was out playing with a group of three or four of his friends. He got very emotional and said: 'That's my son. That's my son.'

He grabbed the youngster who got upset and frightened and began to cry. The child was only about five years old. Noor had a six-year-old son named 'John', the child of his brief relationship with a then sixteen-year-old, mentally retarded Chinese woman, 'Lynn'. He had only seen the boy a handful of times and, after his three-day drinking binge, Noor thought that this Chinese boy was his son.

Kathleen started to lose the head and shouted: 'You're mental, you're bleedin' mental. Leave the child alone. He's not your fuckin' son.'

Farah had been thinking about the child for the last few weeks and had mentioned him a couple of times. He'd made Kathleen go with him to 'Lynn's' house on St Patrick's Day because he wanted to get to know his son. Noor had at least five children dotted around the world and had never shown any interest in being a good father before. Nevertheless he had called around to his former girlfriend's house three days earlier, wanting to meet the lad. 'Lynn' had answered the door and seemed happy enough to see Farah. They hadn't had a relationship as such. Noor had got her pregnant the first time he slept with her and then left when he found out she was expecting his baby. When 'Lynn' had told Farah that the child was not home he handed her €20, turned around and walked away.

The little Chinese boy that Noor was now harassing ran away and the Somalian shouted after him to come back. Kathleen roared at her boyfriend, telling him to stop and cop himself on.

It was about 6 p.m. at this stage and as Kathleen and Farah were fighting, with Linda and Charlotte looking on, a friend of Noor's from Somalia, Mohamed Ali Abubakaar, spotted the group. He was in the central median on O'Connell Street, looking at a festival stall with his Irish girlfriend, Deirdre Hyland. Thirty-six-year-old Ali came from Kismoyo in Somalia and had been in Ireland for the last ten years. He had worked for Dublin Bus for the previous four years and was friends with Farah, regularly meeting him for drinks.

Ali called over to his friend and crossed the road to meet him. They hugged each other and Ali noticed Farah was with his girlfriend, who he knew as Catherine. She told him that the two girls were her daughters but they just nodded at him and didn't shake hands or talk. He thought they all appeared to be drunk but that Farah was by far the worst and was struggling. It looked like they were trying to get him up the road. Ali had met Kathleen a good few times before but she stayed with her daughters, who were carrying cans of beer in a plastic bag. Ali noticed that one of the girls was blonde, looked very gaunt and was wearing a leather jacket. The other woman was darker and heavier. Ali was worried about his friend because he knew he could be aggressive with drink on him. He told him to relax and chill out and not to cause any trouble. Farah said he was fine and that he was going home to Ballybough. Ali noticed that Kathleen did not appear to be in good form and kept on pulling her boyfriend, trying to get him to leave. Ali left the group and the four headed off in the direction of Parnell Square. The bus driver noticed that his friend was wearing his favourite long-sleeved Ireland-away jersey. He had one just like it except that his had short sleeves.

Ali and Deirdre started back walking down O'Connell Street and thought no more of the brief encounter.

They would be the last people to see Farah Swaleh Noor alive.

Linda was getting fed up at this stage and told her sister that they should walk ahead. Charlotte had regularly stayed in the flat since they had moved in the previous December and she knew exactly where it was. Linda had only been out to Ballybough once or twice and probably wouldn't have been able to find the way alone. It was getting dark as Charlotte led Linda in the direction of Ballybough, with their mother and Farah not too far behind.

When the girls arrived at 17 Richmond Cottages, a stone's throw from the Royal Canal, they only had to wait a couple of minutes for Kathleen and Farah to arrive. Kathleen had obviously calmed down her boyfriend and the tension that had been in the air a few minutes previously had disappeared.

The brick-fronted building was nestled in a row of terraced houses beside Summerhill Parade. Divided into four flats, the two-storey house felt cramped and claustrophobic, although the landlord gave his tenants free reign to decorate the flats to their own style and tastes. As they walked in the front door of the house they took an immediate right to get to Flat 1. Kathleen unlocked the door and they walked into the main living room, which contained a three-foot-long table, two wooden chairs, a red settee and two small armchairs. A filthy kitchen was at the end of the same room and empty cans of beer and vodka bottles littered the sticky counters. The kitchen led into a bedroom measuring just eight feet long. The modest one-bedroom Flat 1 had seen better days.

In the bedroom there were bunk beds on the immediate left-hand side of the room, facing against the wall. A mini-double bed was across the room, beside a small window. The only items of furniture were a wardrobe and small chest of drawers, holding all of Kathleen and Farah's possessions. They were used to moving and had stayed in five or six different flats when they lived in Cork, and knew how to travel light. They didn't have that many clothes and used to move their stuff from house to house in sports bags, which were stored under the bunk bed.

As they settled in Charlie put on a CD because Linda wanted music in case the couple started rowing again. They decided to put on Sean Paul. Charlotte had given the CD to Farah as a present a couple of months before. Linda sat on her sister's lap on the red settee, laughing away and singing to the music. They were having great craic and were in good form.

Kathleen prepared vodkas for the girls and a can of lager for Farah. Charlotte got up off the couch and went out to help her mam in the kitchen. As Kathleen was pouring the drinks she took the last of the ten E tablets that Linda had brought and crushed it up on the counter. Charlotte asked her what she was doing and her mam said that she was going to put it in Farah's drink because she wanted him to be on the same buzz as they all were. Farah took the drink from Kathleen and staggered into the living room and sat down beside Linda. He'd been drinking for nearly twelve straight hours at this stage and was very drunk.

Farah got closer to Linda on the settee, put his arm around her shoulder and pulled her towards him. She felt very uncomfortable as he moved his hand towards her back and started rubbing her. He pulled her shoulder again and started to whisper something in her ear. She couldn't understand what he said but knew it was sexual and that it was his sick way of seducing her. She felt ill and knew that what he was doing wasn't right and said, 'Farah, get your hands off me.' But this only seemed to make him more determined.

He pulled her towards him and whispered that she was the image of her mother.

Angry, Linda tried to push Farah away, but he was far stronger than his small 5 ft 6" frame implied and she couldn't get away from him. He pulled her close again and whispered into her ear, 'We are two creatures of the night,' or something like that. Linda was scared at this stage and shouted to her mam, who had come into the room.

'What's he saying about creatures of the night, Ma?' she asked, her voice breaking with fright.

Kathleen told her Farah always said things like that but when she saw that he had his arm around Linda and wouldn't let her go, she roared: 'What do you mean by what you're saying to Linda? What do you mean that we are two creatures of the night?'

Farah seemed to be in a different world at this stage and still had a hold of Linda.

Charlotte had always been very protective of her sister even though she was eight years younger than Linda. She shouted: 'What the fuck are you saying to Linda, Farah? What do you mean about Linda? Let her go.'

Linda tried to get up off the couch again and get away from the demented African but he stood up with her. Farah wouldn't release her from his tight grip. He started chanting 'Linda, Linda ...'

Kathleen was roaring: 'What the fuck are you doing, Farah? What the fuck are you doing? Get your hands off her.'

Linda was on her feet at this stage and had managed to stagger down towards the kitchen sink, but Farah still had a hold of her. She tried to shout at him but no words would come out. He put his hands down to her waist and Linda felt like he couldn't even see Charlie and Kathleen. Farah was acting like he thought she was the only one in the room. She used all her strength to try to prise his hands from her waist but Farah was just too strong. She started crying and said to her mother: 'He would sleep with your daughter just as soon as he would look at you.'

Sean Paul was still playing in the background as Charlotte got up off the settee and ran down to the kitchen.

Noor started whispering: 'You are so like your mammy. You are so like your mammy.'

Charlotte lunged at Noor and told him, 'Get your fucking hands off her now.' Charlie was stronger and more street-smart than Linda. She worked as a prostitute, so she wasn't to be messed with. She started pushing and pulling at him but his grip would not loosen.

Eventually he let Linda go and with a demented look in his eyes, walked towards Kathleen and grabbed her. Farah pushed her down towards the bedroom and made slitting signs with his hand, as if he was going to cut her throat and kill her.

Kathleen started begging her daughters to 'please kill him for me' or she would be dead herself by the end of the year.

Charlotte was furious and frightened and all she could hear was her mother repeatedly asking them to murder Farah, pleading: 'Just please kill him for me; kill him for me.'

Both Linda and Charlotte thought that Farah was capable of anything with the way he was acting, and the younger Mulhall went over to the kitchen counter. There was a Stanley knife on top of it and she grabbed it. She pushed the button to make the sharp blade go up. Noor was still pushing Kathleen at this point and Charlotte went up behind him and grabbed the back of his head. She cut his throat with the blade, as hard as she could. She cut a four-inch gash and the injured man let out a gasp. He staggered forward with a look of disbelief on his face.

Kathleen was screaming, 'Get him away from me. Get him away from me,' as Farah stumbled into the bedroom. He got to about a foot short of the bunk beds, and fell hard, smacking his head off the wood.

Farah managed to get up and cried, 'Katie, Katie,' but Charlotte ran in after him and cut him on the throat again. He was still alive and clutching his throat, as blood oozed from his open wounds onto the blue carpet.

Linda went over to the kitchen drawer and took a hammer from it and followed her sister into the bedroom. Farah tried to get to his feet again. He attempted to pull himself up from the floor but saw the shadow of the hammer Linda was holding in her right hand. He let out a scream before the thirty-year-old used all her strength to bring the tool down on the top of his head.

Linda hit him repeatedly with the hammer and Charlotte stabbed him in the chest with the blade but they still weren't convinced he was dead.

'He's alive, Linda, he's still alive,' Charlotte cried.

Linda was in shock and thought that the dying man was going to get her. She picked up the hammer and started pounding him on the head while Charlotte went out of control with the knife. She stabbed at every bit of Noor she could see through his Ireland jersey, which was left with gaping holes in it.

Charlotte finally stopped stabbing Farah and looked at his lifeless body. Farah was lying flat on the floor, with his head under the bunk bed, in a massive pool of blood. She didn't need to check his pulse to see if Noor was breathing. The condition of the body said it all.

She turned to Linda and gently said: 'Oh my God. He's dead.'

The two women quickly realised the implications of what they'd done – they were now murderers. They hugged each other and cried, trying to console each other and convince themselves that everything would be all right. But they knew that things would never be the same again and that they were facing life behind bars.

After about fifteen minutes they calmed down and remembered that Kathleen was sitting in the front room. She had not come near the bedroom while the murder took place, although she undoubtedly knew what was happening to her lover while she sat in the other room.

The sisters slowly got up, held hands and walked into the sitting room. Both of them were covered in blood and their jeans had turned a dark red colour from kneeling in the pools of Farah's blood. Charlotte was shaking her head as she told her mother that her boyfriend was dead.

Kathleen started screaming and her two daughters joined in. Within seconds all three were crying uncontrollably, as the effects of the alcohol and E tablets began to wear off.

Kathleen finally stopped crying and said: 'Get him out! Get him out.'

They had a discussion about how to get rid of Farah's body. Linda would later tell gardaí that her mother asked, 'How are we going to get him out?' and that Charlotte said they should cut him up and dump his body in the nearby canal. Charlotte tells a different story and later said, 'Me mammy said just cut him up.'

The sisters went into the kitchen and poured themselves a large vodka and coke. They knocked it back, trying to get the courage to carry out an act so unimaginable that it would make anybody physically sick. They had a couple more drinks and then looked at each other before heading into the bedroom where Farah's body lay.

The pools of blood had started to congeal at this stage and the blood on the carpet where Farah's chest rested had spread to a five-foot radius. Charlotte left a large shoe print with her runner as she climbed to the left-hand side of the body and pulled him out from under the bed. She took his left leg and Linda grabbed a hold of his right foot and they dragged him out into the hall and down to the bathroom, about six feet away. A trail of blood marked the route where Farah's body was pulled from the murder scene in the bedroom to the bathroom where his limp body would be chopped up.

The bathroom in Flat 1 was filthy with dirt and grime and the tiles on the floor were thick with months of dust and scum. It was too small for a bath. A toilet sat at the back of the bathroom and a small shower area was to the right of this, about a foot and a half away. The walls were tiled and they hadn't seen a cleaning brush in years.

It took all the women's strength to drag Farah in and

to dump him in the shower, which was barely covered by a curtain. The base of the shower was far too small for the whole body to fit and his legs stuck out the side, lying against the floor tiles.

The girls went into the kitchen and searched the drawers for something sharp to cut the body up with. Kathleen wasn't one for home cooking so they had to make do with a nine-inch bread knife. The brand of knife was Kitchen Devil and both the hammer and knife had been in the flat when Kathleen moved in, nearly four months before.

Kathleen didn't want to see her boyfriend being dismembered so she went and sat in the front room. She hadn't moved during the murder and wasn't going to get involved now.

Linda and Charlotte walked slowly into the bathroom and just stared at the body for a few minutes. Charlotte sat on the toilet and put her head in her hands, before getting up and walking over to Farah. She took the dead man's trousers off and left them on the floor. His two legs were fully exposed now and he was only wearing white underpants.

She picked up the knife and took Farah's right leg in her left hand. She then started to use the knife as a saw and cut through the dead man's right leg above his knee. She didn't think the knife would be sharp enough but was surprised by how quickly the flesh cut, but the bones were more of a problem.

The sound of the knife grinding through bone and cartilage at the top of the knee was too much for Linda. She cried and cried and would not stop.

Charlie was focused on the task at hand and managed to hack through most of the leg after a few of minutes of intense effort. She couldn't completely separate

Farah's kneecap from his thigh so she got Linda's hammer and started hitting the middle of the knee for extra force. Blood splattered all over the bathroom and specks dotted her face. She alternated between the Stanley blade and the bread knife until the top of the kneecap eventually separated from the body. She picked the limb up and tossed it into the shower area, not bothering to remove Farah's white sock. She then started sawing the left leg below the thigh and easily cut through the fatty part but again had problems with the muscle.

Linda had calmed down by then and used her hammer on Farah's left leg. She beat at it furiously until she could hear the weight of the metal hammer crack through the victim's shin bone, shattering it. She must have hit him around thirty times before her arm got tired and she sat back on the toilet seat for a rest.

Charlotte continued to work on the leg as Linda went into the linen press and took out clean white towels. She put a towel over the limb to stop the flow of blood that was seeping out of an artery. The blood was still warm.

As Linda breathed heavily, trying to regain her breath, her sister continued to saw at the left leg until it separated from the rest of the corpse. She was getting better at it now but there was blood everywhere. It was seeping out the side of the shower onto the floor tiles, leaving a horrible mess. Linda used the white towels to soak up the blood from the bathroom floor and they soon turned a cross between dark red and black, as the blood mixed with the filthy floor.

The sisters had to repeatedly rinse out the towels using cold water from the shower. The plughole was blocked with blood and bone, so Linda had to put her hand down to clear a path for the water to escape. After she did this, she finished wringing out the towel and threw it across towards the sink on the other side of the bathroom. The wet towel hit the tiled wall and stuck to it, before slowly sliding to the floor. It left a two-foot long bloodstain.

It was clear that they needed to get rid of the bits of flesh and bone fragments that were blocking the shower and causing a mini-flood on the floor. Charlotte lifted up the toilet lid and they each scooped up flesh and bone, throwing it down the toilet and flushing the chain. Later, tenants remarked that there was always a problem with the sewerage in the flat.

With both Farah's legs dismembered, he could now fit neatly into the shower. It was far too uncomfortable, however, trying to lean in and cut the corpse while trying to avoid the limbs that had already been severed. They would have been there all night if they had to do that. So they pulled the body out of the shower by the arms and laid it on the floor and cut it up there. Linda knelt on the floor for most of the grim butcher's job while Charlotte sat on the toilet. They tossed each body part into the shower as they cut them off and this system seemed to work quite well.

Over the next few hours, Charlotte became tired from cutting and said her right arm was sore. Every forty-five minutes or so she would sit on the toilet seat and rest for a few minutes while Linda took over the cutting. Both women alternated between using the knife to cut the victim's flesh and the hammer to break his bones, by repeatedly chipping at them.

During the rest periods, whichever sister was not disposing of Farah's body would spend their time using the bath towels to clean the excess blood from the floor. There were two large holes in the floor, which had been caused by the hammer slipping when they were beating Farah's leg earlier in the night.

While her children were cutting up the body, Kathleen remained in the living room, leaving her daughters to get on with the grim deed. Charlotte and Linda next cut off both Farah's arms, halfway between the elbow and shoulder blade. This took longer than you would imagine because the dead man was so lean and muscular; there was no fat on him at all. The Stanley knife was used for this and although it was small, its blade was very sharp and was perfect for getting past the difficult muscle. After the arms and legs were removed, they severed Noor's two thighs from below the hipbone.

Thirty-nine-year-old Farah Swaleh Noor had been alive and well only a few hours before but now all that remained of him was the upper part of his body, from his hips to his head. But the sisters were far from finished. They used the knife to cut off his midriff and opened up the stomach in the process. Farah's stomach was already riddled with massive gaping wounds from where Charlotte had repeatedly plunged the knife into his chest. When the stomach was exposed it was almost too much for Linda to bear. She was especially disgusted by what they were doing and regularly used her top to cover her face to shield herself from the stink of the remains. The deep, foul smell of the gut and entrails in an open stomach would be enough to make even the most experienced medical technician retch. She nearly got physically sick. They left the Ireland jersey on the body in a vain attempt to contain some of the smell. In the days and weeks following the murder, Linda could not sleep. She was kept awake at night with the memory of the lingering scent of human flesh being opened up. Somehow they kept to the task at hand and cut the midriff through the spine until it separated, leaving only the upper part of the body from the ribs to the head remaining.

Linda studied the severed midriff and noticed that Farah Noor was still wearing his underpants. She remembered the stories that Kathleen had recently told her about being raped by Farah.

She took her knife and pulled down Farah's underpants. She grabbed the top of his penis and took it between the thumb and index finger of her left hand. Using her right hand, she sliced through the penis section, ignoring the testicles. It had shrunk with the cold mixture of water and congealed blood. She took the two-inch penis and tossed it into the shower with the other human remains.

'There, you little fucking prick,' she whispered. 'Now you will never rape my ma again.'

✂✂✂

The job of cutting Farah Swaleh Noor up took the Mulhall sisters over four hours. The blade on the bread knife was serrated and was not much use for the grim task of dismembering human remains, while the Stanley knife was essentially too small. But after hours of frantic work and intense effort all that remained of Farah Swaleh Noor was his torso and head. Linda and Charlotte were shattered after the night of murder and butchery. This was in marked contrast to Kathleen who had not taken part in either the murder or dismemberment – instead she was watching television.

Farah's eyes were closed and he looked very pale. The mixture of blood and water had made his complexion lighter. His short black hair was covered in thick congealed blood.

'What are we going to do with his head?' she asked.

Linda thought for a moment. She realised that if they didn't cut it off and the body was found, the police would easily find out that it was Farah Noor and would find them all. They'd be sent to prison for life and she'd never see her four kids again. There was nothing else to do.

'We'll have to cut it off,' she declared.

Charlotte took a deep breath and began breathing heavily. Linda composed herself and got one of the white towels and placed it over Farah's face so he wouldn't be looking at her. She picked up the hammer and started raining blows against the battered neck, to try to detach it from the torso. Charlotte took over and pounded the head but it would not dislodge. Linda eventually picked up the bread knife and put her left hand around the dead man's forehead. She put her knee on his torso to steady it and began sawing at the head. Charlotte helped and it took them about ten minutes with the blunt knife to sever his windpipe and get the blade through the back of his neck. The top of Farah's spine stuck out of the back of his head. It was like a scene from a horror movie. His hair was so short and so sticky that Linda struggled to hold the head but she certainly didn't want to put her hand inside the brain and skull, so she just let it drop and it made a thud on the floor.

With the dismemberment of the corpse now completed the girls went into the sitting room and collapsed on the settee, where Kathleen was resting on another chair. They had a couple of drinks to steady their shattered nerves. It was only when they sat down and were away from the bathroom that the enormity of what they had done hit them. They didn't know what to do next. The bathroom of the flat resembled an abattoir and would obviously have to be cleaned. It was hard to know where to even begin.

Linda began to get emotional on the couch and sobbed. Charlotte put her arm around her but didn't join in. Her attitude was what's done is done. All they could do was make sure that the guards didn't catch them. Farah was from Somalia and didn't have any family in Ireland. His only real family was Kathleen and she and the girls would make up a story about Farah running away to be with an ex-girlfriend. He had been known as a ladies' man when he was alive, so if the police checked they would think that the story wasn't too far-fetched. They started thinking about who might notice that Farah wasn't around. Kathleen couldn't think of anybody off-hand. Most of his friends were in Cork and he wouldn't be seeing them anyway now that he lived in Dublin. The Somalian community in Ireland was not that big and they tended to keep themselves to themselves. People wouldn't necessarily think that Farah not being around was a big deal. Finally they agreed it could be done.

The next problem was what to do with all the body parts. Farah wasn't a small man and they couldn't just walk down to the canal and throw him in. They would need to pack him in black bags and transport him to the water. Charlotte thought that walking in the middle of town with black bags early in the morning would arouse suspicion. She suggested that they put the body in the sports bags Kathleen used for her frequent moves. By now it was around 11 p.m. and they agreed that they should clean the place up and pack up the body. The plan was to dump it first thing in the morning, before rush-hour traffic and while it was still dark. Charlotte had been drinking down by the canal before and knew Clarke's Bridge at Ballybough. She decided that it would be as good a place as any. The water was deep and the body would sink to the bottom. You didn't get too many people fishing there so it wasn't too likely that some poor unfortunate would hook an arm when he was fishing for pike.

A lot of clothes and household towels had got covered in blood during the murder and subsequent dismemberment. They had changed colour from the mixture of blood and guts and it wasn't as if you could just put them in the washing machine and use them again. They would have to be destroyed. The duvet on the bottom bunk was splattered with blood from Farah being repeatedly stabbed – that would have to go too. There were also Linda's and Charlotte's clothes to think about. They were drenched in blood and would have to be thrown out as well. Farah also had clothes in the wardrobe. If the guards were to believe that he had run off with some woman, then they'd have to get rid of all his clothes as well. Otherwise it would just make the guards suspicious and lead to them asking questions. There was a major problem though. It was only Tuesday night now and the bin men didn't come until Friday. It would be far too risky to leave bloody clothes in the flat or in the back yard for three days. If the guards did somehow find out what had happened, the first thing they would find would be the bags left for dumping and they'd all be caught. None of the three Mulhall women knew how to drive or had a car. They'd have to contact somebody they could rely on, someone who definitely wouldn't go to the police telling tales of murder. Who can you trust to keep such a secret though? Linda and Charlotte didn't have many friends. Kathleen had left her old life behind when she upped and moved with Farah Noor. The three of them knew that there was only one answer.

There was only one person that would even contemplate covering up Farah's murder. But it wouldn't be fair to drag him into this. It was bad enough that they had got themselves in such a mess without inflicting it on him. But what other choice did they have? It was now 11.41 p.m. Kathleen took Linda's mobile and dialled a number that she hadn't rung in a long time.

'Hiya, love,' said the voice on the other end of the phone.

'It's not Linda, it's me,' said Kathleen.

'What do you want?' came the reply. He would recognize that deep voice anywhere and he didn't want to hear it again for as long as he lived.

'I'm with Linda and Charlotte in me flat. There's a problem here. You need to come over.'

John Mulhall hung up the phone and cursed his ex-wife. She had been out of his life for three and a half years but she was still causing him trouble.

Little did he know that that one phone call would change his family's life forever and that he would be dead nine months later because of it.

2

The Clean-up

JOHN MULHALL WAS furious when Kathleen phoned to tell him about the little problem his two eldest girls were having in Richmond Cottages. He hung up the first time but phoned back a few minutes later because he loved his daughters and would always do anything he could to help them.

Kathleen wouldn't tell him what was wrong at the flat or if Linda and Charlotte were OK, so he eventually agreed to drive over to Ballybough from Tallaght.

While they were waiting the first thing that Linda and Charlotte did was wash themselves. Spending over four hours dismembering a corpse is a messy business and the sisters were covered from head to toe in blood. All their clothes were filthy and caked through with layer after layer of dried, gooey blood. Their hands were also red and thick fragments had got caught under their false nails, while their hair looked like it had been treated with red shampoo. The only part of them that wasn't that bloody was their faces. They were dotted with the odd speck of red but were not as bad as you would imagine. The natural thing for anybody to do when their face gets splashed with dirt is to use their clothes to clean it. This is exactly what the Mulhalls did. When blood spurted up at them while they were hacking the body, they had used the sleeves of their tops to wipe it away – neither girl would ever consider going out without wearing heavy make-up and even during their darkest hours they were not prepared to see their faces spoilt. During the rest breaks they both regularly cleaned themselves in the bathroom sink and dried their faces with toilet roll. They now wanted a good wash and went into the kitchen and filled the sink with water. Charlotte and Linda cleaned away the blood and skin pieces from their hair and skin. They didn't have the option of having a shower at the moment but the sisters made the best of a bad situation. They decided that there was no point changing their clothes yet because they still had to go and clean the flat before dumping the body. It would only ruin a new set of clothes.

They then went to tackle the corpse in the bathroom, having taken a roll of plastic bags from the kitchen to deal with the body parts. There was blood everywhere. The walls had changed colour, with a mixture of dried blood and guts and the blood had gone as high as six feet up the wall from where Farah's arteries were cut and had sprayed out of control. The floor was waterlogged with blood and you could see the impression the towels had left in the large pools as the sisters had made futile efforts to clean while cutting up the body. The toilet and sink hadn't escaped the carnage and the inside of the toilet bowel was now dark red from the bits of bone and brain that had been flushed down it.

Charlotte took charge of packing up Farah's body. She took the torso and midriff and placed them in two black bags and tied a knot on the top of each. She put them in the sports bags and left them in the hall beside the bedroom, ready to be transported to their watery resting places. She did the same with the two arms and packed them in black bags, along with the vest and pair of underwear and put them with the other limbs in the hall.

Linda picked up the left leg but struggled to get it into a bag because of its length. She hadn't opened the refuse sack properly and while she was attempting to get the bag to open wide enough, she dropped the thin black leg. She jumped with fright at the shock of Farah's leg touching her before it struck the ground.

Charlotte took over and packed up the rest of the body until all that was left was the head. She took Noor's head, which by now was unrecognisable because of the ruthless beating it had taken with the knife and hammer. She wrapped it in one of the black bags and was about to put it in a navy sports bag when Linda intervened.

'Hold on. Leave the head here. We can't throw it in the water. The guards will be able to find out who he is if they have his head. Leave it here and we'll get rid of it somewhere else,' she instructed.

The sisters were surprised to see that little or no blood was seeping out of the dismembered limbs. They had expected that the flow of blood in the arms and legs would continue for hours after he died but most of Farah's blood had drained while he lay on the base of the shower. The black bags were still important, however, so the sports bags wouldn't get stained and get them into trouble with the police later.

They discussed when to bring the body down to the canal and decided to wait until later in the morning. It would be better to make a start on cleaning the flat. Although there wouldn't be too many people around now, three women carrying bags would look suspicious. If a squad car went by, they might stop to see what was going on, and how do you explain being out by the canal in the middle of the night with heavy sports bags? If they waited until first light people would be starting to go to work and they would blend in more easily. Granted, there was more of a chance that they would be seen at the canal, but if one of them kept a look out to make sure no one was around when they were putting the body in the water, they would be OK.

At about 1 a.m., they had just agreed on when to go down to Ballybough Bridge when the buzzer of Flat 1 rang. They knew it was John Mulhall. The girls dreaded their father seeing what they had done. They went into the bedroom and closed the door.

Kathleen let her ex-husband in, greeting him with the words: 'Farah is dead; the girls killed him.'

John went ballistic and stormed into the house, past the sports bags and refuse sacks piled neatly near the door. 'What the fuck happened?' he asked.

Charlotte and Linda came out of hiding and looked at their beloved Dad and started to cry.

The glass fitter could not believe his eyes as he looked around the flat. He knew that he didn't want to get mixed up in something as awful as this. He glanced around again and saw the load of black bags in the hallway. He didn't even want to think about what was in them.

'You're on your own,' he shouted and left, getting into his van and driving away. He didn't like abandoning Charlie and Linda in their hour of need but this was way too serious for him to get messed up in.

The girls were devastated when John Mulhall walked

out the door and turned his back on them. They had stood by him when he had an affair and had taken his side during the marriage collapse and now he had walked away when they needed him most. They were genuinely shocked and the events of the previous few hours finally caught up with them. The sisters were exhausted and went into the bedroom and lay on the double bed to get some sleep for a few hours. When they awoke there would still be a lot of work to do.

While her daughters were getting some much-needed rest, Kathleen made a start on tackling the bathroom. She went into the kitchen and took bleach from the press, together with some sponges and cloths. She didn't have a basin and had to fill up two cooking pots that lay on top of the stove. It was about 1.30 a.m. at this point, and, after boiling a kettle of water and filling the pots, she went into the bathroom and put them on top of the toilet. She turned on the shower and took the head off its unit and sprayed all the walls with hot water, using a cloth covered in bleach to remove the stains that the boiling water couldn't clear. She was meticulous in wiping the walls with the cloth, rinsing them off with water, cleaning the cloth and then re-wiping them. It wasn't long before the shower walls looked normal, better than normal, and the plastic base unit was the only thing left that betrayed the fact that a body had just been chopped up there. She washed the remaining bone and skin fragments down the plughole, occasionally having to spray the water directly on the drain to stop it becoming clogged. She poured bleach onto the plastic unit and wiped furiously at it with a J Cloth until the bloodstains started to disappear. She repeated the process a few times until eventually there was no trace of blood at all.

Cleaning the shower had taken well over ninety minutes and her two daughters had woken from their short nap as she had just about finished. Linda and Charlotte weren't really in the mood for sleeping and had just lain in the bed with their eyes closed, not saying anything to each other. All Linda could think about were her children at home. She couldn't bear to live if they were taken away from her again. Charlotte didn't have a family and didn't have very many friends either. As she lay resting, she imagined what life in prison would be like. She lived a nomadic existence and came and went as she pleased, answering to nobody. The thoughts of a life in jail, conforming to rules and regulations didn't suit her at all and she promised herself that she wouldn't be caught. It suddenly dawned on her that it was her birthday today. Last year's shambles of a twenty-first, just having a few quiet drinks at home, was starting to look like the party to end all parties compared with today. Even after everything that had happened over the last few hours, Charlotte couldn't help thinking about her birthday – nobody seemed to have any presents for her and they hadn't even said 'happy birthday'. Knowing her luck they hadn't even remembered.

They got out of bed and took over finishing the bathroom and changed the water in the cooking pots because it was cold at this stage. The pools of blood had carpeted the floor and had started to get hard and dry. They threw a pot of water over the bathroom floor and used cloths and towels to soak up the excess water, rinsing them into the toilet. It was a messy job because the floor was where most of the cutting had taken place. Congealed blood and lumps of skin and bone littered the floor tiles and they had to be picked up by hand and flushed down the toilet. It took about seven or eight pots of water and more clean towels before the dried blood was removed. It wasn't nearly clean yet and, as the water began to dry into the floor, big streaks from where they had been cleaning with the towels started to appear.

Now that the pools of blood on the floor were gone, Linda and Charlie started to clean the wall tiles. The cloths were thick with blood by now and they put some bleach into boiling water in a cooking pot to give them a good clean. Farah's blood had reached nearly six feet up the wall and they started at the top of the tiles and worked their way down. It was easier to mop the wall than the floor because there was far less blood to contend with, but parts of the tiles were in need of serious attention nonetheless. The bathroom was in such a bad state that even the most experienced crime scene cleaner would have had their hands full for days, trying to deal with the amount of blood-staining that Farah's murder and dismemberment had left.

When they had made their way along the whole bathroom wall and had cleaned it to their satisfaction, they got another bottle of bleach from the kitchen. They poured it directly onto a cloth and cleaned in between the wall tiles to get rid of any trace of blood. This took a long time and when they were finished they still had to clean the floor.

They rinsed the cloths and got more fresh water. They got down on their hands and knees and scrubbed and scrubbed. They poured bleach onto the tiles and rubbed it in between them so that you couldn't see any blood with the naked eye.

Cleaning the bathroom the first time took about three hours. They knew that it would need to be done again to make sure that anything they'd missed would be taken care of second time around. Farah's remains were sitting in bags in the hallway but the smell in the bathroom was still indescribable – a mixture of chemicals, sweat and the odour of death filled the air. When the toilet seat was lifted the smell that emanated out of it was far worse than you could ever imagine. Linda would be awake for days on end trying to get the stench out of her mind. They poured bleach and toilet cleaner into the bowl and flushed it, but they had put so much skin and body tissue down that it was now blocked. It was threatening to spill out of the toilet onto the floor. The sisters had no choice but to endure the pungent smell, as they had to leave the toilet to settle down for a few hours and slowly unblock itself.

Kathleen was taken aback when she went into the bedroom she had shared with Farah Swaleh Noor. She hadn't been in the room when the murder had taken place and couldn't bring herself to go in after her daughters had dragged the body from the bedroom into the bathroom. She had expected the bathroom to be in bad shape because Farah had been cut up there but she didn't think that the bedroom would be anywhere near as terrible as it was. There was a five-foot-wide pool of blood on the blue carpet beside the bunk bed. She didn't have to be told that this was the spot where her boyfriend had been stabbed to death. The puddle of blood made a squelching noise when she walked on it because the blood had gone all the way through and waterlogged the thin carpet. Kathleen had no choice but to take the carpet up. She had brought a cooking pot and cloths with her and used them and some damp towels to absorb the blood. It didn't take long before the two towels were soaked through and she rinsed them in the kitchen sink before using them again. By now she had run out of clean towels as they had all been used to cover Farah when he was being chopped up or to clean the blood stains. The girls had used four or five of them cleaning the bathroom and she was using the last two to mop up the blood in the bedroom. There was little else to do, however, except rinse them as much as she could and keep going, although the towels were not much good at absorbing the liquid, which made the job harder than it ought to have been.

The carpet wasn't the only part of the bedroom to be decorated in Farah's blood. The chest of drawers had been drenched from his multiple chest wounds and the blood had even travelled as far as the wardrobe. Kathleen used the cloth and pot to wash these clean but found it difficult to get into the grooves on the pine planks of the wardrobe. The bunk bed was also bloody and it was hard to get underneath it to clean the base because the main pool of blood was on the floor below. The only way to do it was to lie in Farah's blood, which was not an attractive option. An area of wallpaper directly beside the bunk was ruined and would have to be taken off the wall. She removed it using a kitchen knife and some hot water.

When Linda and Charlotte were done in the bathroom they came and helped to remove the carpet. They took the Stanley blade and cut a straight line about a foot from where the last spots of blood were to the left of the bunk bed. They did the same to the area of the carpet to the right of the bed. They took up over six feet of carpet and underlay and were relieved to see that the blood hadn't soaked through to the concrete floor. They brought the carpet to the hall and, using the blade and kitchen knife, cut it up into little strips. They then put it in a black bag along with the wallpaper. Kathleen said she'd leave it in the communal back yard for the bin men to collect and take away later in the week.

They all knew that the bedroom would need to be cleaned again and Kathleen said she'd do it later in the day. She was concerned about Farah's clothes and pulled them out of the wardrobe and put them in the bag with the carpet. Noor hadn't been into the latest fashion and was content wearing old jeans and football jerseys. She took out some tops, a few pairs of trousers, two Manchester United jerseys and other bits and pieces, and his side of the wardrobe was empty. It was important that nothing was left behind if the story about him leaving to live with his ex-girlfriend was to hold up.

Charlotte went through his wallet and took out the few euro that was in it before tossing it in the bag. She also opened his drawer and noticed his rings and chains. She would easily be able to sell these on the street. She took them and put them in her pocket. She asked her mother where his mobile was, saying she would take it home with her and sell it later on. The black bag was now full and Charlotte took it out to the communal yard at the back of the house and put it in a corner where it wouldn't be disturbed.

The only trace that Farah Noor had ever lived at 17 Richmond Cottages was now gone. It was as if he'd never been there at all.

The trio had been cleaning non-stop for nearly five hours at this stage. Once they had dealt with the trail of blood leading from the bedroom to the bathroom, they changed out of their bloody clothes. Linda and Charlie's outfits, specially picked for a day's socialising the previous morning, were now unrecognisable. They were covered with the blood, bone and brain matter of Farah Noor. They stripped off and Kathleen gave them some clothes. Linda had a purple polo neck in her mam's flat that she had been given as a present and she put this on, along with some jeans. Charlotte regularly stayed there so she had lots of clothes in the wardrobe. She put on a black top and a pair of dark denim jeans and Kathleen also changed into fresh clothes. They put their old clothes in a black bag and went and sat down and relaxed in the living room – exhausted and emotional.

Shortly after 6 a.m. the buzzer rang and the three women jumped with fright. Who would be calling to a house at this hour unless it was bad news? Linda and Charlotte were sure it was the guards and thought they were going to be carted off to prison. The buzzer sounded again and they paced around the front room whispering to each other, 'Who the fuck is that?' They were afraid to make any noise in case whoever was ringing at the door heard them. With a bit of luck they might get fed up and go away. The buzzer went for a third time and they knew that the caller was aware that somebody was up. They went to the bedroom window and looked out through a small gap at the side of the curtain.

'It's Da,' Linda shouted, her face breaking into a smile for the first time in hours.

John Mulhall came into the flat but was in no mood for pleasantries.

'What's done is done. I can't believe that you have got yourselves into this awful mess,' he said sadly, the disappointment clear on his face.

He spoke to his daughters about what they planned to do. They told him the whole story, about Farah coming on to Linda and how he wouldn't let her go and that they attacked him with the knife and hammer, killing him. John Mulhall was a decent human being and didn't like the thoughts of anyone meeting such a bloody end, especially not at the hands of his two daughters. He hated what they had done but he felt it was his duty as a father to help them.

He went into the murder bedroom and removed the duvets and pillowcases from the bunk bed and also stripped the double bed down. He took some of Farah's clothes and the bloody towels that had been used to mop up the blood in the kitchen. He also collected the kitchen knife with the black handle that had been used in the murder. When he was finished there were probably three half-packed black bags.

He then made two journeys out to his van and put the black bags in the back to dispose of them later. He wanted to make sure they were never found by the guards. He had wrestled with his conscience for the whole night and found himself back at Richmond Cottages under protest, but he felt there was nothing else to be done. He knew that by removing evidence from a murder scene he was directly implicating himself in the crime but his mind was made up. Two of his sons, James and John, were already in jail; he didn't want his little girls to end up there as well. He hugged Linda and Charlotte and got into his City Glass work van and drove away.

At about 7 a.m. on 21 March 2005 the three Mulhalls left Richmond Cottages, with Linda and Charlotte each carrying a sports bag. But unlike many of the people out at that time of the morning they were not planning to get some exercise in the gym before going to work. Linda's sports bag contained two arms, a vest and a pair of underwear belonging to Farah, while Charlotte held a bag over her shoulder with the heavier torso. Kathleen didn't carry anything but still went with her daughters.

The Royal Canal is less than a three-minute walk from Richmond Cottages. The Mulhalls went out the door, down a laneway that led onto Summerhill Parade and turned left to Ballybough Bridge. There had been heavy rain during the night and they were immediately struck by the 50 km/h winds that blew from the south-east. It felt far chillier than 9° C. Summerhill Parade is one of the main arteries into the city and it would have been bumper-to-bumper at that time of the morning. It was full of commuters travelling into Dublin city centre from areas like Fairview and Beaumont on the north side of the city. The three women looked at each other in silence as they crossed Ballybough Bridge. They looked to the left where they could see the black, cold waters of the Royal Canal flowing slowly below. They trudged down the public walkway and looked up to see the imposing presence of Croke Park to their right. Kathleen started crying and stared at the ground, afraid to see the man she had spent three and a half years with being dumped in such a lonely way into a canal. Linda and Charlotte were cold though and just wanted to get the job done. They had been up the whole night carrying out the brutal and horrific dismemberment – they just wanted the nightmare to end.

Linda unzipped her bag and took out the arms that lay wrapped in the large black refuse sack. She opened the black bag and went over to the water's edge. She gently emptied the two limbs into the water, which was probably about eight foot in depth. The sound of the arms hitting the canal made a pronounced splash but nobody saw the three women, even though dozens of people would have walked over the bridge while they were getting rid of the body.

Charlotte took her black bag out and held the bottom of it and swung the torso into the canal. It landed about three feet into the water and immediately sank. She took her mother by the arm and said: 'Come on, Ma, that's the worst part over now. Let's go home and get the rest and that'll be it.'

They walked side-by-side back to Richmond Cottages. It is not known how many trips they had to make that morning to dispose of Farah's body. Linda later told gardaí they went back and forth six times and Charlotte estimated that it was three or four. It is probable that Kathleen only accompanied them once. CCTV cameras outside the Gala supermarket only observed Linda and Charlotte. Their mother wasn't recorded. Traffic cameras did not pick up Kathleen either. A traffic camera captured the sisters on Ballybough Bridge at 7.23 a.m., just yards from the canal, with the bags on their backs. They went down to the water and when they returned minutes later the bags were empty. However many times they went to the canal that morning, by the time they had finished, Farah Swaleh Noor was lying in the canal in eight pieces, and nobody had seen what they'd done.

After they had finished dumping the body and had returned to Richmond Cottages, the women started to clean the flat again. They had left the cloths and towels steeping in hot water and bleach for a couple of hours and they went over the bathroom and bedroom again with the same amount of effort they had put in earlier. They had all seen programmes about cleaning crime scenes on television and knew that you had to be meticulous if you wanted to avoid detection. They spent the next three hours on their hands and knees, scrubbing the bathroom floor and walls, making sure that people would never think that anything untoward had occurred at the flat. They cleaned the flat with such professionalism that, after spending days combing over each part of Flat 1, a team of trained technical examiners was only able to find a handful of blood specks. Gardaí would later observe that the Mulhalls were so thorough that they could easily have started their own contract cleaning business.

The last area left to clean was the kitchen. They steeped the Stanley knife and murder hammer in bleach in the sink and wiped it clear of fingerprints. Kathleen put the weapons into a backpack and left them in the hallway.

When they were finally satisfied that they had done enough, they gathered all the towels and cloths and put them in a black bag in the yard alongside the carpet, for the bin men to take away.

While they were cleaning, the three women discussed what to do with Farah's head, which was sitting in a black bag in the kitchen. Linda suggested that they should bury it far away from Ballybough so that if Farah's body was found, the gardaí wouldn't be able to use the head to identify him. Hundreds of Africans came into the country each year and promptly left without a trace. It would not be easy for them to identify the dead Somalian. Later on this strategy would make it doubly difficult for garda investigators to determine the identity of the torso in the canal. It was with this in mind that the women decided to get the bus to a park they knew in Tallaght and bury the head in the ground. They also planned to dispose of the knife and hammer they had used to carry out the murder.

The sports bags were damp from being ferried back and forth from the flat to the canal. Even though the black bags had stopped any fluid or blood damaging them they were still quite smelly. The women were afraid that if somebody sat down beside them in the enclosed space of a bus they might be alerted to the fact that something was wrong. Kathleen had no other bags in the flat but remembered that she had a camera bag that her husband had given to her as a present a few years earlier. She went into the bedroom and took the large black bag from the wardrobe. She removed the camera and Linda took the bag and put the battered head in it. They were now ready for a trip across town to Tallaght, where Farah's head would be buried, hopefully never to be seen again.

The three Mulhalls left the house shortly after midday and, as they were walking out the door, Kathleen picked up the bag with the knives and hammer. They took the same route they had walked earlier that morning.

At 12.11 p.m. Linda and Charlotte were captured on CCTV camera entering the Gala supermarket on Summerhill Parade. Charlotte was dressed in a fitted denim jacket, with a pair of dark denim jeans and white runners. She was carrying a dark pink rucksack that looked to be quite bulky. She stayed in the shop for less than a minute before going outside, obviously looking for somebody.

She appeared on camera again thirty seconds later with her mother, and the three women went to the deli counter and queued in line to be served.

The camera footage shows the three Mulhalls in what appears to be an agitated state, as they shuffled their feet and looked nervous. Kathleen was wearing a cream jacket with fur on the collar, a grey polo neck jumper and denim jeans with dark shoes. She had a royal-blue bag over her shoulder and also carried a black handbag. She left the queue and picked up a bottle of water and bought it before exiting the supermarket at 12.15 p.m. Kathleen was a regular in the shop and had been filmed there five days earlier after she collected her social welfare money. She had gone to the household products aisle that day and had bought black refuse bags and bleach, as well as phone credit. It was that same bleach that had been used five days later to clean the Flat 1 crime scene, and Farah's dismembered body parts had been placed in those same black refuse bags before being transported to the canal.

Linda reached the top of the deli queue and ordered a breakfast roll from the shop assistant. She asked for tomato ketchup to go with her sausages, bacon, eggs and hash browns. She was obviously feeling hungry after a hard night of murder and the subsequent clean-up. She also bought six packets of crisps and a packet of Superking cigarettes.

At 12.18 p.m. Linda buttoned her black leather jacket tightly against her purple polo neck and left the shop with her sister, before tucking into her brunch. She didn't even like the polo neck and was only wearing it to please her mother. Her brother John had given it to Kathleen as a present two years before but Kathleen didn't think much of it either and had passed it on to Linda as a gift when her daughter went to visit her in Cork the year before. Linda was carrying the dark camera bag, containing Farah's head, on her shoulder. She put the bag on the ground outside the shop, as she enjoyed her breakfast roll.

Kathleen and Charlotte smoked cigarettes while Linda finished off her roll, and the group then walked towards town to get a bus. As they walked up O'Connell Street, Linda couldn't help thinking about the previous day. If she'd just stayed at home with her children like she'd wanted to, instead of giving in to Charlotte, then everything would be fine now. Why did she even go back to her mam's flat? She knew Kathleen was fighting with Farah and she should have just got a bus back to Tallaght like any decent mother would have done. She realised, however, that there was no point driving herself mad with ifs and buts now and she'd just have to make the best of things.

They crossed the Liffey and turned right down the quays and waited for a 77 bus to bring them to the Southside. One arrived after less than five minutes and they each paid their own €1.60 fare and went upstairs to sit down. It was 1 p.m. and the bus wasn't that busy. Linda and Charlie sat together near the back, with their mother in front of them. The camera bag with the head in it rested under Linda's feet for the journey. They rode along in silence because none of the three felt like talking, each was engrossed in their private thoughts. Little did the dozen or so fellow passengers upstairs realise that they were travelling with the head of a dead African man.

As the bus pulled into the Square Shopping Centre in Tallaght, they got off and walked through the doors, past McDonalds and the cinema complex. They took the escalator up to the second level, stopping briefly to check out the window of a clothes shop. After exiting the shopping centre the Mulhalls walked down the street until they could see Tymon Park North in the distance.

Tymon Park is officially known as Sean Walsh Park and is on the left-hand side of the Tallaght by-pass, in the foothills of the Dublin Mountains. It is a large public park where local people go to sit and read or play football and is described by South Dublin County Tourism as 'the St Stephen's Green of Tallaght'.

The three women crossed over the footbridge connecting the Old Bawn Road to the Square and into the main gate of the park. They started to walk around. The area was so big that it was hard to know where to start. They were looking for somewhere to bury the head and dispose of the murder weapons. Linda would suggest a spot close to trees, only for Charlotte to disagree and say that somebody would notice if the ground was dug up there. This went on for about four hours and they kept walking and walking around Tymon Park, but couldn't agree on a suitable spot to bury Farah's head. There was a bench at the back of the park, up a slight hill and they finally sat down for a much-needed rest. As they relaxed, they looked at the large lake in front of the bench. It would be a nice place to sit to pass a couple of hours but they weren't in the mood for taking in the scenery.

Charlotte began to get frustrated saying they'd been here for hours and still hadn't done anything. She jumped up and went about two feet behind the bench and started digging furiously at the clay with her hands. Linda didn't think they should bury it a few feet from where people came to sit but Charlotte had started digging and wasn't about to stop now.

Kathleen took the Stanley knife out of her bag and handed it to her daughter, who used it to help disturb the earth, but she was having difficulty. Charlie thought to herself that she should have come prepared and brought a shovel. She eventually stopped digging and stepped back to observe her work. The hole was not very deep but the ground was too hard underneath and it was the best she could do under the circumstances.

Linda started having flashbacks to the murder and panicked, shouting at her sister to take the bag off her back.

Charlotte grabbed the camera bag and took Farah's battered head out of the black plastic bag by his hair.

Kathleen and Linda couldn't bear to look and covered their eyes while the birthday girl tossed the head in the shallow grave and started to kick the muck to cover it in. Linda couldn't bring herself to help fill in the hole and sat on the bench sobbing.

It was approaching 7 p.m., and when Charlotte had finished she sat next to Linda and got her breath back. There wasn't much earth covering the top of Farah's head but it wasn't visible to anybody who wasn't looking for it and the three women were satisfied that the job was done.

There was still the question of the murder weapons to be disposed of. The Mulhalls got off the bench and started walking away when Kathleen turned around and headed back towards the large lake. She took the Stanley knife and hammer from her bag and threw them into the water individually, using the end of her jumper to cover her hand so she wouldn't leave fingerprints. They landed about eight feet into the lake and splashed, before sinking to the bottom. They were satisfied that they would never be found because nobody was likely to have any cause to dredge the water. Even if they did, they wouldn't be able to link them to anything because they had cleaned the weapons for fingerprints back at the flat.

After the knife and hammer were disposed of, Charlotte said, 'That's grand now,' and that they could go home.

Linda was furious. She didn't want to hear that everything was grand. They'd killed a man and had just buried his head in a field where kids went to play. There was nothing grand about that and she said this to her sister. Charlotte just shrugged her shoulders.

They walked out of the park and crossed the road in the direction of the Square. They had agreed to stay in Ballybough again that night to clean up some more but Linda announced that she was going home. She was depressed and wasn't able to face it. She walked home to Jobstown, taking the camera bag with her. She said she'd make sure that it was taken care of. Kathleen and Charlotte hugged Linda before she walked away. Charlotte shouted after her, reminding her not to say a word to anybody about what had happened over the previous twenty-four hours.

Linda walked slowly home and when she arrived back at Kilclare Gardens she said hello to the children. They were excited to see their mam but she only wanted to go to bed.

John Mulhall walked into the living room and stared at his daughter before turning around and leaving without saying a word.

Linda went upstairs and had a long shower trying to wash Farah off her but no matter how much soap she used, she couldn't get the dead man off her mind. She went straight to bed and put the camera bag on the floor beside her.

She slept for three or four hours and awoke with a start. She remembered the bag and went downstairs and got some coal and logs and started the fire. She lay on the couch and cried, waiting for the flames to get hot enough. After about half an hour she took the camera bag and put it into the fire. She sobbed as the flames engulfed the bag and soon reduced it to ash. She took another bottle of vodka from the press and poured herself a large drink and didn't even use a mixer. Her hands were shaking and she needed something to calm her nerves. She got through nearly half the bottle and lay down looking at the fire. 'I'm sorry; I'm sorry,' she whispered.

The next thing she remembered was one of her children calling her. Linda looked around and realised she was at home and for a split second thought that she was dreaming about Farah. She looked in the fireplace and saw the ashes from the bag and knew that it was not a dream but very much a living nightmare. She took a plastic bag from the kitchen and got what was left of the camera bag and brought it to the back garden. She lifted the lid of the green wheelie bin, with the No. 31 painted on the side, and left the bag for the bin men. The thirty-year-old went to the bathroom and looked in the mirror.

She saw Farah. His sad eyes stared at her and he shook his head.

She screamed and splashed her face with water.

She glanced at the mirror again but he was still there. Linda wouldn't be able to get the Somalian out of her mind for a long time.

After saying goodbye to Linda, Kathleen and Charlotte walked back to the Square to get a cup of coffee. Charlie was starting to worry about her older sister. She could see that Linda's conscience was already starting to bother her. She'd always been a sensitive soul and would struggle to keep such a horrible secret. She told her mam that they'd have to keep the pressure on Linda over the next few days and weeks to make sure she didn't crack and go to the guards.

They got the 77 bus back into town and walked the rest of the way to Ballybough. Charlotte started drinking vodka, while Kathleen got some cloths and a cooking pot and started scrubbing the bathroom again. Charlotte thought that it looked fine but her mother was like a woman possessed and just kept cleaning and cleaning throughout the night.

She told Charlotte about her life with Farah and said she would have been dead within the year if Linda and Charlie hadn't killed him. That wasn't much consolation to Charlotte – she knew she was the one who would take the bulk of the blame if the guards came calling. The twenty-two-year-old sat on the settee and stared blankly at the TV. She felt dead inside and had no energy left.

Kathleen woke up early on 22 March as there was still a lot of cleaning to do. She used a cloth and bleach to scrub the bedside locker and wardrobe. Then she got under the bunk bed, which could be cleaned now that the blood was dry.

Charlotte wasn't in the mood for sticking around and got a bag of stuff and left without saying where she was going.

Kathleen went back to her frenzied spring clean but the bottle of bleach was empty so she popped out to the Gala supermarket, wearing a white hoody underneath a blue denim jacket. At 10.16 a.m. she bought credit for her mobile phone, a bottle of milk and a bottle of orange. She then made her way to the household products aisle and picked up a bottle of liquid cleaner and a large bottle of domestic bleach. She got back into the queue, and then left it again, putting the cleaner back on the shelf. She paid for her Domestos and left the shop.

The following day, at 11.25 a.m., she left the post office at Summerhill Parade after collecting her Social Welfare and went back into the Gala store next door. She headed straight to the household products and picked up some more black plastic bags and a large bottle of air freshener. She was trying to get rid of the smell of death that would not leave her small flat. She left the shop three minutes later.

All three women were trying to come to terms with what had taken place. Linda started to instantly feel guilty, while Charlotte was a far harder person and had no problem going back to the murder scene to stay there that night. Kathleen had played no active part in the murder and subsequent dismemberment but she had lost her long-term partner and cleaning seemed to be her way of dealing with this.

The Aftermath of the Murder

On 23 March, three days after the murder, Charlotte went to the ATM at the Bank of Ireland on O'Connell Street. It was 7.32 p.m. when she withdrew €60. Exactly one week later, Kathleen did the same thing. At 1.35 p.m. she took out €150, in three €50 notes, from the same machine. There is nothing unusual about this except that Charlotte and Kathleen were withdrawing the cash from the account of Farah Swaleh Noor – the man who had been murdered and dismembered three days earlier.

Noor's account was based at Allied Irish Bank in South Mall, Co. Cork. He was issued with an ATM card, which hadn't been used since August 2004. A replacement card was sent to him in November 2004. Kathleen Mulhall would later claim that she had looked after Farah's card because he wasn't great at managing cash. In later investigations it emerged that she withdrew money from the account on four dates in March. She couldn't tell gardaí where she took the money out, how much she withdrew or what she had used it for. The final time that Farah's ATM card was used was on 30 March 2005. This was ten days after its owner was murdered and the same day that his body was fished out of the Royal Canal.

There was a lot of activity in the account during March 2005. In the ten days before Farah died the card had been used to withdraw money at Bank of Ireland O'Connell Street six different times. He was paid twice in March from Adecco Recruitment, €219.16 and €157.42 respectively. Farah had registered with Adecco Recruitment in Tallaght a few months before he died and was working temporarily in Schmitt ECS in Leixlip. He had failed to show up at work on 18 March because he was on an extended St Patrick's Day drinking session and Deeanne Slade, who works at Adecco, had tried to contact him without success. On 21 March, Patricia Cleary Greene who works as a recruitment consultant with Adecco had tried to ring Noor but couldn't get through to his phone. She did get hold of Kathleen who had told her that Noor was away minding a sick baby and that she didn't know when he would be back. The Adecco staff were concerned that Farah had not come back to work and Patricia Cleary Greene eventually contacted Kathleen again, who told her that Noor 'had moved to Kilkenny with a young one'. Patricia remembered that Noor always referred to his partner as 'the boss'.

After Kathleen and Charlotte helped themselves to Farah's money there was only €16.87 left in the account. Despite Kathleen's later claims that she was 'minding' his money, detectives have little doubt that the two Mulhall women were effectively 'cleaning out' the bank account of the man Charlotte and Linda had murdered. The mother and daughter spent a lot of time together in the immediate aftermath of the murder and Charlotte spent most of the next couple of weeks living in 17 Richmond Cottages. Kathleen became obsessed with cleaning and wasn't satisfied that they had done a good enough job at removing all traces of her boyfriend's violent death. She kept going back over the bedroom and bathroom in the hours and days after Farah died. She also took all the bloody towels, and washed them, with Linda and Charlotte's clothes, and put them in black bags out in the yard. She had left these, along with the bag of carpet and wallpaper and Farah's clothes, out for the bin men. When they collected the bags the evidence was destroyed forever.

While Kathleen and Charlotte were sorting out Farah's financial affairs, Linda was a nervous wreck, on the brink of a breakdown. Farah Swaleh Noor had begun appearing in her dreams each night and she was afraid to close her eyes because of what she might see. She spent most of her days drinking vodka and she neglected her kids, leaving her father to look after them. Something kept telling Linda to go back to Tymon Park and all she could think about was the head sticking out of the ground. The dreams were driving her mental. On 30 March, she eventually picked up the phone and told Kathleen that she had to go back down and dig up the head. She asked her mam to go with her. Her mother wanted nothing to do with it and wouldn't agree to go.

That evening Linda got on a bus to Ballybough to try to convince Kathleen to change her mind.

James O'Connor was enjoying an evening stroll down the Royal Canal. The twenty-three-year-old had spent the day with friends and was heading towards his home at Matt Talbot Court in Summerhill. It was around 6.30 p.m. on Wednesday 30 March 2005 and lots of people were out and about, walking dogs or walking home from work to get some fresh air and take advantage of the lengthening evenings.

He wasn't in a particular hurry and stopped at Ballybough Bridge to watch a group of young lads fishing. As he lingered around, taking in the early evening sun, one of the teenagers shouted up to him that there was a dummy in the water under the bridge. He looked down and saw the group of about three or four fifteen-year-olds gazing intently into the water. He went down the bank and under the bridge for a closer look and was amazed to see an arm and a leg close together, about three feet below the surface of the water. The sun was illuminating the water and you could see right to the bottom of the canal, which was about seven or eight foot deep. He scanned to the right and also saw what appeared to be a torso covered with some sort of green T-shirt. Beside that was what he thought was the top of a human leg.

The limbs were within a foot of the bank and you could have literally reached out and grabbed them and could certainly have hooked them with a fishing rod. James had no doubt that these were human body parts. The arm had a clenched fist and there was a grey sock on the leg. The torso had no head attached to it and a green fungus was oozing out of the top of the leg. He immediately knew that something unspeakable had happened here and told the group of teenagers that it was a human body and they would have to call the fire brigade. Still in shock from the grim discovery, James ran up the walkway to the top of Ballybough Bridge and dialled 999 on his mobile phone and asked for the fire brigade.

Glen Mannelly was on duty at Tara Street Station when he received a call at 6.56 p.m. from a man telling him that he had found a body in the Royal Canal. He immediately sent two fire engines from the North Strand, an emergency tender from Phibsboro Station and an ambulance from Tara Street. He also informed the District Officer, who was based at the North Strand, that a potentially serious situation was developing. Mannelly then contacted the Garda Command and Control centre in Harcourt Street so they could dispatch officers to the scene.

Fifty-two-year-old Derek Carroll was the officer-in-charge of the North Dublin district and received the call from Tara Street at 6.58 p.m. He drove the fire officer's car the short distance to the scene and arrived just four minutes later. James O'Connor was there and flagged down District Officer Carroll's car. He pointed out the spot under the bridge where the body was resting. District Officer Carroll thanked O'Connor and the three teenagers and asked them to move back while he examined the scene. He wanted to make sure that they were real and that the call-out was not a hoax, as is a common occurrence. He walked down to the canal bank and saw what looked like human body parts, clearly on view. The two fire engines and emergency tender had arrived at this stage and he asked fireman Andy Cullen to get a drag from the fire engine to pull one of the limbs out of the water. They needed to determine if it was in fact human. A drag is like a long garden fork, with prongs bent at right angles on a long wooden handle. Andy Cullen got the drag and put it into the canal water, about three feet from the surface – he pulled out a left arm.

District Officer Derek Carroll is a thirty-year veteran of the fire service and knew a human arm when he saw one. He could see bone and tissue on the upper part of the arm and the skin definition on the thumb of the hand was also very clear. He was left in no doubt that they were dealing with a very serious incident. Fire fighters are highly trained and understand the importance of a garda crime scene. District Officer Carroll didn't want to move anything that could jeopardise what would now be a criminal investigation, and he asked fireman Andy Cullen to put the arm back in the water, as close as he could to where it had originally rested. Cullen did this and then Carroll immediately ordered that the scene be sealed off until gardaí arrived. Fireman Mick Cummins taped off the North Strand side of the bridge while Andy Cullen sealed the Ballybough end.

Frank Kiernan is Station Officer at the North Strand and when he realised that the remains were human he radioed the Central Control in Townsend Street and asked them to contact the gardaí. While they waited for them to arrive, the ten fire-fighters at the scene set up lighting equipment on the canal because the light was starting to fade. They also made sure that nobody went anywhere near the canal. Ballybough Bridge is very busy throughout the day and night and a public footpath runs adjacent to the canal. A row of terraced houses at Sackville Gardens and Summerhill Parade overlook the canal where the remains were discovered and within view is the canal end stand of the magnificent Croke Park stadium, the home of the GAA.

Garda Alan Greally was on the 2 p.m. – 10 p.m. shift at the Communications Centre in Harcourt Square. He received a call from the Dublin Fire Brigade around 7 p.m. informing him of the presence of a possible body under the canal bridge. He logged the call onto the Command and Control system – little realising that incident number 050890972 would become one of the highest-profile Garda investigations in decades.

A patrol car based at Fitzgibbon Street was immediately sent to the scene, along with vehicles from the station's District Detective Unit and local Crime Task Force.

Garda Kieran Brady was the driver of the patrol car and was on duty with Garda Niamh McGrath. The pair were ordered to Ballybough Bridge and arrived at 7.05 p.m. They were greeted by members of the fire brigade and Garda Brady was shown the body parts. He immediately contacted Fitzgibbon Street on his mobile phone and told Sergeant Christy Morrison about the body. He then spoke to James O'Connor, who told him how he'd come to see the floating remains.

A large crowd of onlookers had gathered at this stage and Garda McGrath was controlling them. Garda Brady reversed his patrol car onto the canal bank to prevent them getting access to what would soon be declared a murder scene.

An unmarked car from Store Street, driven by Garda Ronan Judge with Gardaí Marc Pender and Justine Reilly then arrived. The three guards could see something suspicious floating in the water about fifty metres from where the body had been found but could not identify it as a part of a body. They sealed the road at Summerhill Parade and controlled the watching crowds.

The scene was now officially under the control of the gardaí, and within minutes detectives and uniformed members began arriving at Ballybough Bridge.

✂✂✂

As Linda crossed the bridge on her way to convince her mother to help her to dig up Farah's head, she couldn't believe it when she saw all the police around the banks of the canal. She instantly knew that Farah had been found and ran to Richmond Cottages to tell Kathleen. The two women started crying as they sat in the front room. They were in a panic over what would happen now. They decided to walk down to the canal the next day to check if the guards were definitely there for Farah. They hoped that a murder or something else had happened but it was too much of a coincidence. They both knew deep down that the game was up. They knew that somebody had spotted Farah floating in the water as they walked along the canal.

On 31 March they left Richmond Cottages and walked towards Ballybough Bridge. There was a cordon up, about 120 feet from the water, so they couldn't see much. They edged forward as far as the police tape would allow them to go. There were dozens of uniformed gardaí around and plainclothes detectives were speaking to the forensic team, who stood out in their white suits.

Gardaí had no idea, as they were removing the body of a man who had been chopped up into eight parts and dumped in the Royal Canal, that two of the people responsible for the grim murder were standing there watching them. Charlotte and Kathleen had also been back to Ballybough Bridge before Farah was found. They had walked up there a few days after the murder and gone under the bridge to see if they could see any body parts – the mother and daughter had been relieved when there were none on show.

Kathleen and Linda were soon positive that Noor was lying in the water, just a few feet from them, but they wanted to be absolutely certain. Linda turned to somebody in the crowd and asked them what the commotion was about. The man told her there was a body all cut up in the canal and the gardaí were pulling it out. She told him that was awful and looked at her mother. They had seen enough and rushed back to the flat to talk about what would happen next. The police had no idea that the remains were Farah Noor's so they were confident enough that they wouldn't be arrested any time soon.

They turned on the 5.30 p.m. news on TV3 and watched live reports from the scene. They did the same thing on RTÉ at 6 p.m. and switched back over to TV3 at 6.30 p.m. Linda stayed in her mother's that night and all they did was watch the news, trying to get more information about what the guards knew about Farah. Charlotte wasn't in the flat as she was staying with friends elsewhere in the city that night. Linda rang Charlie's mobile after watching the news reports and broke the news to her sister. Charlotte was shocked and cursed Farah Noor but she didn't return to Richmond Cottages. She decided to stay in drinking with her friends, instead. Linda and Kathleen stayed in the flat staring at each other. Neither was in the mood for drinking – they were lost in their own thoughts, wondering about the consequences of what the two sisters had done that night.

Linda went back to Tallaght the following morning and spent the next few days with the news on. She saw the murder case featured on RTÉ's *Crimecall* and knew that if the guards were going on TV making public appeals for assistance, they were obviously treating the case very seriously. She realised that now, more than ever, she had to do something about Farah's head.

✂✂✂

In the days after the murder, and even after the discovery of the body, Kathleen played out a charade with people, pretending that her boyfriend was still alive.

Five days after the murder the landlord of 17 Richmond Cottages, John Tobin, had gone to collect his rent from Kathleen Mulhall. A plumber by trade, Tobin bought the large house in June 2004 and divided it into four flats. Kathleen, or Catherine, as she had introduced herself to the landlord, had viewed the flat with Farah Noor and moved in at the end of 2004, paying €190 a week in rent. She had given her former address as 158 Lower Glanmire Road in Cork and listed her previous landlord as a reference. Tobin had found that Kathleen and Noor kept to themselves and didn't cause much trouble. There had only been one incident when, after a minor disagreement, they called the guards about a fellow tenant.

As Kathleen was giving John Tobin the rent on 25 March, she told her landlord that Farah had run away to be with another woman, who'd had a child for him. She said that the girl only lived around the corner and that she'd only found out about it because Farah was meant to be working nights as a security guard in a shop in town. He'd told her he was spending all his time working but she'd discovered that he was actually seeing another woman and had spent hardly any time in work. She told her landlord that she had put Farah's stuff into black bags and left them under the stairs. John Tobin did see two or three black bags in the house but in reality they probably contained bloody carpet, rather than clothes.

John Tobin wasn't the only person to whom she spun the cock-and-bull story about Noor leaving her for another woman. In one incident Kathleen bumped into Farah's friend Ibrahim Mohamed in the city centre. She asked him if he had seen Noor and told him to tell her boyfriend that she was looking for him if Mohamed happened to see him.

Farah's cousin, Lulu Swaleh, had phoned her on 10 March to ask if a parcel of clothes sent from Kenya had arrived in Ireland yet. Even though Farah was still living with her at this stage, Kathleen had told Lulu that Farah had left her for a former partner and hung-up the phone.

Farah's family would later make numerous attempts to contact Kathleen. She eventually told them that Farah had left her for good and was living with another woman. Then one day in July Kathleen rang Lulu Swaleh. The mother of six was in a very distressed state about Farah. She was in tears, ranting and making no sense. She eventually hung up the phone and never spoke to Noor's family again.

Kathleen also had a second story that Noor had suddenly left her and she'd heard nothing from him. In early April, Kathleen rang Ali Suleiman Abdulaziz asking if he had heard from Farah. Abdulaziz and Farah were quite close but he had not seen the Somalian and asked Kathleen whether the pair of them were still going out. Kathleen became upset and wouldn't answer and hung up on him. He tried ringing Noor's mobile over the next few days but kept getting a message that the number was not in service. Ali had spent the previous Christmas Eve drinking with Farah, Kathleen and Charlotte at Richmond Cottages and was genuinely worried about his friend. He could not get the missing man out of his mind. Three or four days later he rang Kathleen to see if Farah had changed his phone number and she sobbed, 'Ali, I'm finished with Farah.'

She also met and chatted with Karen Tobin, the landlord's wife, and told her she 'did not know what it is like to give somebody three years of your life and for that person to then walk out on you'. Mulhall told Karen that gardaí knew that Farah had 'gone off' and was 'not legal' and was using an assumed name. Karen Tobin later stated that she felt that Kathleen was trying to give the impression that she had been in a committed relationship with Noor and was devastated that he had left her.

In the second week of May, Kathleen ran into a man she knew from drinking in the Parnell Mooney pub on Parnell Street. She had not seen him since Farah Noor had attacked him during an incident in the pub. It later emerged that she said he would not see the man who had tried to beat him up again because the police had deported him.

On 23 May 2005 Kathleen Mulhall made one of her regular visits to the community welfare office at 77 Upper Gardiner Street. She spoke to Community Welfare Officer Dermot Farrelly who, in later investigations, made the following statement to gardaí: 'Last month Kathleen Mulhall came into the office and I spoke to her at the counter. She was by herself. She was worried about Farah Swaleh Noor. She didn't know about his whereabouts. She was asking me to tell her from the records on file if we knew where Farah was, if we had any address for him. She wanted to know if we knew if he was all right. I told her that we weren't in a position to give out the information to her. She then said that Farah might be using his real name. She said she didn't know how to spell the name but it was Sheila Swaleh Shagu. That's how she pronounced the name. She wasn't very clear on the exact pronunciation. I have put variations of the name into the system but there is no match that is similar to the name at all on our computer files. I know from the information on Farah on our computer, his mother's name is Sumeha Shigoo.'

Kathleen was going to great lengths to inform as many people as possible that she was looking for Farah. Some time after going to see Dermot Farrelly and enquiring about Noor, Kathleen ran into the community welfare officer in the Gala shop on Summerhill Parade. Farah's body had still not been identified at this stage so Kathleen spoke to him again. Mr Farrelly was on his lunch break and didn't really want to talk to her outside work but he didn't want to be rude either. They exchanged small talk before going their separate ways.

As well as sorting out her cover story in the weeks and months following the murder, Kathleen was still obsessed with cleaning up the crime scene. She had removed quite a large area of carpet from her flat that needed to be replaced. On 26 March she paid a visit to Carpet Mills on Thomas Street. She gave a shop assistant the measurements of the bedroom and front room and was quoted €365 to re-carpet both rooms. Kathleen couldn't afford anything like this. She walked around the showroom wondering what to do and was looking at a large piece of lino when the owner, Thomas Eustace, offered her help. She said she wanted to buy a piece of vinyl but was short on cash and couldn't afford much. She then examined some Threadford carpet, which is usually fitted in schools and offices and wouldn't be suitable for domestic use. Kathleen knew she had to come up with a story to explain why she had just removed certain sections of carpet and not the whole lot. She said that her flat was infested with cockroaches and handed over €50 for the blue carpet. It measured about 6 feet by 10 feet and was delivered by Carpet Mills' deliveryman and fitter, Joseph Tackaberry, three or four days later. She told him she could fit it herself and took it from him at the door of Flat 1. It was too small to fit the whole bedroom so she cut an area off with her penknife. This would at least replace the pieces she had taken up because they were covered in blood.

There had been a problem with bugs at 17 Richmond Cottages between February and mid-March 2005. John Tobin had hired the company Pest Guard Environmental Services to deal with the problem. Lee Kelly, a surveyor with Pest Guard, visited each flat and found evidence of a major infestation in one of the upstairs rooms. The experts thought that the cockroaches had been brought into the house from abroad. To explain the problem with the carpet, Kathleen cleverly dwelt on the cockroach story. She knew that if the gardaí ever had to ask her why she had removed carpet from a house, just days after a violent murder, she would then have a plausible explanation. Kathleen's flat, however, only had a very minor cockroach problem and all four flats were sprayed on four separate occasions, effectively eliminating the infestation. Another Pest Guard employee, Kevin Conroy, had visited Flat 1 a couple of times. He later said that he thought there was no problem with bugs of any sort in the flat.

Proceeding with her plan, Kathleen rang John Tobin on 30 March and said she had seen another flat and wanted to move out. He told her that she had to give him two weeks notice but if she paid the following week's rent, they would call it quits. She wasn't willing to do this and said that she had lifted the carpet in her bedroom and found cockroaches there. She told him they had laid dozens of eggs. The landlord knew that the pest control people had only been in the flat two weeks before and had given it the all clear. Tobin asked Kevin Conroy to go back and check the flat again. The pest expert found no evidence of any bugs and said that it would be very rare for cockroaches to be living in bedrooms. They favoured the warmth of kitchens, with easy access to leftover food.

A day or two later, the landlord called around to collect the rent, which Kathleen always left inside the door. John Tobin let himself in and noticed that all Kathleen's belongings were packed in black bags. It looked like she was ready to move out.

He discovered that the blue bedroom carpet had a piece the size of a door cut out of it and he could now see the concrete underneath. Another piece was lying against the wall in the bedroom. Tobin tried to ring Kathleen over the next few days to see what had happened but couldn't get through to her.

Kathleen eventually made contact with him on 7 April to say that she had changed her mind about moving out and now wanted to stay. She claimed that one of her daughter's kids had broken her phone so she couldn't contact him. She said that she had got a new piece of carpet fitted in her bedroom for €90. Tobin told her that Flat 4 was free and she agreed to move in there. The landlord met her two days after she changed flats and helped her to take out four black bags for the binmen.

Kathleen moved into Flat 4 on 10 April and shared with two Russian men, who did not speak English well. Around this time Kathleen became quite friendly with her neighbour, Donna Fitzsimons, who lived in Flat 2. Maintaining her story, she told Donna that Farah had gone to live with a Chinese girl who'd had a child with him. She said that her old flat was too big now that she'd split with Farah and Donna later remembered thinking that this was a strange reason to move. Kathleen also confided in Donna that Farah was brutal towards her and used to give her bad beatings. Donna had seen her neighbour remove the carpet from the flat and had been there when the new carpet was delivered. Kathleen also showed her a robe that she was using as a tablecloth on the small kitchen table. She put on the robe, which covered her head and face and only allowed her eyes to be on show. Kathleen said that when she was with Farah in his own country she had to be covered from head to toe because he was a Muslim. Donna didn't really speak to Kathleen when Farah was around. She had only previously called to borrow some milk and Farah had always ignored her. She recalled that the couple obviously liked to drink.

Donna felt that Kathleen 'wouldn't be allowed by him to say hello or anything like that. He was a Muslim and wouldn't let her talk to us or open the door or anything like that. If I ever called to the door when he was in, she would only barely open the door and would hardly speak. She only spoke to me after he left.'

A woman called Catriona Burke moved into Flat 1, with her three-year-old son. Kathleen told her that she'd had to leave because she could not afford the rent by herself. Catriona was struck by the 'big blue ring' on the floor at the bathroom door, which was caused by a combination of cleaning chemicals and Farah's seeping blood and brain matter. When she moved the double bed in the small bedroom there was no carpet, just concrete. Patches of carpet had been placed at the side of the bed to give the impression that the whole area was covered and the carpet at the bedroom window looked like it had been hacked. Catriona never noticed any other blood stains in the flat but she later said there was 'a very bad sewerage problem'. This could have been as a result of flushing skin and bone fragments down the toilet. She never saw a single cockroach and was surprised when gardaí told her that Kathleen claimed that Flat 1 was infested.

Catriona subsequently found an Irish passport, in a foreign name, in the flat and gave it to John Tobin, and his wife, Karen, then handed it in to Dunboyne Garda Station.

✂✂✂

A few days after the murder, Charlotte visited her family home in Tallaght and started drinking very early in the day. Her twenty-one-year-old sister, Marie, came in from work at about 6.30 p.m. and found Charlie crying in the bedroom. She went in to see if everything was OK but Charlotte was very upset and weeping uncontrollably. She initially wouldn't say what was up with her but eventually turned to the apprentice mechanic and said: 'We're after killing Farah Noor.'

Marie later gave a statement saying: 'I did not believe her at the time as Charlotte was in the habit of telling wild stories, particularly when she was drunk. She told me that herself and my mother, Kathleen, were after killing Farah Noor. She did not say when. I just let her talk. She said my mother, Kathleen, and herself were in a chipper and returned to a house they were sharing with Farah Noor. She did not identify the location of the house. They said they found Farah Noor trying to rape my sister Linda. Charlotte then said she hit him and he turned and caught her but she did not say where. At this stage my sister Linda hit him and he did not get back up. She did not describe the items used to hit Farah, nor did I enquire. She then told me that they then cut Farah Noor into two halves and buried him either side of the canal. She did not identify the canal, nor did I ask her.

'I honestly did not believe her. Charlotte was very upset at this stage and I was shocked, to put it mildly, by the story she told me, even though I did not believe her. I left the house and went for a drive and returned some time later and Charlotte was sitting on the couch talking to my father. She had calmed down at this stage and appeared to be having a normal conversation. I went to bed and did not give her story any further consideration, nor did I discuss the story with my sister Linda or my father, John Mulhall.'

At the time Marie didn't know that her mother lived in Ballybough, beside the canal, but she thought of the strange conversation a few days later, when a body was recovered from the water. The twenty-one-year-old didn't know what to do but she eventually decided to let it rest and not to tell anyone.

Charlotte's admission to her sister seemed to be an uncharacteristic blip – other than that outburst she seemed to be coping quite well with the gruesome events of 20 March. Not only was she happy to take money from a dead man's bank account, she also met a few people she knew from the streets and sold them Farah's rings, watches and other jewellery, in order to make some extra cash. While Linda and Kathleen had spent the day the body was discovered crying, Charlotte was getting on with her life. On 31 March, just a day after the Somalian's remains were found in the canal, she met a man and started a relationship with him. She hooked up with a Russian called Dilmurat Amirov. He lived in Flat 3 at the cottages and that's how they met.

Over the following weeks, Charlotte spent many days sitting at the side of the canal, drinking cans with her new boyfriend. They sat on the benches at Summerhill and regularly walked under the bridge where Farah's body had been discovered. Charlotte showed no emotion as she strolled by.

Amirov also got to know Kathleen over the next few months. Charlotte's mother followed her daughter's lead and had a fling with Dilmurat's friend, a Russian named Alex, who also lived in Flat 3. She started going out with Alex only a few weeks after her boyfriend was murdered. It didn't seem to have taken Kathleen too long to get over Farah.

Three weeks after Kathleen had moved upstairs she invited her neighbour Donna up to her flat for a drink. When Donna arrived at Flat 4 Charlotte was there, along with the two women's boyfriends, Dilmurat and Alex. Donna had one glass of vodka before her taxi arrived, as she was going out for the evening.

Donna later stated that she was on decent enough terms with Charlotte and Linda and that Charlotte had called into her for a chat a couple of times. Donna also spoke to Linda once or twice while she was around Richmond Cottages. She said she got the impression that Linda was not very close to her mother and had taken her father's side when the couple had separated. She was a shy person who kept herself to herself and didn't mix with other people like her mother and sister. Linda suggested that they should go out drinking together. Donna agreed that it would be a good idea but never had any intention of spending a night out with any of the Mulhalls. It never struck Donna that Kathleen acted as if she had been involved in Farah's murder. She seemed very normal to her friend and neighbour.

Neither Charlotte nor Kathleen ever mentioned Farah or the horrible events that had taken place in the downstairs flat. Alex and Kathleen's relationship soon fizzled out and Charlotte's relationship with Dilmurat didn't last long either. Dilmurat and his three friends were thrown out of Flat 3 and then moved into Kathleen's flat. They lived there for a while but were caught and were thrown out of Richmond Cottages altogether.

As the weeks passed, Linda was still having terrible trouble sleeping and Charlotte thought it would be wise for her to spend time around Richmond Cottages so she could keep an eye on her older sister. Around Easter time, Linda moved in for a few nights with her four children. The group would arrive back to the flat with cans and neighbours would hear them up drinking all night. The three women spoke about the murder a few times but didn't dwell on it. They did discuss what to do if the police began asking questions. The Mulhalls decided they would say that they knew nothing about what had happened to Farah and stick to their story. Charlotte told her sister that they should 'keep their mouths shut' – no matter what happened.

Towards the end of March 2005, Robert McGovern and Brian Molloy, two park rangers were working at Sean Walsh Park in Tallaght when they saw a strange object sticking out of the ground. The rangers are responsible for patrolling the park and picking up rubbish. They were on foot patrol, emptying a bin beside a park bench in front of the lake, when they noticed what looked like a dead animal buried behind the bench. The men stopped to have a smoke and examine the object. The 'animal' had short black hair and was sticking out a few inches from the ground. Brian Molloy walked behind the 'animal' and started kicking at the ground with his foot. Bits of grass and chipping came away and when he saw the black hair Molloy thought that it looked like a human head. It was round in shape and appeared to have a wound in the middle of it. He called Robert McGovern and for a couple of minutes the two men had a conversation about what it might be. Eventually they decided that it was a dog's belly. They also considered whether to dig it up or to just ignore it. In the end they agreed to cover it with a bit of clay and forget about it. They were both convinced that the object was an animal and nothing more.

McGovern thought nothing more about what had gone on and would only remember the strange 'animal' when the gardaí eventually cordoned off the area.

Brian Molloy noticed that the object was there for about a week or ten days after he first saw it. He had decided not to dig the remains up because he assumed that they would just rot in the ground, but then one day they had just disappeared. A few people also contacted him to report that something was in the ground, including a man who he knew as Lar. Molloy knew Lar because he spent a lot of time in the park drinking.

'Lar' is Laurence Keegan, a retired army private from Tallaght who goes to Sean Walsh Park with a book every day and has a drink and a smoke. He sits at the same bench and enjoys a few quiet hours keeping his own company. A few days after the remains were recovered from the Royal Canal Laurence looked up from his book and saw something black on the ground beside the bench. He thought it was a dead bird. He got up and started kicking it with his boots but it didn't move. Then he realised that it wasn't lying on the ground and was in fact buried in a hole. He saw that there was hair sticking out the top of whatever was buried. Laurence then realised that it could be the top of a head, with short dark hair. He had steel toecaps on his boots and tried to dig up the ground around the thing to move it. He thought he'd dig it up so he could see exactly what it was. It was lodged solid though and wouldn't budge at all. He had read about the headless corpse taken from the canal and it immediately struck him that the 'head' he was digging up could be the same head for which gardaí were desperately searching the city. He went and reported the find to park ranger Brian Molloy and asked him to get rid of it. Molloy told him it was only a dog buried there but Laurence insisted that the object was human. He said it was the head of the body that had been found in the canal near Ballybough. Keegan thought that the park ranger didn't believe him and wasn't taking him seriously because he drinks in the park.

Laurence Keegan returned home and met his daughter Carol Kelly. He told her he'd seen what looked like a buried head in the park. He said it could be 'the black fella' found in the canal. He asked her if she would go back and help him to dig it up but she refused. He went back to Sean Walsh Park as usual the following day and it was there in the same position. Keegan became convinced that the head was human because of the crown sticking out of the ground. He could clearly see that it had black hair but couldn't see enough of the face to make out the skin colour.

It was the same for the next three days as well. The second last time he saw the head, he noticed that blue bottles had started eating into it.

Two days later it was gone, and Keegan assumed that one of the park rangers had dug it up. All that remained of it was a large hole. He saw Brian Molloy and asked him if he had dug the object up but Molloy said he had taken nothing from there. Once the head was gone, Laurence didn't think much more about it and thought that it was none of his business anyway.

It later emerged that Linda had dug up the head. After the body had actually been discovered she had started to get worse. Farah would not leave her mind, even when she was awake. She was in a constant state of drunkenness and was teetering on the edge of insanity. Her dreams started to get darker and the demons were telling her to dig up the head.

Some time in early April she was in the house drinking when she had got the urge to go to see the head. It was after 10 p.m. but she walked down to Tymon Park and sat on the bench, just feet from where they had left Farah, a few weeks earlier.

She was suffering from hallucinations and Farah started to talk to her, thanking her for coming to see him. She thought he had shaved his hair off since he'd been in the ground. She dug up the clay with her hands and picked up the head and put it in a black bag. It was badly decomposed and there was a good chance that rats and other wildlife had feasted on it while it lay exposed.

Linda picked up the bag and left Tymon Park. She walked to Killinarden Park in Tallaght, which was just a short distance away. She hid the bag in some thick bushes where she was sure it wouldn't be discovered and went home to Jobstown. She spent the rest of the night drinking vodka and only went to bed for a couple of hours.

She got up early and went back to Killinarden Park and took the bag from the bushes, after making sure that nobody was around. She took the black bag and put it in a carrier bag she had brought from the house. It was her son's schoolbag and she had taken his pencils and sharpeners out of it that morning – school copy books had now been replaced by a human head. As the mother-of-four walked home, she was determined to get rid of Farah's head permanently.

When she reached the house, she rang Kathleen. She told her that she had Farah's head with her and was going to bury it in a safer place. Her mother didn't want to know about Linda's plans. The thirty-year-old went to the extension in the back garden of the empty house. She took a hammer out of the toolbox and put it in the schoolbag, beside the head. She was about to walk back out the door when she remembered there was a litre bottle of vodka in the kitchen press. She took this too and also put it in the bag.

She walked in the direction of an area in Tallaght known as Killinarden Hill. It was about forty minutes' walk from Kilclare Gardens and Linda knew the area well because she used to live close by. When she got to Killinarden Hill, she climbed over a locked gate into a large field with burnt-out cars dotted around it. She turned right and walked for about 300 feet to the back of the field, before sitting down on the grass close to a ditch.

She took the bag off her shoulder and kissed it.

'I'm sorry, Farah; I'm sorry,' she said and sat for over an hour, thinking about just where her life had gone so badly wrong.

She took out the bottle of vodka and drank it straight. It was empty before long. Linda was drunk and highly emotional by now and she started hitting the bag with the hammer. She smacked it dozens of times and could hear the skull shatter as the heavy tool repeatedly connected with the bones.

She fell asleep for a few hours and woke up shivering. It was getting dark and she decided to re-bury what remained of the head. She walked towards the ditch and found an area of the field that was soggy and dug a small hole with her hands. She took the black plastic bag out of the schoolbag and tipped the fragments of the head and skull into the hole and covered it with the wet soil.

'I'm sorry Farah. It should be me ma in there and not you,' she whispered, as the last bit of muck filled the hole. She took a lighter out of her pocket and set fire to the plastic bag. It was soon consumed with flames and she put it on top of her child's schoolbag and that went on fire as well.

Linda waited until all that remained of the bag was ashes, and she threw them into the ditch. She got the hammer and threw it into the ditch and left the empty vodka bottle in the field. With that she ran across the field, jumped over the gate and ran all the way home to Kilclare Gardens, not stopping once. She thought she'd never get to her house and just wanted to be as far away as she could get from Farah Noor and his talking head.

When she got home she didn't say a word to anybody and went straight to bed. Farah didn't come to see her in her dreams that night. She eventually went to the Heatons department store in the Square and bought two school bags for €20. Charlotte had already taken her other son's bag and the two children had to go to school with their books in plastic bags for a few weeks.

Linda's mental health had not been helped by the fact that she'd had a pregnancy scare. She had met a man a few weeks before the murder and had been involved in a casual relationship with him. In early April she'd informed her mother and sister that she was pregnant and intended to go to England to have an abortion. The three of them met in Richmond Cottages and decided that they should all go to the UK for a while, to try to get over what they had done to Farah. They decided to get the ferry over four days later, after social welfare day. While they were waiting Linda went to see doctors in the Coombe Hospital and was told that her pregnancy scare was a false alarm. As she was no longer expecting a child, she decided not to go.

Charlotte and Kathleen, however, were determined to go anyway and booked the ferry. They got the boat over to Holyhead, carrying changes of clothes in two schoolbags. They went on the Irish Ferries crossing and the weather was so bad they couldn't go onto the top deck. When they got to Holyhead they stayed in a homeless hostel, which was a ninety-minute walk from the train station, for a night. They ended up sleeping rough in a park for two or three nights before going back to the hostel. They had enough money for the train fare to Manchester and when they arrived in the city, they went drinking.

Charlotte met an Englishman named George Gray in a pub and they ended up staying in his room at the Grattan Arms hotel. She later said it was 'not a proper relationship, just going for a few drinks, staying for a few days'. At the time she was going out with Dilmurat, her Russian boyfriend, but she never contacted him while she was away. Instead, Charlotte was happy to sleep with another man and let him pay for drinks for herself and her mother.

After they'd been there for about a week, Linda agreed to go to England to meet up with them but she then changed her mind. She was supposed to bring them over money, as after their ten-day holiday the two Mulhalls had decided they'd had enough of England. They wanted to go home, but without Linda they had no cash. They contacted the social welfare who arranged tickets for the two of them to travel back to Ireland. When they returned, Kathleen told Donna Fitzsimons that she had been staying down the country with a friend.

Each of the women had changed in their own way since Farah's murder and they were all battling internal demons to one degree or another – Linda was on the brink of suicide, Kathleen was running away from her problems and Charlotte was in denial that anything was wrong at all.

The two eldest Mulhall brothers, James and John, were both serving prison sentences in Wheatfield Prison, in Clondalkin. Kathleen, Linda and Charlotte paid them several visits in the three or four months after Farah's murder. Both men were serving sentences for road traffic offences. Thirty-three-year-old James was in the middle of a three-year term for dangerous driving, causing the death of a fellow motorist in January 2002. John Mulhall Jnr, who was nearly five years younger than his brother, was on remand on two counts of being a passenger in a stolen car in Cork. An arrest warrant had been issued for him after he failed to appear in court. Charlotte went to see her brothers with Kathleen two or three times but Kathleen also went alone most weeks and was a regular visitor to the jail. Linda was especially close to James, as they were the two eldest in the family, and she saw him on several occasions. The brothers also had access to a mobile phone in prison and were probably in telephone contact as well.

Some time between April and July 2005, Kathleen, Linda, and possibly Charlotte, confessed to John and James about the murder. Kathleen went to visit the pair one day and broke down. She told James that Linda and Charlotte had murdered her boyfriend after he made a move on Linda. She went into minute details about the murder and told him about the body being dumped in the canal and said that their father had come over in his van and removed bloody clothes from the flat.

James Mulhall didn't believe her and thought she was telling lies. Linda then went to see him and confirmed the story but did not go into any great detail. She asked him to look after her kids if anything happened to her.

Charlotte hasn't admitted telling her brothers anything but detectives believe that she could also have got the murder off her chest.

The Mulhall women didn't realise it at the time but opening up to John and James would prove to be a very costly mistake.

The Garda Investigation

BY 8 P.M. on the evening of 30 March, senior gardaí attached to the Dublin Metropolitan Region (DMR) North Central Division had been informed of the discovery of the body. They converged on the scene to take control of the investigation. The headquarters of DMR North Central is Store Street Garda Station in central Dublin but the body was found in the area covered by Fitzgibbon Street Station, which meant that the investigation would operate from that station. The detective then in day-to-day charge at Fitzgibbon Street was Detective Inspector Christy Mangan. DI Mangan (now Detective Superintendent) is a highly experienced and respected officer who would go on to take charge of the investigation into the Dublin Riots in February 2006. When he arrived at the scene he saw the limbs floating in the canal and directed that a murder inquiry be commenced. He ordered that the area be preserved as a crime scene.

Garda Ronan Hartnett is a member of the street crime unit at Fitzgibbon Street Garda Station and was on mobile patrol with Garda Tom O'Brien when they were called to assist at the scene. He spoke with Garda Kieran Brady and Fire Station Officer Frank Kiernan and was brought down to the water's edge to examine what were now clearly human remains. The firemen were pointing lights and torches at the scene and Garda Hartnett observed two arms cut from the body at the shoulder, two parts of a lower leg cut from the body just above the knee, two thighs and a part of a pelvic area covered with white clothing. He noticed that the skin was very discoloured and it was hard to make out if the remains were those of a black or white person. All the body parts were lying submerged in the water close to the canal wall. A vest and pair of underwear were lying beside a torso that was covered with what appeared to be a white football jersey. The two legs had socks on the feet and all the body parts covered a distance of about ten feet. Garda Ronan Judge told him that they'd found another object around 150 feet up-water. Garda Hartnett could just barely see something visible protruding from the water further down the canal and went to check it out with fire fighter Pascal Proctor. They climbed down the ladder from the fire tender and onto the railway side of the canal. About sixty feet past the bridge a bag was visible in the neon light. Fifty-four-year-old Proctor had a drag tool with him. He slowly pulled the bag about five feet, towards himself and Garda Hartnett. Before the package reached dry land the contents spilled out and the fire fighter was horrified to see a torso floating on top of the water. He picked up the plastic bag and was struck by the terrible smell coming from it. He gave the bag to Garda Hartnett and they labelled it with yellow plastic markers and left the torso where it was. It was very discoloured and it was impossible to make out whether the victim was black or white.

Detective Sergeant Colm Fox from Mountjoy Garda Station rang Garda Control in Harcourt Square at 7.42 p.m.

to inform them that the Garda Technical Bureau and Water Unit would be required at the Ballybough scene. A garda technical team arrived at 9.07 p.m. and at 9.55 p.m. Detective Gardaí Geraldine Doherty from the ballistics section of the Technical Bureau and Liam Lynam from ballistics and photography arrived. The two officers were shown around by Detective Sergeant Mick Macken from the fingerprints section. All three stayed to assess the crime scene and realised that they would need to return the next morning.

Dr Y M Fakih, who has a doctor's practice in Whitehall, received a call from Fitzgibbon Street requesting that he come to the canal to examine the remains and pronounce the victim dead. He was brought to Ballybough Bridge where he met with Detective Sergeant Gerry McDonnell. He was shown the mutilated limbs and pronounced the victim dead at 9.30 p.m.

Three gardaí took it in turns to monitor the canal for any movement of the body parts while they waited for first light to come and a murder probe to begin. The locations where the eight body parts had been found were marked using white A4 sheets on the bank, in case any of them moved with the flow of water.

Gardaí preserved four areas around the murder scene in the days following the discovery. Summerhill Parade/Ballybough Road, beside the canal bridge, was closed until the evening of 1 April. The bridge on the Croke Park side was closed until 2 April. The scene at the Royal Canal Bank was patrolled by uniformed gardaí until the beginning of April and Sackville Gardens, which overlooks the canal, was also preserved as a crime scene.

Over the next few hours gardaí began the standard procedures that take place during all murder investigations.

Everybody at the scene who witnessed anything was preliminarily interviewed and their names and address were noted so that they could be contacted about formal statements. Uniformed officers carried out house-to-house inquiries to see if local residents had noticed anything unusual in the last few days and weeks. The scene was also policed throughout the night to prevent anyone contaminating the crime scene.

The two gardaí in overall charge of DMR North Central were Superintendent John Leahy and Detective Superintendent John McKeown, who were based at Fitzgibbon Street and Store Street respectively. At 10 p.m. on the night of the 30 March 2005, gardaí held the first of well over fifty conferences about the murder. The investigating team discussed the day's events and decided on how the investigation should progress. All were in agreement that a lengthy and difficult inquiry lay ahead. They knew that the key to solving it was to find out the identity of the man who had met his grisly end in the lonely waters of a canal in the centre of Dublin.

At 1 a.m. all the investigators went home for a night's sleep and planned to reconvene at the scene at 8 a.m. the following morning.

✂✂✂

Although the remains of the man who would eventually be identified as Farah Swaleh Noor were not officially found until 30 March 2005, it later emerged that they could have been discovered many days before, because several, possibly even dozens, of people had inadvertently seen them.

A local woman, forty-three-year-old Margaret Gannon, who lives near-by with her husband and three children, was bringing her seven-year-old son, Evan, to school at North William Street on Monday 21 March. She stopped at her sister's house to collect her two nieces and was walking over Ballybough Bridge just before 9 a.m. when little Evan said, 'Ma, look at that.' Margaret looked into the water and saw a black bag with plastic and lots of brown tape wrapped around it. The bag was between two trees, close to the bank, and was resting against a grassy area towards the North Strand. Margaret immediately thought it looked like a body with no head. She was sure it wasn't a dog drowned in a bag, something she often saw in the canal. Her niece, said, 'Oh Margaret, is that another body?' but she said it wasn't and they continued on to school. She saw the bag again the following morning but the kids never mentioned it after that, so she forgot about it. She later remembered the date she had seen what could have been Noor's body because it had been her husband's birthday the day before. After she heard about the discovery of the dismembered body, Margaret contacted the gardaí and told them what she'd seen.

Twenty-four-year-old Paul Kearney, a local man, was cycling along the canal from Jones Road towards Ballybough at around midday on Good Friday, 25 March. As he approached the bridge, he saw what he thought was a right arm in the canal. When he stopped to take a closer look, he saw other body parts, including a leg. The arm was sticking out of the top of the water and he could see fingers and nails on the clenched fist, but it was the same whitish colour all over so he thought it was a dummy. He rang his dad, Paul Snr, who was sitting at home, and said: 'Da, you're not going to believe me. I was walking along the canal when I saw part of a body.' He told his dad he was worried, but his father thought he was joking and started laughing, telling him to 'go away out of that'. Paul hung up the phone but a few times over the next week thought about his find. He contacted Fitzgibbon Street when the body was eventually discovered.

On the day that the remains were finally uncovered, fourteen-year-old Christopher Leech was fishing in the canal with his pal Sean Tighe. The teenagers were on their Easter holidays and were sitting on the bank of the canal beside Ballybough Bridge. At about 2.30 p.m. Christopher saw a black bag with see-through Sellotape around it, floating down from the Croke Park side of the canal. The closed bag wasn't moving very quickly and was being carried back and forth around a small area by the current. Christopher later told detectives that half the bag was under the water, with the other half floating on top, near the bank. He was looking in the water for pike but didn't see any fish and didn't notice any body parts either. The boys thought nothing more of what they'd seen and continued fishing for another hour or so. Then they went back to Christopher's house, which was across from Ballybough Bridge. When they looked out his window later in the evening they saw a large crowd at the bridge, with police cars and fire engines.

At about 4 p.m. that same afternoon Ballybough man David O'Connor was out for a walk on the canal with his two daughters. His girls were looking at a football that three or four kids had just kicked into the water. David was on the Williams Street side of the canal and saw a bag lying on the bottom of the water, under Ballybough Bridge. It was white and medium-sized like a plastic shopping bag, with something in it that looked round. He didn't pay much attention to it and his daughters never saw it at all. They continued on home and David only thought about the incident when a garda called to his home later.

At the same time Linda Staunton from Ballybough was returning from dropping old clothes to a recycling centre near Westwood Gym in Clontarf. She sat down on the bench nearest Ballybough Bridge to have a cigarette. She stayed there for about five minutes with her two-and-a-half-year-old daughter, Jade, who was asleep in her buggy. She saw Christopher Leech and Sean Tighe fishing and also saw three other youngsters throwing rubbish into the water. She noticed a black plastic bag floating on the canal at the bridge and assumed that the children had thrown it in. She paid no more attention to it.

Linda also told gardaí that on or around St Patrick's Day she had seen a group of young people in their early twenties around the canal. She described how they 'looked like college students – they were respectable'. There were two males and two females in the group and one of the girls was trying to remove a big plastic bag that looked 'packed out' from the middle of the water. Linda went home without seeing anymore but the incident stuck in her mind because 'you don't normally see college students along the canal but they had an interest in the bag'.

✂✂✂

At 8 a.m. the following morning, Det Gda Geraldine Doherty arrived back to Ballybough Bridge to carry out a technical examination of the scene. Before she met the dive team that was en route from Athlone, she collected a number of samples and packaged and numbered them. As gardaí did not have any idea of the victim's identity she was very thorough in collecting and bagging anything that might potentially be of evidential value. She took samples of paper that lay beside faeces under the bridge, three swabs from the faeces, as well as collecting cigarette butts and chewing gum. These would all be tested for DNA to hopefully identify the victim.

The garda sub-aqua team arrived at around 8.30 a.m. to carry out the unenviable task of removing the limbs from the canal waters. Sergeant John Bruton from Athlone Garda Station headed the team of four. Sergeant Bruton was acting as the dive supervisor while Garda Eamon Bracken, who was also stationed in Athlone, set up and tested the equipment that would be used to film the dive. The two gardaí whose job it was to recover the limbs – Gardaí Eoin Ferriter and Brian Breathnach – were both from Santry Garda Station and were experienced divers.

Sergeant Bruton was briefed by Detective Sergeant Mick Macken from the Technical Bureau, who was acting as the crime scene manager. Superintendent John Leahy also talked the dive expert through what had happened the previous day, so he could prepare his two divers for the job ahead.

Gardaí Ferriter and Breathnach put on their diving gear while Garda Eamon Bracken was finishing setting up the Colourwatch, a state-of-the-art underwater video system. Before they even got started, the two divers, Ferriter and Breathnach, removed the torso that was floating in water close to a wooden jetty, 150 feet past the bridge in the direction of Croke Park. Garda Brian Breathnach lifted up the torso and scooped it into a body bag held open by his colleague. Both men could clearly see that the victim had suffered multiple stab wounds to the chest area. The head and both arms had been removed and the torso hacked off across the midriff. They got the torso out of the water using a stretcher and placed it on the wooden jetty, where it was handed over to Detective Garda Geraldine Doherty.

The dive then got under way at 9.55 a.m. when both divers entered the freezing water. Garda Breathnach held the Colourwatch camera, which relayed video images that were recorded and watched on the surface by Garda Bracken. This underwater video survey took about forty-five minutes and seven body parts were located, at a depth of about 1.8 metres, under the bridge, close to the canal wall.

A part of a lower leg was the first limb recovered, followed by a thigh, a full leg, an arm and the midriff, followed by a second arm and finally, another section of thigh. Each limb was placed in a separate plastic evidence bag under the water before being handed over on the surface to Sergeant Bruton, who passed each bag on to the Technical Bureau. The video footage clearly showed that the pelvis was wrapped in a green and white Umbro football jersey.

Senior gardaí supervised this important dive and Sgt John Bruton offered instructions from time to time, making sure that the video footage would be of sufficient quality to be used in any later court case. The underwater search team continued to scour the canal in search of other body parts, from the lock gates under Ballybough Bridge up as far as Croke Park, a few hundred feet away. It soon became clear that the victim's limbs had all been dumped in the one spot and that the torso was the only body part that had floated away from where it had been dumped.

At 11.10 a.m. both gardaí were called out of the water and got dried off before going back to their stations. Garda Bracken labelled the videotapes of the morning's work and handed them over to Det Sgt Colm Fox. Over the next few days other searches of the canal took place, including one from Crossguns Bridge back to Ballybough, but nothing more was found.

After the divers had left the scene, the work of the Garda Technical Bureau was only just starting. Members of this elite section, based at Garda Headquarters in the Phoenix Park, are trained to work methodically and routinely spend hours trawling crime scenes. As well as gathering chewing gum and old cigarette butts from under the bridge, Detective Garda Doherty also took samples of canal water and drained water from the recently recovered torso. She took swabs from bloodstains found close to where the body parts were recovered under the bridge. Items of clothing removed by the divers, including a pair of jeans and a tracksuit top, also had to be bagged up and sent to the lab for testing.

Stafford's Funeral Directors, who are based at nearby North Strand Road, were contacted by the City Coroner's office and agreed to remove the victim's body to the City Mortuary in Marino. Nevin Stafford arrived at Ballybough around midday and was directed to the two body bags that contained the remains. He loaded them onto a stretcher and placed them in an ambulance. He was accompanied to Marino by Garda Cliona Beirne. Karl Lyons, the Mortuary Technician, met him and took delivery of the body bags.

Later that afternoon, Malachy Fallon from Stafford's picked up the body bags and brought them to Beaumont Hospital. The limbs were X-rayed before being brought back to the morgue for the post-mortem.

Dr Michael Curtis, the Deputy State Pathologist, carried out a post-mortem examination at around 7 p.m. that evening. He had been at the scene at 9 a.m. that morning when his preliminary examination revealed that the victim had most likely died from stab wounds.

Dr Curtis determined that the body parts found in the canal were probably those of a healthy black male, aged between twenty and thirty years old. It had originally been thought that the remains were those of a white man because they'd been in the water so long that most of the skin had separated from the limbs. The body had been contaminated with silt and fresh-water prawns and he thought that it had probably been in the water for in excess of a week. When he looked beneath the white underpants it was clear that the man's penis had been amputated, along with the anterior part of the skin of the scrotum. The testicles were still present, as was the victim's pubic hair.

When the body parts were laid out on the mortuary table their combined length measured 5 ft 4", which meant that allowing for the head, the body would have probably been in the region of 6 ft. The victim appeared to be of an athletic and muscular build.

According to the post-mortem, 'There was considerable water-logging of the skin of the wrists, hands and fingers, producing a so-called washerwoman appearance.' The hand was found in a clenched position with the fingernails short and ragged. There were no defensive wounds to the hands or fingers and the way the bones of the body were fragmented indicated that they had probably been cut by a sharp instrument. Some of the fracturing was not very clean though, which suggested that a blunter instrument had also been used.

The victim had been stabbed a total of twenty-two times, with eighteen of these wounds being made to the middle of the chest, between the nipples and neck. Many of these wounds measured 3.5 cm, such was the ferocity of the assault. There were two injuries to the lower chest. The stomach had suffered four wounds to its front and was empty when examined. There was also trauma to the large intestine and colon. There was a 22 cm wound on the victim's back which had penetrated deep into the flesh, while another wound to the shoulder blades was also detected, as was a stab wound to the lower left-side of the back.

The liver appeared pale and there was a superficial V-shaped wound on it, as well as a 2 cm long cut to its posterior. The left kidney bore a small amount of surface damage, which had most likely been caused during the dismemberment. The bladder had been pierced a number of times and was empty. There was significant damage to three ribs, caused by the knife cutting through the stomach. The victim's stomach contained traces of blood and blood clot. Two attempts had also been made to penetrate the heart but these stab wounds only caused damage to the heart muscle, the organ itself was not penetrated. The dead man's lungs had been penetrated five times. All of the victim's vital organs were healthy and Dr Curtis believed that the dead man had a history of good health and had not been in any way sick.

Alcohol was detected in the blood but the level could not be quantified. Drugs were not initially detected.

Dr Curtis's report concluded: 'This man's body had been dismembered. Dismemberment would have occurred after he had succumbed to multiple penetrating wounds. In the course of the dismemberment, the soft tissues had been cut relatively cleanly with a sharp knife or similar implement, while the bones had been severed relatively clumsily by repeated chopping actions from an instrument or instruments such as an axe or a cleaver. The head and neck had not been recovered at the time of post-mortem examination. The penis had been amputated and was not recovered.'

He determined that the victim had died as a result of 'penetrating wounds to the trunk'.

Detective Garda Geraldine Doherty was present while the examination took place and was in charge of handling samples taken from the remains. Samples of the victim's pubic hair, nail swabs and anal swabs were taken. Bone marrow, muscle tissue samples, as well as blood and toxicology samples, were also gathered and handed over to Dr Hillary Clarke of the Forensic Science Laboratory in Dublin. Dr Clarke was also responsible for testing the soccer jersey, vest, underpants, socks and tea towel that were found with the remains.

Mr Neil O'Brien, a biochemist at the Toxicology Department in Beaumont Hospital, took delivery of the toxicology samples. Detective Garda Glenn Ryan of the Bureau's fingerprint section took a set of palm and fingerprints from the body. They would be checked against the National and Asylum Fingerprint Databases to see if the victim had applied for asylum as a refugee. Europol, Interpol and international immigration authorities' records would also be checked.

While Dr Curtis was determining the cause of death, a massive garda inquiry aimed at identifying the remains swung into action. Hundreds of residents in the Summerhill and Ballybough areas were canvassed and each filled out a questionnaire with the help of gardaí. The results were collated at the incident room in Fitzgibbon Street.

Gardaí realised that the help of the media would also play a key element in identifying the murder victim. The media took an immediate interest in the grizzly case and in the few weeks following the discovery scarcely a day went by when it wasn't mentioned in the national press. The day after the remains were found, a press conference was held at Fitzgibbon Street and was attended by dozens of newspaper, TV and radio reporters. Detective Inspector Christy Mangan and Superintendent John Leahy put the items of clothing that were found with the remains on display. Gardaí especially focused on publicising the white long-sleeved Ireland-away jersey because it was so distinctive.

There was also a huge interest in the case among members of the public, and Superintendent John Leahy made an appearance on RTÉ's *Crimecall,* appealing for public help in the case. Little did he realise that Linda Mulhall was watching the programme. It was around this time that she moved the head from its original resting place so the guards would never find it. Officers made special pleas to landlords to check their accommodation for missing tenants and many did come forward offering potential names. Crimestoppers, an anti-crime agency funded by the Department of Justice and working in co-operation with An Garda Síochána, put up a reward of €10,000 for anyone who could help identify the body. Gardaí assured members of the public that all information they received would be treated in the strictest of confidence.

Members of the African community were also heavily canvassed for information, with special pleas being issued to immigrant media outlets, such as the *Metro Éireann* newspaper. These publications ran articles on the discovery of the body parts and also printed posters in a number of different languages, featuring the distinctive soccer jersey found with the victim. Gardaí also made church appeals and spoke with the pastors of all the African Churches in the Greater Dublin Area. African community leaders were later praised for the co-operation they gave in trying to identify the remains. It would be an African man who read a newspaper article about the body, who would give gardaí their first breakthrough.

Much of the newspaper reporting focused on the possibility that the victim had been murdered as part of a ritual sacrifice, and gardaí did give this theory real consideration in the absence of anyone coming forward to identify the body. Investigators were conscious that members of the African community were flocking to Dublin and little was understood about their religious beliefs or traditions. Ritual sacrifices are relatively common in parts of West and Southern Africa where it is thought that an increase in wealth or brainpower must come at the expense of others. The most powerful way of acquiring another person's wealth or intellect is to consume medicine made from their body parts and this belief has existed for centuries. Certain parts of the body are believed to offer different benefits. Testicles are thought to bring virility, fat from the breast or abdomen brings luck, while a tongue will smooth the path to a girl's heart. A businessman might sacrifice a hand in order to attract more customers. The organs have to be removed while the victim is still alive and their screams enhance the power of the medicine. Human sacrifice is thought to please the gods and gives special powers to those conducting the ceremony.

On the face of it, the discovery of a dismembered corpse with the head and penis missing would set the alarm bells ringing in any police force. But many detectives privately felt sceptical that they were dealing with black magic, or *muti* as it is known. Only two ritual murders have taken place in Britain over the last forty years and none have been recorded in Ireland. The lack of a head and penis were seen as a possible attempt by the murderers to throw investigators off the scent and to divert time and resources away from discovering the real motive for the crime.

Despite these reservations, gardaí examined similarities between the Ballybough case and a 2001 case involving the discovery of a body floating in the River Thames in London. An unidentified torso of an African boy, who was named 'Adam' by British police, was found in the river. His head and limbs were severed and the calabar bean (a toxic plant found in West Africa), pellets and gold particles, were found in the child's gut.

Detectives also spoke to an Irish priest who had spent several decades on the Missions in Nigeria. His opinion was that the canal murder bore remarkable similarities to cases he had encountered in Africa. Gardaí then made official contact with Detective Superintendent Gerard Labuschagne of the South African Police Service's Investigative Psychology Unit (IPU) based in Pretoria. Dr Labuschagne has a doctorate in clinical psychology and has studied serial killers since 1994. He is a renowned international expert on *muti* killings and has had plenty of practice dealing with cases involving black magic. He estimates that there are between fifteen and three hundred ritual killings in South Africa each year. Most deaths go unreported or are treated as ordinary murders. As well as black magic, his unit also investigates mass-murders, baby-rapists, extortionists and all the unusual crimes that baffle detectives. Dr Labuschagne's three-person unit has been in existence for over ten years and has been responsible for putting some of South Africa's most dangerous criminals behind bars. Its main job is to profile the offenders. The unit conducts research into psychologically motivated crimes and has the largest database of serial murderers in the world. The South African Police Service (SAPS) has a 100 per cent success record in solving serial murder investigations in which Dr Labuschagne's team has been involved. The SAPS also catches serial murderers faster than any other police force in the world.

The Detective Superintendent is in regular demand throughout the world and has assisted agencies such as Scotland Yard, the Finish National Bureau of Investigation, the Royal Swazi Police and the Netherlands National Police Agency. During his brief contact with gardaí he told them that it is usually quite easy to distinguish a *muti* murder because body parts are removed in a functional manner, while the victim is still alive. This is in contrast to serial murderers, who take a sick pleasure in torturing and mutilating their victims. It is far more difficult to track down the people behind *muti* killings because the culture of silence around those who believe in and practice black magic is so strong. He confirmed that the removal of the genitals is a strong characteristic of a *muti* murder, because they are seen as a source of good luck. In many ways the body in the canal case did not really seem to fit the *muti* criteria but Dr Labuschagne nevertheless agreed to assist detectives in their investigation. Arrangements were being made to fly Detective Sergeant Gerry McDonnell to South Africa to interview him, when the identity of the corpse was discovered.

Another theory scrutinised was that the dismembered body could have been that of Paiche Onyemaechi's husband. Her headless remains were found at the side of a riverbank in Kilkenny City, in July 2004. Chika Onyemaechi has not been seen since his wife's disappearance. Paiche was the daughter of the Malawian Chief Justice and had lived with her thirty-three-year-old husband and two children in Waterford before they separated. The remains loosely fitted the description of Chika Onyemaechi, and gardaí were open to the possibility that he was murdered by associates of his dead wife, but they quickly ruled out any link in the cases. Nobody has ever been charged with Paiche's brutal murder.

In the early part of the new millennium hundreds of asylum-seekers managed to sneak into Ireland, taking advantage of our lax immigration laws. Most of these refugees lived within their own communities and never came to the attention of the authorities. They were effectively invisible. The number of African men in their twenties and thirties who had come to Ireland and then vanished was so vast that gardaí were offered sixty-two names of possible victims matching the description of the body found in the canal. All these individuals' families and friends had to be interviewed and it was a time-consuming exercise that involved a massive amount of garda manpower. Specialist detectives from the National Bureau of Criminal Investigation (NBCI), whose job it was to investigate serious crime, were also drafted in to help the dozens of gardaí from Fitzgibbon Street, Mountjoy and Store Street stations who were involved in the case. Most of the names on this list were not even in the country but every lead had to be checked and every line of inquiry ruled out.

CCTV footage also proved to be very important. Hundreds of tapes, containing thousands of hours of footage were handed over by local businesses around the north inner-city. Garda CCTV footage and traffic cameras also had to be scrutinised in fine detail. A special unit with around twenty video monitors was set up and gardaí viewed the footage around the clock. Charlotte and Linda Mulhall would later be identified on a number of traffic and security cameras around Ballybough, and Farah Noor's last hours were filmed by a camera on O'Connell Street.

The incident room at Fitzgibbon Street was manned by Detective Gardaí Daniel Kenna and Michael Quinn. They received literally hundreds of calls from helpful members of the public, offering leads and suggestions as to who the canal victim might be. All these suggestions, however unlikely, had to be checked out and investigated thoroughly.

As the victim was a non-national, who might only have entered Ireland a short time before his death, gardaí had to liaise closely with their colleagues on the continent. Fingerprint and DNA databases were checked through Interpol, the worldwide policing agency. A description of the dead man was also issued and checked through Interpol. The gardaí also contacted police forces in the UK, Nigeria, Kenya and South Africa for help and assistance.

Detectives attempted to establish the victim's identity through isotope analysis, which was undertaken by a forensic scientist who was based in Belfast. Every garda station in Dublin collected a sample of water from their area and the investigation team forwarded the samples to the scientist for analysis. From examining the density of the victim's bones and the minerals present, the scientist was able to determine, with near certainty, that the dead man had lived in the area covered by Fitzgibbon Street Garda Station for the last six months of his life. Gardaí did not take these results as definitive and kept an open mind, but the scientist would later prove to be accurate in his findings.

The first breakthrough in the case came on 16 May, when a Somalian man living in Dublin, Mohamed Ali Abubakaar, made a statement to gardaí. He reported that his friend and fellow countryman, Farah Swalah Noor, had been missing for well over a month. Abubakaar and his girlfriend Deirdre Hyland went to Malahide Garda Station where they informed Inspector Eddie Hyland, Deirdre's cousin, of their suspicion that Farah Noor could be the canal murder victim. Inspector Hyland passed this information on to the Fitzgibbon Street investigation team who interviewed the Somalian.

Abubakaar told detectives that he had last seen Noor in the company of his girlfriend, a woman named Kathleen Mulhall, and two other women on O'Connell Street on Sunday 20 March. It was St Patrick's weekend and Farah Noor had appeared very drunk to Abubakaar, while the other three also looked like they had been drinking heavily. He had known Noor from working with him on fishing boats in East Africa and was sure he had seen him at about 6 p.m. that Sunday. Abubakaar said that the group accompanying Farah had bags of cans and that his friend seemed very unsteady on his feet.

He told gardaí, 'I call him to talk to him because I know after a few drinks anything can happen to him.' Kathleen Mulhall had intervened and told Abubakaar that Farah was fine and the group kept on walking. Ali knew Kathleen from his job in Dublin Bus. He was a driver there and operated the 77 route from the city centre to Tallaght. He'd met her two or three times on the bus and had been on nights out with the couple, including one night in Shooters bar on Parnell Street. Ali was certain that he'd run into the group on the Sunday of St Patrick's weekend, because he and his girlfriend had been in town to visit a multi-cultural fair they were interested in that was being held on O'Connell Street.

That was the last he saw of Noor.

Ali explained that over the next few weeks he had tried to ring his friend but the phone was mostly switched off. It was answered by an Irish voice on one occasion but the caller said he had the wrong number. He also began asking mutual friends in the Irish Somalian community if they'd seen Farah, but nobody had. On 9 May 2005, just over a month after the remains were found, Abubakaar had seen an advert placed by gardaí in *Metro Éireann*, looking to identify a man whose body had been found in the Royal Canal. Abubakaar recognised the white Ireland-away jersey that was pictured in the advert as belonging to his friend. He also remembered that Noor had been wearing it on O'Connell Street the last time he had met him. He started to fear that the man found in the canal might be Farah. All the pieces of the jigsaw seemed to fit and when he told Deirdre she had advised him to contact the gardaí.

Officers were initially sceptical that it was Farah Swaleh Noor who ended up in the canal, because he did not match the profile of the victim given in the post-mortem report. The post-mortem had determined that the man was in excess of 6 ft in height and aged between twenty and thirty years old. Farah Swaleh Noor was 5 ft 6" and was aged thirty-nine. Nevertheless, a post-mortem result is only an estimation, so Farah Swaleh Noor's name was added to the list of possible victims.

Garda inquiries into Farah Noor revealed that he had arrived in Ireland from Somalia in late 1996 and had had a son with an Irish woman from South Dublin. On 20 May officers interviewed the woman who was the mother of Noor's six-year-old child.

This woman, called Paula to protect her identity, had

ended her relationship with Noor in April 2001 because he was violent towards her. She hadn't seen him since September 2002. Paula told the guards that Noor also used the name Sheilila Said Salim and post had arrived for him in that name. Four days later she gave permission for detectives to take buccal swabs from her son for DNA comparison, which would be tested against the remains. The results of the DNA tests would not be known for about six weeks and investigations into Noor continued.

The investigating team discovered that the last known address of Farah Noor was 17 Richmond Cottages, Ballybough, where he shared a flat with his partner, Kathleen Mulhall. On 21 May Detective Inspector Christy Mangan and Detective Sergeant Colm Fox called to Richmond Cottages and spoke with Kathleen Mulhall and her flatmate, a twenty-four-year-old Russian named Alex Ibramimovich. Alex spoke no English but one of his friends confirmed that he had only been in the country for about four weeks and gave details of his whereabouts during that time. Kathleen told the two men she had only recently moved into Flat 4 in the building, having previously lived downstairs, in Flat 1. She was asked about her boyfriend Farah Swaleh Noor and said she didn't want to talk about him in the flat. She said she would get dressed and call down to Fitzgibbon Street.

Kathleen arrived at the station shortly afterwards and told Det Sgt Fox that she hadn't seen Farah since February. She said that he came to her flat one night and took all his stuff and said he was leaving. Kathleen said she didn't know where he was or who he was with and she'd had no contact with him at all since then.

This struck gardaí as being very suspicious, considering

that she told them that she had left her husband of twenty-nine years to be with Farah and had moved to Cork to live with him.

Kathleen said she was happy to see him out of her life because she'd had enough of his violence and had ended up in hospital three times when they lived in Cork. The couple had had to move 'a good few times in Cork because Farah caused trouble everywhere'. She said: 'He was on heroin, grass, hash, crack cocaine, E. He had a bad habit. He did not get on with people when he had drink or drugs taken and would fight with anybody.'

Gardaí already knew that Kathleen Mulhall did not tell her landlord that Noor had moved out of the flat until 25 March and her story did not make much sense. They took a statement from her and decided that her background deserved further scrutiny.

On 26 May Detective Garda Geraldine Doherty accompanied Detective Sergeant Mick Macken, also from the Garda Technical Bureau, to Flat 1, 17 Richmond Cottages, Farah Noor's last known address. They recorded that it was a two-roomed, ground-floor flat, consisting of a kitchen cum living room, a bedroom with shower and an en-suite toilet. In the bedroom the concrete floor was covered with pieces of carpet and rugs. It looked to the gardaí like the original carpet had recently been removed. The tenants in the flat, Caroline Hanley and her niece Martina Norton, gave their permission for the gardaí to carry out the technical examination. Eight swabs were taken from the dressing table and two swabs from the bunk beds. A further swab was taken from a stain on the edge of a mirror behind the bunk beds, which had originally been part of the dressing table unit. All the exhibits were handed over to the Forensic

Science Laboratory for testing but it would be a number of weeks before the results were available.

Gardaí went to Dublin District Court and applied for permission to examine a bank account held under Farah Noor's name at AIB in Southmall, Cork. The assistant manager at the branch, Catherine Lynch, subsequently gave the details to Garda Ian Brunton. The records revealed Noor's financial transactions for the last four years. They were surprised to discover that Noor's bank account had been used only twice in the last few months, the last time being on 30 March. If Noor was alive and well he wasn't taking any money out of his bank account.

Gardaí also determined Farah Noor's mobile phone number and contacted Vodafone to check whether it had been used. The phone had not been used from the end of March up until June 2005. In early June it was used a total of eight times in the first few days of the month. Detectives tracked down the individual who was using the phone. It was not Farah Noor but a man named Florian Williams. At the end of May, Williams had bought a phone and SIM card in good faith from his work colleague, John Mulhall.

John Mulhall was interviewed and told the officers that at the end of March he had been given the mobile phone by one of his daughters. He didn't know who had previously owned the phone. Further detective work revealed that John Mulhall was the estranged husband of Kathleen Mulhall, Farah Swaleh Noor's girlfriend. John Mulhall had somehow come into possession of the missing man's mobile phone. Detectives immediately knew that something was out of place.

In the meantime other friends and associates of Noor had also begun contacting the authorities, saying they had not seen him. Mohammed Ali Noor knew the Somalian and had last seen him on St Patrick's Day. He'd meet Farah most days around town and had become very worried when he hadn't encountered him over the previous few months. He told his friend Rashid Omar Ahmed of his concerns and asked Ahmed to make enquiries about Noor in Cork, where he had lived for over two years. Ahmed was close to a Somalian named Hamed Salim Miran who had moved into Noor's old flat in Cork. Miran was in Dublin three weeks after the body was pulled from the canal and met Ahmed and Ali Noor. They began talking about the missing Farah and agreed that if any Somalians living in Ireland had seen Farah anywhere in the country they would have heard about it. They feared that it could have been Noor's body that was pulled from the canal. Lots of Farah's friends in Dublin were saying the same thing. Ahmed eventually contacted the guards with his suspicions.

On 8 June, Sergeant John Malone was working in Abbeyleix, Co. Laois when he received a call about a suspicious car at the local petrol station. The blue Nissan Micra was listed as stolen and he stopped it at about 8 p.m. The three African men in the car agreed to go to Abbeyleix Garda Station. They told Sgt Malone that they'd bought the car in good faith. Their story checked out and while they were talking, the men said they knew the identity of the body that had been recovered in the canal in Dublin. They named the victim as a Somalian, Farah Swaleh Noor. The way Farah's name kept coming up was beginning to intrigue the garda investigators.

Betrayal and Arrests

ON 11 JULY 2005 the investigation into the torso in the canal murder, which had been ongoing with only limited success for 102 days, suddenly sprung to life and was effectively solved in four days. A combination of forensic science and family betrayal led to the confirmation that Farah Swaleh Noor was the man who had ended up with the waters of the Royal Canal as his final resting place. Gardaí were determined to establish who was responsible for putting him there.

Garda Damien Duffy was on duty at the Communication Centre at Harcourt Square on 11 July when he received a call from the Dublin Emergency Exchange at 7.47 p.m. The male voice at the end of the line told the operator that he had information about the so-called 'body in the canal' case and wanted to talk with gardaí. He said his name was John Mulhall and he was serving a prison sentence in Wheatfield Prison with his brother James. He said he was in a position to name the victim of the canal murder. He claimed he could also identify who had carried out the crime and where it happened. When Garda Duffy finished talking with Mulhall he rang the Dublin emergency operator. The supervisor informed him that the 999 call had come from a mobile phone. He immediately entered the details of the conversation on the Garda Command and Control system.

Both John and James Mulhall were well known to gardaí in Tallaght and had amassed a series of convictions. Thirty-four-year-old James first got into trouble in 1991. He had three convictions in as many years and was given the benefit of the Probation Act. He had largely remained clean until a road traffic accident in 2002.

At the time of the murder investigation, James Mulhall was serving a three-year jail sentence for dangerous driving causing the death of a fellow motorist in January 2002. Mulhall had pleaded guilty to causing the death of fifty-two-year-old Tony O'Brien. He crashed Mr O'Brien's BMW into the wall of a house on the South Circular Road, Dublin, in the early hours of the morning. The pair had been drinking in a city centre hotel and were going to drive home together, but after O'Brien could not turn off his car alarm he had agreed to let Mulhall drive them home. Following the fatal accident, James Mulhall fled the country and went on the run to England, which prolonged the torment for Mr O'Brien's wife and family. The court heard evidence that there was a high level of alcohol in the dead man's bloodstream and he was probably asleep in the back of the car when the accident happened. Garda Laurence Collins gave evidence that after arriving on the scene he realised that Tony O'Brien was dead in the back seat because the Dublin Fire Brigade crew were concentrating their efforts on the front. They were tending to Mulhall and his girlfriend, Tanya Whelan, who had been travelling in the front passenger seat.

James Mulhall had no tax or insurance and caused significant damage to the passenger side of the car and also demolished a garden wall. Judge Frank O'Donnell said he 'must have been driving at considerable speed to have lost control'. The judge took into account Mulhall's previous convictions, which included assault causing harm and a string of other road traffic offences. Judge O'Donnell jailed James Mulhall for three years and banned him from driving for twenty-five years, saying that James had a 'disregard for the structures of road traffic legislation'. James began his prison sentence on 12 November 2003.

Twenty-eight-year-old John Mulhall had over twenty convictions for a huge variety of offences, including assault and theft. In early 2005 he was given a two-year suspended sentence for assaulting a man on a bus in Tallaght in April 2004. John was a regular heroin user and often spent hundreds of euro a day on his addiction. He moved between various addresses and stayed at Kilclare Gardens for long periods.

John Mulhall was in Wheatfield Prison as a result of his failure to appear in court in Co. Cork. He was due to appear before a judge on 29 November 2004 because of an incident involving a stolen car. When he failed to show, a bench warrant was issued. He was arrested in Dublin on the same day but was subsequently bailed. He was back in prison on remand on 4 March 2005, two weeks before the murder took place. He was then sentenced to eight months' imprisonment on 30 May 2005, on conviction of two counts of being a passenger in a stolen car

On the morning following the mobile phone call, two uniformed gardaí, Sergeant Bobby Cooper and Garda Kevin O'Connell, went to Wheatfield Prison in Clondalkin and spoke with the two Mulhall men. The pair claimed that their mother and two sisters had murdered their mam's boyfriend, an African by the name of Farah, and had cut his body up and dumped it in the canal.

Gardaí at the Fitzgibbon Street murder headquarters were immediately informed and Detective Sergeant Colm Fox and Detective Garda Terry McHugh went to the prison, where they met with Sergeant Cooper and Garda O'Connell. The uniformed men told the two detectives that the prisoners had potentially vital information about the canal case.

John and James Mulhall were taken from their cells to an interview room where they were introduced to Det Sgt Fox and Det Gda McHugh. The brothers told the detectives that their mother, Kathleen Mulhall, and their sisters, Linda and Charlotte, had murdered Kathleen's boyfriend at her flat in Ballybough. They had then cut up the body, before dumping it in the Royal Canal. The pair said that their mother had come to them in jail a few weeks after the murder and confessed that she had spiked Farah's drink with ecstasy and that her daughters were forced to kill him, after he made a pass at Linda. They claimed Kathleen could not keep the killing a secret from them. She had broken down and said she had to tell them what happened. The brothers said that it was Kathleen who had planned the murder and she had got her daughters drunk and given them drugs so that they'd be willing to kill her boyfriend. Kathleen told her sons that Linda rang their father, John, after the murder and that he went 'ballistic' when he found out what had happened. He still drove his work van to his ex-wife's flat, however, and took carpet and towels away to dump so that the gardaí would not find them. The pair claimed their father also took bedspreads, clothes and other items away from the murder scene. The prisoners said that it took the three women hours to clean up the flat and that they were now pretending that Farah was still alive but that he'd left Kathleen for another woman. They stated that Kathleen had bought new carpet for the flat and redecorated it so that the bloodstains would not be obvious.

John and James told the detectives that they were 'disgusted' by what their family had done. The brothers said they wanted to get the truth about what happened to Farah off their chests. James said it was Charlotte who cut off the head, so Farah couldn't be identified, and that Linda had chopped off his penis, as punishment for raping Kathleen.

Det Sgt Fox and Det Gda McHugh interviewed the two prisoners for about half an hour. After they had finished, the investigators immediately went back to Fitzgibbon Street, where a case conference was held to dissect the spectacular information. The following day, the two detectives went back to meet the Mulhall brothers at 2.45 p.m. and they had a forty-five-minute conversation. Det Gda McHugh transcribed what was said into his official notebook. The brothers repeated the allegations about their family's involvement in the murder. At 8.29 p.m. the same day, Det Sgt Colm Fox received another call on his mobile phone from John Mulhall. He told the detective that he and his brother had discussed going on the Witness Protection Programme but had opted against it and instead wanted a transfer to another prison. The Mulhalls were worried about their safety. Det Sgt Fox told John that he had been looking into getting the pair moved to another prison so they would be secure.

The next day, 14 July, Det Sgt Fox got a text from the same mobile number, even though the use of mobile phones is forbidden behind bars. He rang John Mulhall back and had another conversation with him on 15 July. The brothers were asking for a move to medium-security Castlerea Prison in Co. Roscommon. If they could not go to Castlerea together, then they wanted to move to Shelton Abbey open prison in Co. Wicklow. Det Sgt Fox told them that he did not have the authority to promise them any transfer but said the possibility was being looked at. The brothers said they were going to talk to a solicitor.

John Mulhall rang the Detective Sergeant again the following day, confused about why they hadn't been moved yet. He then said he'd changed his mind and now wanted to stay in Wheatfield because it would be obvious that they had touted to the gardaí about what their family had done if they were both suddenly transferred. The pair did not want any other prisoners knowing that they had spoken to the police. John said they had extra information on the killing but would not tell gardaí and would not make official statements. They did not want their family to know that they had talked to the gardaí. Nevertheless they continued to keep in contact with Det Sgt Colm Fox.

On the same day Dr Dorothy Ramsbottom of the Forensic Science Laboratory confirmed to a 99.9 per cent certainty that the canal remains were those of Farah Swaleh Noor. The DNA tests taken from his son six weeks previously were positive. Dr Ramsbottom also told gardaí that the blood swabs extracted from the flat at Richmond Cottages on 26 May matched Noor.

Gardaí were convinced that Flat 1 at 17 Richmond Cottages was the murder scene. They arranged for a more in-depth forensic examination of the flat. This took place over the last two weeks of July and arrangements were made with the landlord, John Tobin, that the two tenants from

Flat 1 would be housed elsewhere. Detective Sergeant Mick Macken and Detective Garda John Higgins were in charge of the search, which involved members of the Garda Technical Bureau and the Forensic Science Laboratory. During the search a chemical called luminol, designed to show up the presence of minute levels of blood, was used for one of the first times in Ireland. The luminol examination revealed splatters of arterial blood throughout the bedroom. The bloodstaining was consistent with a serious assault having taken place. There was evidence of blood present in the grooves of the pine planks of a wardrobe in the bedroom but not on the surface of the planks. This meant that the area had probably been well cleaned. Gardaí now knew, with scientific certainty, that the man found in the canal was Farah Swaleh Noor and that he had been murdered at Flat 1, 17 Richmond Cottages, the home of his partner, Kathleen Mulhall. All the pieces of the jigsaw were starting to fit nicely into place. In the days after the double breakthrough Detective Sergeant Colm Fox and prisoner John Mulhall had a number of further conversations. Then, on Tuesday 19 July, James Mulhall rang. He told the detective that he wanted a transfer to Shelton Abbey and that his brother knew about it and didn't mind. He said he didn't feel safe in Wheatfield and was worried he would be attacked. Det Sgt Fox told him that he'd have to check with the authorities and ring him back but the brothers suddenly stopped co-operating with the investigation.

In the end the brothers completely refused to co-operate with gardaí and would not give statements implicating any of their family in the murder. They were never transferred out of Wheatfield. Their informal statements against their parents and sisters, however, were more than enough.

The brothers' crisis of conscience had resulted in detectives making massive progress in the case.

Gardaí had now built up a reasonably strong case against the Mulhalls. The DNA linking Farah Swaleh Noor's death to 17 Richmond Cottages was significant, as was the witness statement placing the three Mulhall women with Farah Noor on O'Connell Street on the night he died. Combined with the fact that Farah's phone had ended up in the hands of John Mulhall Senior and the new information from John and James Mulhall, detailing the alleged roles their mother and two sisters had played in the crime, detectives now had enough evidence to arrest Linda, Charlotte, John and Kathleen Mulhall.

Detectives had a case conference on the afternoon of 2 August 2005 and it was decided that Linda, Charlotte, Kathleen and John Mulhall would all be arrested for questioning the following day. It was agreed that four teams of detectives would swoop simultaneously and that the Mulhalls would be questioned in two separate city-centre garda stations. Some members of the media had been tipped off in advance about the imminent arrests and the *Evening Herald* had planned to run the story about the breakthrough in the case on its front page on the morning of 3 August. A senior garda involved in the case requested that they pull the story in case one of the suspects was not at their address when the gardaí called looking for them. The *Evening Herald* subsequently led with the story in its later editions, and the arrests, which took place at around 10 a.m., were the main story on RTÉ's *News at One.*

At 10.40 a.m. Detective Sergeant Walter O'Connell from

Store Street drove to 31 Kilclare Gardens with Detective Gardaí Kevin Keys, Adrian Murray and Garda Muireann O'Leary. They arrested Linda Mulhall under Section 4 of the Criminal Justice Act, on suspicion of murder.

The mother-of-four was taken to Store Street Garda Station for questioning and was processed at 11.25 a.m. by Garda Paul Caffrey, supervised by Sergeant Karl Mackle. She was fingerprinted, photographed and also provided a sample of blood and saliva to a doctor. She declined to have a solicitor present but said she wanted her father informed. Linda didn't know that at this stage John Mulhall, as well as Charlotte and Kathleen, were all being detained and that her father was also in Store Street.

Over the course of the next twelve hours, Linda Mulhall was interviewed on four separate occasions by two teams – Detective Gardaí Kevin Keys and Adrian Murray and Detective Gardaí Larry Duggan and Mark Jordan. Linda told her interviewers that she was not in Ballybough on the day that Farah Noor was murdered. She insisted that this was the truth, even though she was told that two witnesses had put her with Noor, her mother and sister on O'Connell Street on 20 March. She was shown CCTV footage from the Gala supermarket taken the day after the murder. Linda admitted that it was her captured on the film but said she couldn't remember being in the shop or being out drinking on the day of the killing. The detectives put it to her that she had denied being in O'Connell Street with her mam and sister on the day of the murder to conceal her role in the crime.

She told them: 'It's not that I tried to distance myself; I honestly can't remember being there. Unless I must have been drinking. I'm not supposed to drink when I take these tablets.' At the time Linda was on medication for her blood pressure.

She was shown Farah's Ireland-away jersey and told: 'Now I just want to point out the numbers one to ten. Now these are all holes we believe were caused by a knife when Farah was stabbed. Do you see them? What do you have to say about that?'

She said she didn't know anything about Farah's jersey and didn't even know he had been murdered until today. She couldn't offer any information about his death.

She conceded that she had been in her mother's flat in Ballybough on two occasions and was given pictures of the bunk bed, which had bloodstains on it. 'God, I don't know anything about that,' she replied.

She started to lose her composure when gardaí produced photos of the scene at Ballybough Bridge where the body was found. They asked if she recognised anyone there.

'No, no, no, no, no, no,' she shouted.

The detectives then asked: 'You do know that Farah was cut up into eight pieces?'

'I knew there was a body found but I didn't know the way it was cut up. Was it really Farah? I would like a solicitor because I just can't believe any of this.'

Linda asked for a solicitor at 8.31 p.m. and she spoke to Kevin Tunny, who is based in Tallaght, by phone. He then came to the station and spoke to her in person.

When the interview resumed, gardaí played Linda the tape of her brothers making the 999 call from Wheatfield Prison telling the police about their family's involvement.

After hearing it she said, 'That doesn't sound like my brothers.'

The tape was played again for her but she insisted: 'That's

not my brothers; that's not my brothers. That sounded like a junkie to me. My brothers don't sound like that.'

The detectives told her that they were hardly making it up and that John and James Mulhall had rung them because they wanted to get what they knew off their chests. 'Do you not believe that your brothers would tell about the murder?' she was asked.

'They don't know anything to tell about murders. I don't know anything. I don't believe what you're saying to me, I don't believe any of that,' she replied.

The mother-of-four also denied ever seeing the Sagem V55 mobile phone that belonged to Farah, which her father had said one of his daughters had given to him. She claimed, 'I've never seen that phone before in my life,' and also said she knew nothing about money that had been withdrawn from Farah's account after he died.

Garda Paul Caffrey, who was based at Store Street Station, went into the interview on two occasions. He wanted to check that everything was all right with the prisoner. During one of these visits Linda asked the detectives if her father was in the same station. Apart from this, she did not ask about her family.

Before she was released from custody that night, after the twelve-hour interrogation, Linda was asked if she wanted to reconsider anything she had said during the day. Gardaí first summed up the evidence against her: 'So your two brothers call the gardaí and tell us that you and your mother and Charlotte killed Farah at Flat 1, 17 Richmond Cottages. We go to that address and search the same. This is where your mother lived and we find splatters of blood everywhere and the indication we have is that there was a violent struggle or assault there. Farah's body is found in the canal very close to the flat. You are the last people seen with Farah. He is found wearing the jersey he had on when last seen with you. You were in the Ballybough area after he was last seen and your father states that you or Charlotte gave him Farah's phone and Charlotte takes money out of his account after he goes missing. We can prove all these allegations very well indeed. What do you say to that?'

Linda said she didn't know what to make of the evidence. She was asked if she wished to make any alterations to the notes that gardaí had made of the interview and replied, 'About the shop, where I said I wasn't in the shop, I must have been in the shop.' She was then released without charge after twelve hours in custody and went home to Tallaght.

Sergeant Liam Hickey had arrested Charlotte around Kilclare Gardens, just fifteen minutes before Linda was picked up from their family home. Charlotte was taken to Mountjoy Garda Station. Gardaí had difficulty in getting a doctor to the station to take hair, blood and saliva samples from her and there was a short delay while one was found. During her twelve-hour detention, she was interviewed on five occasions by Gardaí Niamh Coates, Ian Brunton, Nichola Gleeson, Fergal O'Flaherty and Detective Garda Tom Feighery.

The twenty-two-year-old insisted that she knew nothing about Farah Swaleh Noor's murder. She said that she had no involvement and neither did her mother or sister. She denied carrying out the killing and dumping the body in the canal. She told them that her dad didn't get rid of the evidence in his van. She said that her brother was telling lies when he said that they were involved and he 'must be fucked in the head'.

Gardaí knew immediately that Charlotte was a hard nut and wouldn't crack easily. They decided to ask her a series of difficult questions, to try to get her emotional so that she would be more inclined to tell the truth.

They asked her about cutting off Farah's penis, enquiring if 'it [was] a sexual thing, or was it pure spite on your part?' Charlie didn't bat an eyelid and they continued with: 'Your mother, Kathleen, she was the one being badly treated by Farah. Did she get enjoyment when his penis was cut off? Was that the ultimate revenge? To clean up – I'd say that was great fun. When you were hungover after your birthday, was it a treat for you to clean up the mess?'

Charlotte was well used to dealing with the police and she had no respect for them. Questions such as, 'Did ye enjoy cutting him up?' or 'If you say you didn't cut him up, did you enjoy watching others cut him up?' or 'When you cut off his head did you talk to it? Do you find that funny?' didn't bother her in the slightest.

She said that the last time she'd seen Farah was in Eamon Doran's pub in Temple Bar when she met him and Kathleen for a drink around mid-February. She claimed they had three or four drinks and then she got a taxi back to Jobstown. She said she never saw him around St Patrick's Day and that she was very drunk at that time. Her mam had told her that Farah went off with a Chinese girl around mid- April and she didn't ask many questions because it wasn't her business. She said she wasn't interested who her mam was seeing but she had known that Farah had had a child with the Chinese girl.

She told gardaí that she thought 'not a lot' when she

heard on the news that the remains had been discovered in the canal. When gardaí put it to her that the crime was very gruesome, she said, 'God, yeah.'

The detectives said they had CCTV footage of Kathleen and Farah on O'Connell Street taken on St Patrick's Day. He was wearing the Ireland-away jersey but Charlotte said she'd only ever seen him in a Manchester United shirt. She told them she was drinking on 20 March because it was the day before her birthday but she couldn't remember if she was with Farah and her mam and couldn't remember if she saw a friend of Farah's on O'Connell Street.

She claimed: 'I can't remember any of my birthday this year because all I done was drank.'

'Surely you must have woken up at some stage, sober?' she was asked.

'Not if ya drank as much as I do,' she responded.

'Did you always drink a lot?'

'Yeah,' she said and claimed that she regularly suffered from memory loss because of drinking but denied that she was an alcoholic. She admitted, 'I don't really do much but drinking so there's not much to remember.'

She said she couldn't even remember where she woke up on the morning of her birthday, but it was in either Tallaght or Summerhill. She thought she'd spent the previous day drinking in a pub and her mam might have been with her, but she couldn't be certain. Charlotte maintained she could remember absolutely nothing of March 2005, except for the fact that she met her boyfriend at the end of the month, on the thirty-first.

Gardaí said that they thought it was 'very strange that you remember 31 March 2005 and no other days in your life.' They asked her: 'You don't remember your birthday but know the day you met your boyfriend. Did you feel guilty on your birthday?'

'I'd nothing to feel guilty about,' she coldly replied.

Charlotte said she never took drugs, except for the odd E tablet and had never taken them with Farah and didn't think that he was a drug user either. She couldn't explain how a work colleague of her father's had come into possession of Farah's phone. She denied taking the phone after he was killed. She said she never changed the voicemail greeting on it and didn't know who did.

The prostitute didn't recognise Farah's Ireland jersey or a pair of socks or a number of bags and other evidence exhibits that were shown to her. She identified Farah and Kathleen from CCTV stills taken in the Parnell Mooney pub on St Patrick's Day and recognised pictures of the beds and dresser from her mam's flat. She said she didn't know why the wallpaper was removed from beside the bunk beds and said that the carpet was probably taken out because it was infested with cockroaches. She knew there had been a problem with cockroaches since Kathleen moved into the flat in December 2004.

Charlotte also claimed that she never saw blood in the flat in Richmond Cottages. She told the guards that she loved her mam and sister but wasn't protecting them. She was certain that Kathleen never asked her to murder Farah because as she put it: 'Well, I think you'd remember something like that, wouldn't ya?'

The interviewing gardaí spent a lot of time asking Charlotte about the violence that her mother had suffered at the hands of Farah Swaleh Noor. She told them that she had seen Farah push her mam once and knew that he probably hit her but she didn't have any details and didn't ask. She then recalled one conversation with Kathleen where her mam had claimed that a scar on her leg had been caused in 2003, by Farah beating her up. They asked her if she was concerned that the man who was supposed to be her mother's boyfriend was beating her up. Charlotte answered, 'Obviously it concerns me; everyone has arguments though.' She added that she wasn't concerned about her mam's safety. Just because he pushed her once 'that doesn't really mean how the general relationship was, does it?' Although she had heard and suspected that Farah was violent towards Kathleen, she didn't have a clue about how he treated her because: 'I wasn't there twenty-four hours, was I?'

Charlotte was asked if she had discussed worries about how her mother was being treated by Farah Noor with Linda at any time throughout the month of March. She answered that she hadn't mentioned anything to her sister: 'Why would we speak about me mother? Ya don't speak about your mother, do ya?'

The twenty-two-year-old admitted that she had gone to see her brothers in Wheatfield during April and they had asked her how Kathleen was getting on. She didn't tell them that their mother had split up with Farah and didn't mention the small fact that he was beating her up because 'it didn't come up in conversation'. She didn't like to talk about 'other people's problems' on the visits because she didn't want to upset John and James and there was nothing they could do about it anyway.

The fact that her two older brothers had contacted the guards and ratted on their whole family was also a topic of conversation during the interviews. Charlotte acted like she didn't know what they were talking about and claimed not to know anything about Kathleen confessing about the murder to her sons. She said that she usually went to visit her brothers with her mother but there were times when Kathleen went on her own and she could have, in theory, told the two boys, but she did not think this was the case.

'Well, how, apart from your brothers being psychic, which I take it they're not, how on earth would they have known about all this?' she was asked, but couldn't offer an answer.

'Your brothers rang us and told us that they've been told, so you see we've a serious problem here. Why did your brothers ring us up from prison to tell us what had happened? Why do you think that happened? Did they fall out with your mother or the rest of the family? Something happened, didn't it, to change your brothers' minds?'

Charlotte played dumb and insisted that she knew nothing about any murder.

Despite not revealing anything about the murder during her twelve hours of questioning, detectives were sure that she was lying. They were convinced that she was probably the main instigator of the murder. The guards felt that they would have a difficult job in getting her to come clean, however, and had to release her without charge – for the moment. When Charlie walked out of Mountjoy Garda Station she was nearly two months pregnant.

✂✂✂

On 3 August forty-nine-year-old Kathleen Mulhall was staying at Ardfert House on Nelson Street in Dublin 7. At 10.15 a.m. she was arrested at Summerhill Parade by Detective Sergeant Gerry McDonnell, along with Detective Gardaí Terence McHugh, Pat Keegan and Garda Sheelagh Sheehan.

She had been waiting outside the post office to collect her social welfare payment. She told the gardaí that there was no need to arrest her because she was on the way up to see them at the station anyway and she wasn't going anywhere. She was taken to Mountjoy Garda Station for questioning. Detective Superintendent John Fitzpatrick of the National Bureau of Criminal Investigation gave permission for her to be photographed and finger and palm printed. Officers also took samples of her blood and hair.

The four officers who had arrested Kathleen, along with Garda Sean Earley, interviewed her on six occasions during the twelve hours that she was held in custody. She contacted her solicitor, Daragh Robinson from Garret Sheehan's office, and spoke to him by phone and in person during the course of the day.

When gardaí asked if she was involved in her partner's murder, she completely denied having any hand in Farah's death, saying: 'That my kids may die I did not hurt a hair on his head.' She added, 'Do you think if I did anything I would still be in the country? Why would I stay here? I have a passport. I could have left.'

When asked if she was upset that he was dead she replied: 'Yes. I was waiting for him to come back to me. Three years of my life I gave to him.' She said to the gardaí: 'I can't understand that you'd think I'd hurt him. Farah was harmed enough times and what did anyone do? Irish lads beat him and they [the gardaí] did nothing. He has enemies: his so-called friends who gave him drugs.'

Kathleen said that Farah was often violent towards her but she never contacted the police. She thought that he would be capable of murdering somebody and had made her life hell at times while they were together. She denied that she murdered him for revenge and said he didn't deserve to die 'with no head and his body cut up'.

She stated that she had no idea how he ended up mutilated in the canal and insisted: 'I didn't do nothing; I don't know how he ended up there. I never murdered Farah; no one touched Farah, no one in my family. You're looking in the wrong place.'

Kathleen claimed that she was seeing somebody else and didn't even know that Farah was dead until the guards told her on the day of her arrest. She said their relationship was over when he died and she saw him 'like a friend, a companion'. Kathleen claimed that Noor was staying with her for two nights a week over the two months before he died but she didn't know where he was when he wasn't at Richmond Cottages. She spoke with gardaí about Noor's history of cruelty to women but she totally denied that he had ever raped her, saying: 'He did get sex. He never forced me. He never raped me.'

She said that Noor was a heavy drinker who used to polish off two large bottles of vodka a day, and always went out drinking, even though Kathleen always pleaded with him to stay in. He would fall into deep comas when he drank heavily and wouldn't be able to defend himself if anybody attacked him. The mother-of-six also alleged that Farah took drugs but did not sell them.

On the day of the murder Kathleen said that she was drinking with Noor and her two daughters. She said the four had been drinking heavily for the whole day and had also taken drugs, including ecstasy tablets. She said the two girls went home and that she and Farah parted at an off-licence on O'Connell Street that evening: 'He went his way and I went my way.' Her way was in the direction of Baggot

Street, where she spent the evening working as a prostitute.

She claimed: 'Farah went to see his other girlfriend, the Chink. He went to see the Chink; I was drinking, drinking vodka. I can't remember. I was on the street that night, with a man that night. I was with a man, someone I went off with.'

Kathleen couldn't remember who the client was, if he was Irish, where she stayed or what time she got home the following morning. She did say she hailed a taxi on the side of the road and arrived back very early but she couldn't guess at what time. The guards asked her what she thought could have happened to Noor but she didn't have any ideas, although she said, 'He was so drunk with drugs and that when he was with Charlotte and Linda that he could fall asleep.'

The two of them often attended house parties with Noor's friends throughout the city and she said it was possible that he'd gone off to one of these. He had a key to the flat and came and went as he pleased, as did she. They had the kind of relationship where they both came and went without telling each other.

During the interview she complained about having breathing problems and Dr Y M Fakih who practices at Whitehall was called to the station. Dr Fakih was the man who had pronounced Farah Swaleh Noor dead on the evening his body parts were pulled from the canal. Kathleen told him that she was suffering from asthma. She said she'd had chronic obstructive airways disease for several years and was using two inhalers. She told him she had lost one of them on the way to the Garda Station and had left the other one in her flat. She didn't have any regular GP and couldn't remember the name of the chemist where she got her inhalers. She did not have any specific medical complaint for the doctor and put simply, there was nothing wrong with her at all. Dr Fakih advised the gardaí to go to her flat and get her spare inhaler in case she needed it during questioning. They did this and resumed interviewing her.

After seeing the doctor the questioning continued and Kathleen admitted to buying bleach and bin bags in the Gala store the day after the killing. She said that the bleach was for cleaning a pair of white cords that Charlotte had given her. She said she spilled a glass of cranberry juice on them and used the bleach to try to clean them. She also agreed that she had bought black bin bags and aerosols for the flat after Noor was murdered, but said, 'Everybody buys bin bags.'

Despite the fact that they had lived together for over three years and that countless witnesses had remembered seeing Farah Swaleh Noor in his Ireland jersey, Kathleen said she never saw him in the soccer top: 'I didn't recognise the top he was wearing. I never washed the top. I wasn't interested in what Farah was wearing.'

Kathleen couldn't explain how blood splatters were under the bunk beds in her flat and on the bedroom floor and wardrobe. She commented: 'I don't know; I'm not going to tell you bullshit.' She was surprised when she was told that blood found in her flat matched Farah's and said that if he was murdered at Richmond Cottages, 'it must have happened when I wasn't there'.

She took a photograph of Farah in her hand and shouted: 'I did nothing to that man. That man knows I didn't kill him. I never hurt a hair on that man's head.'

Kathleen was shown Farah's mobile phone but did not

recognise it and said she never saw him with it. She didn't know anything about how one of her daughters had given it to her husband, who had then sold it on to a work colleague.

During the interview DS Gerry McDonnell asked Kathleen if he could examine her mobile phone and she agreed. He noticed that she had a missed call at 1.11 p.m. that day, from a number saved on her mobile as J. It was the same number as the mobile that had been used by her son John to contact gardaí from Wheatfield to tell them about Farah Noor's murder. She initially said that the number belonged to a close friend but eventually, reluctantly, admitted it was her son's number and said he used a phone from jail.

Detectives played the 999 call and Kathleen first denied it was her son's voice. Then she said her two boys were telling lies: 'I never told my sons anything. My sons know nothing about me. When I do see my sons I will tell them that my boyfriend Farah is dead, something I only found out today.'

Detectives said that the two Mulhalls had informed on their family because they were 'genuinely horrified at what happened'.

'Not as horrified as I am,' she replied, before adding, 'My sons told you nothing. They would tell you nothing because they don't know anything.' The only reason she could give as to why they would wrongly ring the guards with such an extraordinary story was that her sons must have been looking for a reward. As Kathleen had made no admissions while in custody, she was released without charge at 10.10 p.m., twelve hours after being arrested. She commented, 'All I could do was wish to God that I could help you. I can't help you.'

✂✂✂

John Mulhall was fitting windows in Terenure College, when a car pulled up alongside him at about 10.55 a.m. Detective Inspector Christy Mangan got out of the unmarked garda car and told John Mulhall that the guards wanted to question him about the murder of Farah Swaleh Noor. Detective Gardaí Adrian Murray and Dave O'Brien were also present, as was Garda Ronan Hartnett. Det Gda Dave O'Brien arrested him and drove him back to Store Street Garda Station. He was processed and searched at 11.12 a.m., before being placed in a cell. He was taken to an interview room at 12.10 p.m. He was interviewed three times while in custody. He also declined to have a solicitor present.

When he was questioned, John Mulhall offered no information to the gardaí. He said that he had not had contact with his wife since she had walked out on him in 2002 to go and live with Farah Swaleh Noor. He did not know Noor and had no dealings with him. He said he did not feel anything for him either way, although it was sad that anybody would die in such a brutal fashion. The fifty-three-year-old denied ever threatening the African and blamed his wife for the break-up of their marriage, not Farah.

John Mulhall said he did not know what the detectives were talking about when they told him about his sons coming forward to claim that he had removed items from the house where Farah was murdered. He said he was never in Kathleen's flat and that John Junior and James were mistaken.

When gardaí pointed out that a white Berlingo van, with the registration number 97 D 11647, had been filmed near Richmond Cottages on 21 March, he confirmed that he drove a van with that registration number. He said, however, that the van belonged to City Glass, the company he worked for, and a few other people had access to it. Over the next few days, investigators went to City Glass to get statements from all John Mulhall's work colleagues to eliminate them as being the driver of the van that morning. It was subsequently determined that nobody else had been driving the vehicle that day.

John Mulhall did admit to detectives that he had sold a work colleague a Sagem mobile phone that turned out to belong to Farah Swaleh Noor. He said that either Charlie or Linda had given it to him. He had no idea that it had belonged to the dead man or how one of his daughters came to be in possession of it.

Of the four Mulhalls detained, gardaí had nothing on John and this didn't change after his arrest. Where Linda, Charlotte and Kathleen came across as being very hard during their initial interviews, John Mulhall struck the guards as being different. He had not come to their attention over the years and seemed genuinely shocked that he was being caught up in a murder investigation. His two brothers had come to Store Street Garda Station looking for him and John Mulhall was released without charge, just after 9 p.m.

Life for the Mulhall family started to disintegrate following the arrests. Kathleen effectively disappeared and cut off all ties with her daughters and did not contact them at all. Charlotte continued to work as a prostitute, even though she was pregnant and spent weeks at a time away from home. Linda went off the rails and started drinking heavily and using heroin, while John struggled with the burden of holding everything together.

After the four Mulhalls were released, gardaí met at a

late-night conference to review the progress of the investigation. None of the prisoners had made any admissions while in custody and the gardaí were not in a position to prepare any files for the Director of Public Prosecutions. Nevertheless they had gained some valuable information that could be investigated further. They had also developed new insights into the demeanour of the family while they were being held. The detectives working the body in the canal case were all experienced investigators and, after reviewing the records of the interviews, agreed that Linda Mulhall was a potential weak link. She had gotten very emotional when they had mentioned the discovery of the body under Ballybough Bridge and she was clearly not being forthcoming with the truth. Kathleen and Charlotte were both cold fishes, who would lie through their teeth and probably believe they were telling you the truth. John Mulhall seemed like a decent man and it was also decided that they should keep on top of him, in the hope that he would crack.

All the investigators were aware that something significant would have to happen if they were to break this case quickly.

In the meantime the detectives continued to work any leads they had. Det Sgt Gerry McDonnell had been assigned to liaise with the African authorities and members of Farah's family after he was identified through the DNA of his Irish son. The guards wanted to find out as much as possible about Noor and his background. Det Sgt McDonnell discovered that Noor had made an Irish asylum application in 1997. Through further investigation he also learned that Farah's wife, who according to the application had supposedly been executed during the civil war, was in fact alive and well, living in Mombasa in Kenya. Farah's three children, who he had claimed were missing, were also in good health – they were being cared for by their 'dead' mother.

On 12 September 2005 Det Sgt McDonnell spoke to Farah's former wife, Husna Mohamed Said. Husna logged onto the garda website and identified Farah Swaleh Noor's photograph as being that of her husband Sheilila Said Salim. She faxed the detective a copy of her late husband's birth certificate. The Kenyan birth cert showed that Salim was born on 7 July 1965 in the Lamh District in the Coast Province. His mother was listed as Somoe Abubakar and his father's name was Seyyid Salim. Farah Noor was not Somalian at all, as he had claimed to everybody he'd met in Ireland over the last eight years.

Farah had kept in constant touch with his 'dead' wife Husna since his arrival in Ireland in 1997 and they spoke regularly. Husna faxed the detective a letter that her husband had sent her on 6 November 1999. It had an address in the south of the city and was written in Bajun. Farah signed the letter as Sheilila S Salim and in it told his wife about his new partner and even sent her pictures of his Irish son. Husna was not bitter about this and was on good terms with Farah.

It was apparent to Det Sgt Gerry McDonnell that Farah Swaleh Noor and Sheilila Said Salim were in fact the same person. Farah Swaleh Noor was an assumed name Salim had used to get into Ireland under false pretences.

His wife would also later fax gardaí a copy of another letter Farah had sent to her, signed with his real name and dated 26 July 1995. He noted his address as 43 Eversleigh Road, East Ham, London E06 1HG. The letter begins in

Linda and Charlotte Mulhall on their way into the Central Criminal Court in Dublin.
© *Courtpix*

Farah Swaleh Noor on holiday with friends, in happier times.

The front of Flat 1, 17 Richmond Cottages, where Farah Swaleh Noor was murdered.
© *Sunday Tribune*

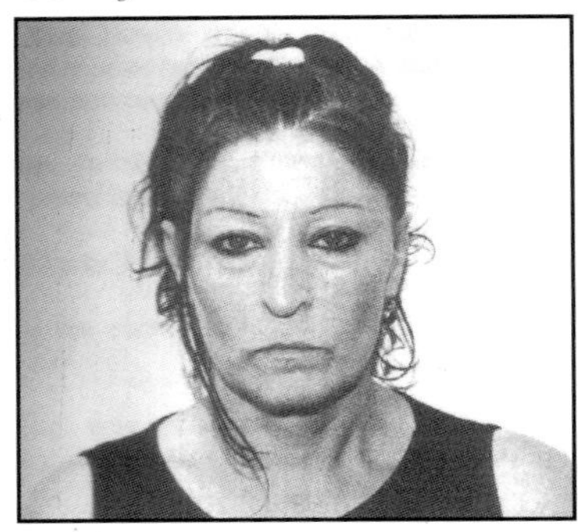

Kathleen Mulhall.

Charlotte Mulhall, captured on CCTV camera on her way to dump Farah Noor's body in the Royal Canal, at Ballybough Bridge.

Linda Mulhall, filmed with Farah Noor's remains in her backpack.

A CCTV image of the Royal Canal on the morning after the murder, 21 March 2005.

A team of detectives look on as Farah Noor's remains are recovered in eight pieces from the Royal Canal, Dublin.

Gardaí search for evidence on the banks of the Royal Canal, at Ballybough Bridge.
© Kyran O'Brien/Evening Herald

A garda patrols the crime scene at Ballybough Bridge.
© Gerry Mooney/Evening Herald

Gardaí spent hours searching the grass beside the canal, looking for evidence.
© Kyran O'Brien/Evening Herald

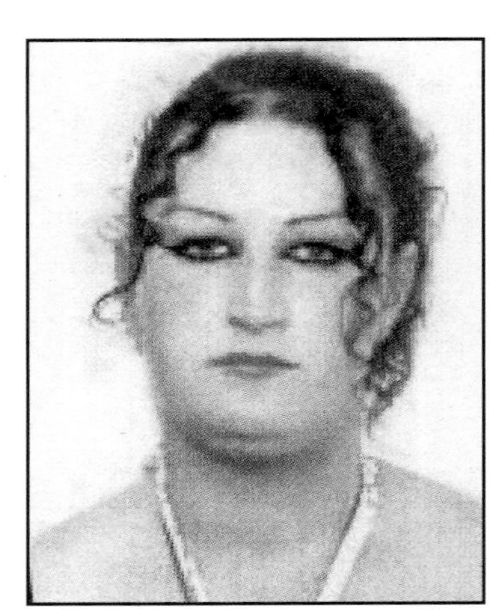

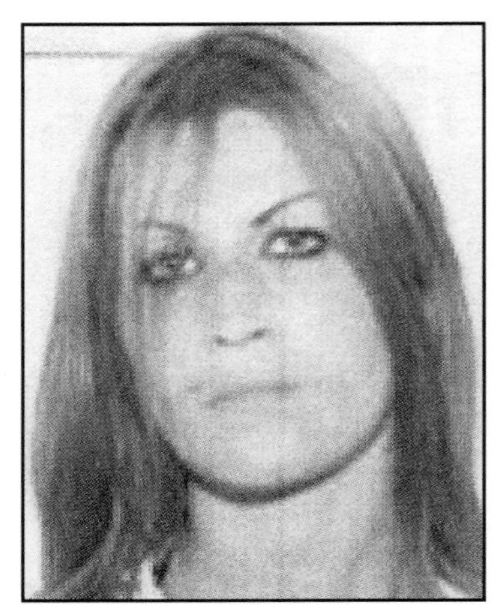

CCTV images of Charlotte (top) and Linda Mulhall, which were examined against their garda mug shots.

The Crimestoppers poster that led Ali Abubakaar to come forward and suggest that Farah Noor was the man whose remains had been found in the Royal Canal.

Superintendent John Leahy and Detective Inspector Christy Mangan (now Detective Superintendent) appeal for the public's help in identifiying clothing found with the remains in the Royal Canal.
© David Conachy/Indpendent Newspapers

The photograph of Farah Noor released by gardaí after he was identified.

Farah's remains are lowered to their final resting place in Glasnevin Cemetery.

English before changing to Bajun. It reads: 'To the one I love Husna Mohamed Said. I want to tell you that me I'm well but I miss you for long time you and my babies. How are you, me I am fine.'

It is thought that Noor may have lived in London for a number of years prior to arriving in Ireland and had a job as a butcher, but this theory has never been verified.

It later emerged that Noor also maintained regular contact with his family and phoned his mother almost every week. He also sent home money to his wife and, although he did as he pleased in Ireland, he made sure his children had food at home. His family relied on the small sums that he sent to them.

Det Sgt McDonnell contacted Interpol and asked them to run the names Farah Swaleh Noor and Sheilia Said Salim through their immigration records. They came back negative for both names. Interpol's Dublin office then contacted their counterparts in London to see if Noor or Salim had any previous convictions. They subsequently received an email with the following message: 'Please be advised that checks on Farah Swaleh Noor on our criminal, intelligence and immigration databases has also been negative. Lastly, all of the above subjects have been circulated to the PSNI for checks. These checks have also returned negative results.'

Despite these findings, which make it unclear if Farah had ever actually lived in London, it was obvious to Det Sgt McDonnell and the entire investigation team that Farah Swaleh Noor was not what he seemed. It was clear that the history of the victim deserved closer scrutiny.

The True Life of Farah Noor

The plane from Rome touched down at Dublin Airport on a bitterly cold morning on 30 December 1996. As the passengers disembarked, many looking forward to spending New Year's Eve back in Ireland with their friends and family, one passenger faced an uncertain future. Sheilila Said Salim had turned thirty-one that year and had left his wife and three children back in Kenya to set himself up with a new life in Ireland, the land of the céad míle fáilte, a hundred-thousand welcomes. Sheilila had heard about the laxity of Ireland's immigration laws. He was confident that if he could get into the country there would be little that the authorities could do to get him out again. The Irish economy had turned itself around from the terrible brain drain of the early 1990s when our great and good had to emigrate to Britain and America to find work. The country was beginning to prosper and the Celtic Tiger was in its infancy, a phenomenon that would soon bring previously-unthought-of prosperity to Ireland's five million residents.

Sheilila Said Salim later claimed that he had paid $1,600 to a man who specialised in illegally transporting people into Europe. The man arranged for Salim to get on a flight from Mombasa in Kenya to Rome and on to Ireland. Salim had decided to change his name and hide his past once he got to Dublin. He presented himself to customs officials as Farah Swaleh Noor. He said he was a Somalian national, born on 2 July 1967. He told detectives from the Garda National Immigration Bureau (GNIB) that he had arrived from war-torn Somalia and was seeking political asylum. He carried no passport and few personal belongings and GNIB staff – who were well used to such claims by wannabe refugees – routinely processed Salim. He would have been interviewed and asked where he had come from and how he had managed to get into Ireland. GNIB staff would then have photographed and fingerprinted him. It was then arranged for him to be housed in temporary accommodation until a Department of Justice official could interview him. It was noted that Salim was approximately 5 ft 6" in height, of a thin, lean build with dark hair and black skin. Staff noticed a scar on his right wrist and on the back of his head.

Although Salim had decided to be dishonest with the authorities in Dublin Airport to try to get asylum in Ireland, his family back home in Mombasa missed him and wondered if they would ever see him again. As Det Sgt Gerry McDonnell later discovered, Salim had actually been born in Kenya in 1965, but as Farah he claimed he was almost two years younger. His father, Seyyid Salim, was a Somalian who was born in the mid-1940s. He had died in Mogadishu when Sheilila was a young man. His mother, known as Somoe Bakari Shigoo, a fifty-two-year-old Kenyan native, was still alive and living in Mombasa. Salim had one brother, Mohemedi Abuu, who was three years older than him and had emigrated to Toronto, Canada, in 1991. The young Salim had set up a life for himself in Kenya, marrying his wife Husna Mohamed Said, when she turned eighteen. They had three children together: Somoe, a girl, was born in 1989, Mohamed, his only son, came along the next year and Zuleh, the couple's second daughter, was born in January 1991. Sheilila Said Salim did not have many friends in Kenya but was close to a cousin, Lulu Swaleh. As the years passed, Salim believed that there was no future for him in Kenya. He wanted to live in Europe. He told Husna that he would go to Europe and establish himself there, before flying his whole family over to start a new life. Secretly, however, Farah Noor as he later became, had no intention of ever seeing his wife and children again. He'd heard stories that some countries in Europe were soft touches when it came to refugees. If you turned up at a border and told a convincing sob story they would welcome you with open arms, give you free houses and cash in your pocket. You didn't have to work and you could spend the days partying and hunting down women. This sounded like a sweet deal to Salim. He saved hard to come up with the $1,600 needed to smuggle him out of Africa and into a life of new and exciting opportunities.

When Salim arrived in Dublin seeking asylum, and while he was waiting to be assessed and processed by the Refugee Asylum Commission, he was sent to Tathony House in Dublin 8. At the time it was designated accommodation for asylum seekers. He spent a couple of nights there, before being transferred to the Brewery Hostel at 22-23 Thomas Street.

On 14 January 1997, Salim made his way into the Asylum Section of the Immigration and Citizenship Division of the Department of Justice at St Stephen's Green to complete his application for refugee status. He filled out his name on the official form as Farah Swaleh Noor, born 2 July 1967, in Mogadishu, Somalia. He gave his nationality as Somalian, wrote that he was widowed and that his religion was Muslim. He claimed to be from the Bajun tribe and said that he spoke 'Bajun, English, a little Arabic and Italian'. He gave his address in Somalia as PO Box 25, Shagari, Mogadishu, and he did not have any documents to prove his nationality. He claimed he had married his wife 'Hajila' in 1988 but that she was now dead. He gave the true details about his three children but he noted that he did not know where his children were now. He gave real names and addresses for his parents and said that his father was a businessman in Mogadishu, running a shop, and that his mother was a housewife.

Under the Education section of the application form he claimed that he had been privately educated between 1974 and 1978 but that he had gained no qualifications. He stated that he had worked as an assistant in his father's shop for five years, until 1982, when he moved to live with his grandfather. He then got a job in the Italian Fisheries Department as a fisherman from 1982 until he left when the war started in 1991. When asked to explain why he had no identification or passport he wrote: 'I had no time to get these documents before I had to flee from Somalia.' He said he had left Somalia in May 1991 and travelled to Kenya. He claimed he had lived there until late 1996, in a refugee camp, until he gathered enough money to get him to Ireland. He told them he got a flight from Nairobi to Rome, where he then boarded a two-hour connecting flight to Dublin. It is likely that he didn't stay in Rome because Italian immigration laws were far tighter and their system does not simply hand out free money to asylum seekers.

Farah saw Ireland as a far nicer proposition. The only other possibility is that in reality Farah flew to Rome from London where he may have been living before he arrived in Ireland, seeking asylum.

Refugees are supposed to claim asylum in the first country they reach after fleeing their native land, usually because it is in the grip of civil war. Authorities around the world frown on people cherry-picking where they run to and asylum seekers must have a good reason to explain why they didn't seek refuge in the first country they escaped to, in Farah's case Kenya. His reason was: 'Kenya is not a good country for a refugee. No food in camp. Giriyama tribe people do not like Somali people. Kenyan police do not like Somali people. Police steal from Somali people.' On the application form he described his life in Kenya from 1991 to 1996, saying he: 'Stayed in a refugee camp called the Wayoni camp in the Magongo region of Kenya. There was Bajun refugees mainly staying at this camp. Bad conditions, no water, nowhere to sleep.'

Farah claimed to have registered with the United Nations High Commissioner for Refugees (UNHCR) in Kenya when he was staying at the refugee camp. He denied that he had ever been in police custody or was a member of a political organisation or a trade union. Noor stated that he had a brother living in Toronto but that he wanted to stay in Ireland.

The final section of the Asylum Application Form enables those wanting to seek refuge in a country to give the reasons why this request should be granted. The following are Farah's own words as they appear on his application:

'My name is Farah Swaleh Noor. I was born in Somalia on 2-7-1967 in Mogadishu. My father and my mother they all Somali. I have one brother; I'm second born in my family. I used to be a fisherman in Kismayo. I was work with Fisheries Department. I start work from 1982-1990. From 1982-1990 there was no problem but from 1990 the war start to spread. So the war was worst, more than worst then I decided to go back to Mogadishu and see my family. When I reach Mogadishu I went to my family house. The door was open, when go inside nobody was in. The only thing I saw was the dead body of my wife, she was having a bullet in her chest. Then I start panic and I was afraid then I didn't know what to do because the war was spread all over the country. Then I decided to take some few stuff. I start to walk towards Port Mogadishu when I arrive there I got a small boat to go back to Kismayo. When I reached Kismayo I saw a lot of people which they were leaving the country with a big boat. I rush there and I ask where's the boat going. One of them tell me is going to Kenya. We spend three days to Mombasa, Kenya. We registered with UNHCR then they take us to the camp. I stay in the camp for five years. We face many problems at the camp. There were no doctors, no food, no water and overcrowding. There were many refugees from my country and also there were Kenyan people. They don't like Somalia people to be in their country. Sometimes to come to camp night time and start to attack us and sometimes kill some refugees so I was afraid with that, also I was lucky to find agent. Then the agent ask me if I have 2000 US Dollars he can arrange me a trip to go abroad, then I told him I don't have that amount but I have 1600 US dollars. Then the agent agree with me. I was very happy to leave the camp it was a terrible life at the camp. Before the war I was having a good life but the war affect me very much. It may be you refuse my application, I don't know what to do because the war destroy my house and I don't know where's my family are they live or dead. No government to protect me. Even if is reach 20 yrs Somalia it will be never like before. The war affect my country as well. No hospital, no houses, no water, no animal, no light, no road and no food. So I will be very happy if you allow me to stay in this country.'

On June 2, 1998, Noor was interviewed, through an interpreter, by an officer from the Department of Justice. He said he had no information about the whereabouts of his wife and children because all his friends had fled Mogadishu as a result of the political situation there. He stressed that he had not wanted to leave Somalia but he'd had no choice. He said he then fled to Europe from Kenya because of the tough conditions at the refugee camp – when he got the chance to leave he took it.

Noor was interviewed again on 17 September 1998 and claimed that scars on his wrist and head were inflicted by a group of bandits or soldiers from one of the defeated tribes during the war in Somalia.

In early December Farah Swaleh Noor's application for refugee status in Ireland was rejected. He was informed of the decision on 2 February 1999, over two years after his application was submitted. Nine days later he appealed the decision and that appeal was heard on 3 June 1999. The Appeals Authority recommended that his appeal be granted and he was officially given refugee status in Ireland on 30 July 1999. This meant that he was now legally entitled to be in the country and could claim social welfare payments, under his assumed name. Friends of Noor say that he was proud to be legally living in Ireland. They said that he was happy in the country and, for the most part, that he got on with people. He owned several Ireland soccer jerseys and was a big supporter of the national team. On 21 August 2003 Noor made an application for Irish citizenship and this was still being considered when he was murdered.

While Farah Noor's application for refugee status had been going through the slow and bureaucratic system, he lived in quite a few flats around the city, including one in 47 North Strand Road in Dublin. He spent most of 1997 there and the owner, Leah Morahan, remembers Noor as being 'very friendly and charming'. He never caused trouble or problems for her 'except for late night partying or dope smoking'. He also had a flat at 573 North Circular Road in Dublin 7 and spent quite a bit of time housed in the Rosepark Hotel on Baker's Corner in Dun Laoghaire in South Dublin.

Farah Noor spent most of his days in Ireland drinking. He was a serious alcoholic who would get through three or four large bottles of vodka a day without any problems. He was a friendly man when sober and was well known around various pubs in Dublin city centre and Dun Laoghaire. Alcohol wasn't his sole vice though. Noor was an occasional user of a variety of hard and soft drugs including grass, hash, cocaine, ecstasy and possibly even heroin. As well as the names Farah Swaleh Noor and Sheilila Said Salim, he also occasionally went by a third alias, Shilelagh Swaleh Shagoo.

Noor loosely socialised with the Somalian community in both Dublin and Cork. He would turn up in a pub and go in every day for months on end, before disappearing and not being seen or heard from for a year or more. He was the same with his friends. They would see him occasionally and then he would up and leave without a word to anybody.

He spent a lot of time drinking with friends around the Blessington Street area and would spend every second night or so there, drinking with other men who'd come to Ireland from Somalia. His Somalian friends didn't know that in reality Farah was from Kenya and was using an assumed name.

Noor's friends knew him by quite a few nicknames including Sheilila, America and Abawa. Farah was a massive football fan and religiously followed the English Premiership. He was a big Manchester United fan and had three or four Man United jerseys and two tracksuits, as well as other clothes bearing the emblem. He even wore a Man United sovereign ring.

In August 1997 Farah met a Chinese girl in Dr Quirkey's amusement arcade on O'Connell Street. 'Lynn' was just sixteen and was mentally disabled. She was playing pool with a friend when Farah went up to her and asked her to be his girlfriend. He told her that he wanted her babies. He had never seen or spoken to her before and Lynn refused. She did agree to go back to his flat, however, and when they arrived Noor sat beside her on the couch and then forced her to have sex with him. It was the only time that the pair had sexual intercourse. Lynn found out she was pregnant one month later and when she told Farah he said he wasn't interested. He wanted nothing to do with her or the baby. She rarely saw Noor after that and he didn't try to meet his son 'John' until he had drunkenly called to Lynn's city-centre flat out of the blue, on St Patrick's Day.

Lynn later told gardaí: 'Farah was not violent to me. We had a nice relationship. I was with him for nine months and I only had sex with Farah once. Farah lived by himself in the flat down the road. When John was born Farah never saw him. I think he was six years old when Farah first saw him. Farah called to the house here to see him. I don't know if John saw Farah on 20 March 2005. He didn't tell me that he saw him. John would know what Farah looks like and he knows that Farah is his dad. When I first met Farah we used to play pool together. Sometimes Farah would phone me to meet with him. I didn't have a phone number for him. He would phone me 'cos he had my number. The last time I saw him before March 2005 was last year. I was walking near Jury's on Parnell Street when I heard someone call me and when I looked I see Farah. He stopped but he told me he goes to work. He told me he stayed in a hotel and that's where he lived. He didn't tell me the name of the hotel.'

Although this statement doesn't portray Noor as nasty or violent, Lynn would later give a far different version of events during Linda and Charlotte's court case, claiming that he was a brute.

Noor's life changed in April 1998 when he met and fell in love with 'Paula', who was out celebrating her sixteenth birthday. She was in third-year in secondary school and the courts have since asked that Paula's real identity should not be revealed. Paula was walking through town with her friends when Noor approached her and started talking to her. He told her he was twenty, even though he had told the authorities he was born in 1967 and was supposedly thirty-one. They started going out and she became pregnant less than three months later.

Paula gave birth to their son in March 1999. They were very happy at first. Farah was a devoted dad who spent a lot of time with his son and loved and cared for his partner. He stopped calling round to most of his Somalian friends and was very close to Paula's family. He used to go fishing and hiking with her father and moved into her family home in South Dublin.

When the baby was about three months old, however, Noor began to drink a lot and his behaviour and attitude changed. He would often disappear for days on drunken benders and he started hitting his girlfriend. Paula would later describe to detectives how Noor was a 'lovely man' at first but changed when he started drinking.

Noor and Paula were given accommodation by the council and over the next three years moved into three different houses in the same area as Paula's family. Farah put his ex-girlfriend through years of hell. She spoke to gardaí on a number of occasions and shocked officers with her harrowing accounts of life with the alcoholic Kenyan. She told detectives how she had feared that it was only a matter of time before Noor murdered her.

The first time he hit her was during a night out with one of her friends. He accused the woman of being a lesbian who wanted to sleep with Paula. His girlfriend stood in shock as Noor abused her pal in graphic sexual terms. Paula was so afraid of him that she didn't go home that night. The following day she turned her key in the door and Noor attacked her, giving her a vicious beating. She did not go to hospital and subsequently returned to Farah because she was young and naïve. When he said he'd never do it again the seventeen-year-old believed him.

Farah regularly beat her black and blue after that, for no other reason than that he was drunk. He would pull her hair and punch her on the head so he did not leave marks. She was forced to call the guards three or four times because of his violence towards her and others. Paula made a number of complaints to Tallaght Garda

Station about her boyfriend but still did not have the courage to leave him.

Noor used to burn himself with cigarettes and threatened to do the same to his girlfriend. The violence against her started to occur every single day and he eventually started to rape her. Paula later stated he had had 'very brutal sex anytime and anywhere he wanted it and wouldn't take no for an answer'. Eventually rape and domestic violence became an everyday experience, living with Farah Swaleh Noor. Paula, who was only a young girl, thought at the time that this animalistic behaviour was normal. Nevertheless she left him on two occasions but Noor came and begged her to get back with him, promising that he would change and be a better father. She gave him the benefit of the doubt and went back to him but the beatings always continued.

He didn't just take out his aggression on Paula but regularly became involved in fistfights for no reason at all. She said he was 'someone who'd get into a row at the drop of a hat'. Paula also spoke to gardaí about Noor's obsession with knives. He pulled one from his pocket one day and threatened, 'he'd cut me up like a chicken'. Noor said he had once been a butcher in England and always carried a Swiss Army knife and a large dagger. Paula was very worried about the dangerous knives he carried around. She stole a few from him and destroyed them so he could cause no harm with them.

Noor spent each day drinking several large bottles of vodka and often accused Paula of cheating on him, even though he wouldn't let her out of the house and monitored her phone calls and text messages. When he was extremely drunk he would stumble to the front hall of their South Dublin council house and have two-way conversations with himself in the mirror. He wouldn't speak in English and pretended to be two different characters, talking to himself for minutes at a time. On good nights he'd then fall into bed and sleep the booze off, but more often than not he'd destroy the front room of the house, overturning tables and chairs and breaking ornaments. When the demons were present he'd beat Paula, rape her in the front room and tie her up while his son slept, oblivious in an upstairs bedroom. He'd then get his camera out and force her to lie in degrading sexual positions while he photographed her, laughing demonically.

A woman called 'Avril' moved into the same house as Noor and Paula in early 2001 and later described him as being an 'unstable' control freak. Avril is a fake name used to protect her identity. The twenty-five-year-old only lived with the couple and their twenty-two-month-old son for three weeks but saw enough during that time to convince her that the Kenyan was an aggressive brute who had a 'serious drink problem'. Paula showed Avril the negatives of pornographic photographs that he had taken of her naked, where she was bound up and blindfolded in sick sexual positions. Paula was forced into posing for these photos and beaten if she refused. Noor caught her trying to destroy them one day and went ballistic. He badly thrashed her in front of their young son.

Avril saw Noor bully Paula, both physically and emotionally, and found the eighteen-year-old 'very vulnerable and naïve'. She said she was 'directly under the control of Noor at all times. She couldn't do anything without his permission and he was constantly checking on her.'

On 11 May 2000 Farah had decided that he needed a job to earn some extra cash and registered with Adecco

Recruitment Agency in Tallaght. He supplied them with copies of his identification card, issued by the Garda National Immigration Bureau, to prove that he was legally allowed to work in Ireland. He got a job five days later with Sydney Cooper on the Ballymount Road, Dublin 22. Farah worked there for just two weeks because the job was only temporary. On 13 June he got another job with DFDS Transport Ltd at Toughers Business Park, Nass, and spent about seven weeks in employment there. Adecco transferred his pay cheque directly into Paula's bank account in the Irish Permanent, as he continued to work for the agency over the next few months.

While Noor was out working during the day, Paula used to break down and complain to Avril about her life with him. She wasn't allowed leave the house to see anyone and she couldn't even pop to the local shop without asking first. Avril witnessed Noor's violence towards his girlfriend on several occasions and later said in her statement: 'He would beat her by slapping her across the face and knocking her to the ground. She would curl up on the ground to protect herself and he would kick her. He would even do this when she was holding the baby. He had no scruples whatsoever and when he was drunk he would do this in front of anyone, both in public and back at the house. The main motivation for this was jealousy and possessiveness on Noor's behalf. There was never any reason for him to be this way but he would never believe her. It was like he was looking for an excuse to beat her.'

Avril witnessed Noor go through Paula's phone to see who she had been texting. She regularly heard stories about the daily rapes that her friend suffered at the hands of the monster who was supposed to be her partner and who was the father of their son.

Just a few weeks after Avril moved in with the couple, Noor also started to become abusive towards her. He believed that Avril was trying to convince Paula to leave him. She began to fear for her own safety and left at the first available opportunity, asking Paula to go with her, but the eighteen-year-old refused.

Avril remained in almost daily contact with her friend and a couple of weeks after she fled the house she received a call from the young mum, begging her for help. She went to the house with a male friend just after midnight and encountered a drunken Noor who had wrecked the place in a fit of anger. Paula was on her hands and knees, cleaning broken mirrors and glasses on the living room floor. The Kenyan didn't even think about helping her and cursed, demanding more drink. Noor eventually calmed down and started laughing and joking as if nothing had happened. He eventually collapsed asleep on the bed. Avril and her friend tried to convince Paula to leave with them but she was too scared. The teenager was also worried that she had nowhere to go and that Noor would follow her.

Avril rang her friend's parents the next morning and warned them that their daughter would be killed if she didn't get away from the domineering African. Paula's dad went to the house that day and collected his daughter.

Paula had eventually got the courage to leave Farah Noor for good this time. While she was recovering with her parents, she took a barring order out against Farah in the courts. She won full custody of their son in April 2001. 'He abused me so I just got up and left him,' she said.

Farah Swaleh Noor, however, was not a man who was put off easily. The fact that Paula had walked out and wanted to build a life without him only made him angrier. He was determined that he would get her back. From the end of February 2001, and for the next nine months, Noor stalked Paula. He made abusive phone calls in the early hours of the morning, turned up outside her parents' house and threatened to kill her. He followed her when she went outside and also phoned Avril, warning her that he would kill her for taking his child away from him. Farah used to take pleasure in following the two women into town on the bus. He would sit there grinning maniacally at them, making them both feel uncomfortable and in fear for their safety. He was very aggressive and threatened both women, saying he would murder them. The pair had met and began dating two South African men in the meantime and this made Noor even more jealous. He bombarded both women with telephone calls, leaving them with little option but to change their numbers.

One night in May 2001 the two friends were drinking in a Southside pub when Noor arrived in a drunken state just five minutes after they'd walked in the door. He bought himself a drink and sat down beside them uninvited.

Farah started shouting and abusing the women. He told Avril that she had ruined his family and lost his temper completely when she tried to ring her boyfriend for help, pushing his face into hers and screaming loudly so the whole pub could hear him. He then picked up the glasses on the table and started smashing them on the floor. The girls got up and ran away but he followed them, saying he would kill them both.

By chance, Avril's father happened to be meeting a client in the same pub and witnessed what was going on. He went over and called Noor to one side. He warned him to behave himself and leave his daughter alone or there would be trouble. The drunken African apologised profusely and left.

He didn't end his sick campaign of intimidation, however, and a couple of months later he followed Paula into Dame Street where she was meeting Avril and a male friend from South Africa. The South African had heard all about Noor's unacceptable behaviour. He confronted him in the middle of the street and ended up punching the Kenyan. A brawl ensued, with Noor taking a bad beating until the gardaí arrived. They arrested both men for public order offences.

Avril moved away in October 2001 and the harassment stopped, but Paula was still regularly stalked by the violent alcoholic. Although Farah was officially out of Paula's life he still had parental access to her son. She became very concerned that her boy might be getting abused while on these unsupervised visits, which took place every second Sunday. The youngster came home from one two-hour visit with what his mother thought were cigarette burns on his body. The round burns were causing her son serious discomfort but Noor couldn't explain them. He said he didn't know what had happened. The Kenyan had a history of self-harm and often burned himself with cigarettes to 'relieve the pain and the stress'. If he was having problems at work, in his relationship or if he missed his family back home he would put a lit cigarette to his arms and chest and let it burn through the flesh. Every time someone he knew passed away he would slice a mark into his wrist to remember them by.

Worrying marks to her son's body were not the only thing concerning Paula about Farah's relationship with the lad. Her son came home from visits 'overly sexualised and acting in a sexual way'. Paula had never spoken with her son about sex and believed that her former partner was putting sexual ideas into the young boy's head.

After a few more months of stalking her, Farah eventually accepted that Paula had met a new man and he finally left her alone. Farah never again attempted to see his child and didn't contact Paula again either. He contacted Adecco Recruitment Company and informed them that he was leaving Dublin to go to Cork and would not be available for any more jobs. Farah had met somebody else – Kathleen Mulhall.

✂✂✂

While he was still going out with Paula, Farah Swaleh Noor's name had been linked to one of the most infamous and serious murders in Ireland – the unsolved slaying of seventeen-year-old Dublin teenager, Raonaid Murray. At one stage Noor was a bona fide suspect and he even admitted carrying out the murder, during drunken ramblings. He seemed to match all the hallmarks of the Murray suspect – he carried knives, was familiar with the Dun Laoghaire area where the killing occurred and had shown a propensity for violence towards females.

Raonaid Murray, a pretty blonde teenager, was viciously murdered after leaving Scott's pub in Dun Laoghaire on the night of 4 September 1999. She left her friends at around 11.30 p.m. and started the fifteen-minute walk back to her family home in Glenageary. She was going to collect some money and return to meet some old school friends at Paparazzi's nightclub in Dun Laoghaire Shopping Centre. The student was seen by witnesses arguing with a man on Corrig Avenue at 11.55 p.m. A local woman heard a scream fifteen minutes later, which was probably when Raonaid saw her attacker and realised that she was about to be killed. The mystery man lay in wait for her in a dark lane between Silchester Road and her home at Silchester Park, a plush middle-class estate. She was brutally stabbed four times, with a one-and-a-half-inch sharp knife. The attack was extremely violent. Her murderer escaped into the safety of the dark night on foot, and Raonaid desperately staggered about 200 feet before she collapsed and died from her injuries. Her body was found by her sister Sarah, less than thirty minutes after the assault. Sarah and her two friends had got a taxi home after a night out and they were devastated when they made the grim discovery. She ran the short distance to her parents' – Jim and Deirdre's – house and raised the alarm.

A huge garda investigation was immediately launched. Detectives feared that a random psychopathic killer was on the loose because the contents of Raonaid's Sally West bag were untouched and her clothing had not been tampered with, meaning that rape was not the motive. The overwhelmingly middle-class community of South Dublin demanded a quick arrest and a team of fifty experienced detectives were assigned to investigate the case.

The day before the Raonaid Murray murder, Farah Swaleh Noor was out in Dun Laoghaire with Paula and one of her friends. They spent the afternoon drinking cans of beer on Sandycove beach and, as usual, Farah had a fair amount to drink. At about 5 p.m. the group headed back to Farah's accommodation at the Rosepark Hotel in Dun Laoghaire. Paula went into the communal bathroom to have a shower and she got undressed and started to wash herself. Noor came into the room a minute or so later, got undressed and climbed into the shower, trying to have sex with his girlfriend. She rejected his advances, saying that their son was only down the hall. The Kenyan became angry and snapped, throwing her into the bath and attempting to force himself on top of her and rape her. Paula started screaming and Noor punched her in the face and body with a closed fist and wouldn't stop. He shouted at her, calling her a slut, but she managed to get out of the bath and grab her clothes and make it to Noor's bedroom. Her friend heard all the commotion and was waiting at the door with the couple's five-month-old son. Paula was in floods of tears. She got dressed and gathered her belongings, before leaving the hotel and jumping on a 46A bus that was passing by. Farah Noor came running out of the hotel and chased the bus, shouting that he was sorry, but Paula was in no mood to make up. She went into the city centre and caught a bus back to her South Dublin home.

She arrived in shortly before 9 p.m. and received a call from Noor who sounded very drunk. He apologised for trying to rape her and said he was sorry and it would never happen again. He told her he was drinking in Dun Laoghaire town but she hung up the phone and told him their relationship was over.

She didn't talk to him again for a few days. Paula remembered reading about the Murray murder in a newspaper over the next few days while she was deciding whether to take Farah back for the sake of their son. She met up with him a day or two later and he was in good form again. He matter-of-factly told her that he had been questioned by the guards about the teenager's murder. He had a big grin on his face and was boasting about the fact that he was a suspect in the murder. He told her he had spent the night of the killing drinking in a pub in the middle of Dun Laoghaire with two men. He used to spend many evenings doing this. Paula also remembered that Noor spoke about losing his dagger around the time of the murder but she thought no more about the sad killing of Raonaid until the couple broke up in April 2001.

Paula was out with her brother and her friend Avril in the Pennyblack Pub in Tallaght one night when Noor came in looking for her. Avril had been in school with Raonaid Murray in St Joseph's Cluny, in Killiney. She had been in the same class as Raonaid all the way through their secondary education from 1993 onwards. They were good friends and socialised together outside school and would have moved in the same circles. The two girls had lost contact after Raonaid left to study in the Institute of Education on Leeson Street but a few weeks before the tragic killing in September 1999 they had bumped into each other in Dun Laoghaire. On the Saturday before Raonaid's murder, Avril had met her friend in Scruples with four other girls. They'd had a few drinks together and said they'd meet to go out again but left without making any arrangements. Avril was devastated when she heard about the murder but didn't make any statement to gardaí because she didn't know about Raonaid's private life and had no information that might help catch her killer. She put the shock of the tragedy behind her and met Paula in January 2001, through a friend of hers who was living with Paula and Farah. After Avril had moved into their house and one day after an article about Raonaid had appeared in the paper, she had confided in Paula that she had known the dead girl.

Noor started shouting at Avril in the pub telling her

that she was the reason why Paula had left him. He said that Avril was also responsible for her 'friend's murder in Dun Laoghaire'. The group took this to be referring to Raonaid Murray and Avril ran from the pub in floods of tears. Paula left as well and they went to Tallaght Garda Station and reported Noor for breaching the barring order she had taken against him. They didn't tell them about what he'd said about the dead Glenageary teenager. Paula had never told her former boyfriend that Avril and Raonaid had been close. Following the incident in the Pennyblack pub, Avril thought that Noor had been trying to hurt her by saying things that he knew would get to her. She didn't think that the Kenyan had killed her friend even though she had seen the results of Farah's violent temper first-hand. Paula never actually believed that Noor was responsible either. It wasn't until September 2002 that Avril phoned the gardaí with her concerns about Noor. She did not give an official statement but warned them that she and her friend had their suspicions about him. In late 2005 she again contacted the gardaí when she heard reports that Noor had been a suspect for Raonaid's murder, before he himself had been brutally butchered.

The Murray investigation was one of the most extensive ever seen in An Garda Siochána's history. Some of the country's most senior and distinguished detectives were assigned to it, including Detective Superintendent Martin Donnellan, who would go on to be one of the senior officers in the Noor case. The investigation was based in Dun Laoghaire Garda Station and some of the most experienced investigators in the force, such as Assistant Commissioner Tony Hickey and 'The Sheriff', Detective Inspector Gerry O'Carroll, worked countless long days trying to get justice for Raonaid. Over 8,000 people were interviewed and more than 3,000 witness statements were taken and it took a long time to eliminate all the various suspects named by concerned members of the public. Nevertheless, when Farah Swaleh Noor's name came up again it had interested gardaí. When the murder had occurred he lived in the vicinity and was known to have a propensity for violence. He had even been arrested in Dun Laoghaire with a knife. It was decided that he should be interviewed again about his movements on the night of the murder. He had originally offered gardaí no information about Raonaid's death.

On 29 May 2003, Detective Gardaí Don Griffin and Dominic Hearns travelled to Cork to interview Farah Swaleh Noor about the Raonaid Murray murder. He was picked up in his house at 9 Wellington Terrace, taken to Anglesea Garda Station and interviewed under caution.

Noor seemed surprised to be quizzed about the killing and told the officers, 'I have never killed anybody, either in Ireland or Somalia.' He said that in September 1999 he was staying in the Rosepark Hotel in Dun Laoghaire. He said he remembered back that long because 'that was when the girl Raonaid Murray was murdered. It was all over the papers on the news. I didn't kill Raonaid Murray. I didn't know her; I have never met her and I have never even seen her. I can't really remember that well but I think that on the day that Raonaid was killed I was out at my girlfriend's house. I think I got the bus to the Rosepark Hotel. It was the last bus leaving at 10.30 p.m. and it is about forty-five minutes on the bus. I went straight into my room in the hotel. I was on my own. I went direct to my room and didn't speak to anybody. It was a long time ago so I am not fully sure but I think that's what I did. I didn't go back out until morning time.'

Noor's story did not tally with either Paula's or her friend's and the detectives asked why would two people lie to them about such a specific date.

Farah changed his story and said he remembered going to Sandycove beach to drink with his girlfriend and her friend, stating: 'I don't think it was the day that Raonaid was killed but it might be; I don't remember. Anyway I never had an argument with Paula that time. I was not drinking in Dun Laoghaire that night either. I don't have the money anyway. I was not drunk in Dun Laoghaire that night and I didn't ring her at her home that night from Dun Laoghaire to say I'm sorry. I have met a friend of Paula's called Avril. She is a fat girl. I don't like Avril. Avril made Paula leave me for a South African man. I know that Avril knew Raonaid Murray because she told Paula that they were friends and Paula told me.'

The two Dublin-based detectives asked Farah Noor why he had boasted about committing such a brutal act of murder if he was innocent.

He claimed that he did it because he was jealous that his girlfriend was moving on and had met somebody else: 'Before me and Paula split up I met Paula in the Pennyblack pub in Tallaght. It was our son's birthday. He was two years old. Paula's family were there and so was Avril and two South Africans. I was upset because I didn't want the South Africans there but they had all the money. I had an argument with Paula because I didn't want them there. I told Paula to be careful because Avril was a bad girl and her friend was killed. I mean Raonaid Murray, and I don't know how. Did Avril know something because she was her friend? I don't know. Avril then left with the South Africans, and me and Paula went home. A couple of months later we split up. She has married one of the South Africans. She broke my heart and I never see my son now. All I know is that I didn't kill Raonaid Murray. I was arrested last year in Dun Laoghaire with a knife. The garda has the knife now. I got the knife as a present from my girlfriend. Before I used to go climbing and fishing with Paula's father.'

Farah had boasted to other people about his involvement in Raonaid's murder and regularly warned Kathleen Mulhall that she would end up the same way. During one of her interviews Kathleen said: 'He told me he killed someone, some girl in Dun Laoghaire. I 100 per cent believe it. He told me he stabbed her; she was a friend of an ex-girlfriend. He told me I would end up the same way. He said he was too good to be caught. He told me it was somewhere down a laneway and he killed her with a knife. When he told me he killed a girl in Dun Laoghaire he told me that if I told the police that he would get my family, my children and kill them and said I would be the first killed.'

She said that Farah was very drunk when he confessed about the murder but a week before his death he brought it up again during an argument, telling her: 'I am going to fucking kill you just like I did with the whore in Dun Laoghaire.'

After Kathleen Mulhall told gardaí about Noor's confession, investigators at Dun Laoghaire were immediately informed. They accepted that he was 'a nasty piece of work' but were satisfied that he was not the killer. Gardaí believe that he brought up Raonaid's murder in the pub in Tallaght on the spur of the moment, while under the influence, in order to upset and hurt Paula's friend. Although Farah Swaleh Noor was initially a bona fide suspect in the slaying, investigators eventually ruled him out of having any involvement. No witnesses saw a black man near the scene and there wasn't a shred of evidence – except for Noor's own tenuous admissions – that he was responsible.

Despite the thousands of garda hours put into tracking down Raonaid Murray's killer, the crime has never been solved. There were twelve arrests in the case but no charges. There have been a number of what looked to be very promising leads but all of these have come to nothing. One woman came forward four years after the killing and said she had given a false alibi for her then boyfriend on the night of the murder. She said the man had threatened to stab her during an argument but he was eventually eliminated because there was nothing to link him to the crime.

Another suspect lived in Dun Laoghaire and had displayed violence towards women in the years before Raonaid's death. He was once regarded as the chief suspect but was able to present a watertight alibi and this line of investigation hit a dead end. A second local man who was detained was obsessed with knives and swords and lived in a fantasy world. His hobby was making drawings of women suffering extreme acts of violence. Another suspect arrested and quizzed was a convicted rapist who had been released from prison just months before the murder. Again, his alibi checked out.

Most detectives who worked the case agree that the man who callously stabbed Raonaid Murray to death was the 'Noel Gallagher look-alike'. Several witnesses had come forward and told gardaí that they saw Raonaid having a row with a man in the minutes before she was murdered. This individual was described as being in his late twenties, of average height and wearing a beige jumper. He had blonde hair and wore it in the style of Noel Gallagher from the band Oasis. This man was probably responsible for murdering Raonaid but to this day nobody knows who he is or why he did it. Some investigators believe he was a visitor to Ireland and caught the first ferry out of Dun Laoghaire, after carrying out the ghastly deed. The authorities have offered a €207,000 reward for information leading to the conviction of the killer but unfortunately the money remains uncollected.

The head of the Dublin Metropolitan Eastern Division, Chief Superintendent Pat Culhane, described the murder as 'a motiveless, very savage, vicious attack', saying: 'It is an investigation that we must solve and one we will solve.'

At the inquest into the death Detective Inspector Eamon O'Reilly apologised to Raonaid's family for not bringing her killer to justice and promised that the hunt would go on. 'Someone out there knows some little thing. It is a big jigsaw and we're missing a few pieces,' he said. 'We would renew our appeal for anyone who knew Raonaid Murray and who has not come forward to please come forward now.'

The lives of Raonaid's parents, Jim and Deirdre, have been torn apart since that terrible night in 1999. They cannot understand what would motivate anybody to murder their vivacious daughter or how it happened in an area where people expect their children to be safe. In a poignant appeal for their daughter's killer to be brought to justice the family said: 'While Raonaid lies in her grave, her murderer is free to walk the streets. We know nothing will bring Raonaid back to us but the thought of her vicious killer roaming free adds to our agony.' The murder the case remains open and several detectives still work on the unsolved murder. They will continue to do so indefinitely.

✂✂✂

Paula had tried to put Farah out of her mind but then late one night during 2003, a woman called Kathleen Mulhall rang her for advice on how she should deal with Farah. The two women had never met and Kathleen said she'd got her number from Farah's phone. She described how Noor was beating her up and she wanted to know how to stop him. Noor was displaying the same violent tendencies with Kathleen that Paula had experienced for three years.

Paula later said: 'She was looking for advice. I advised her to leave him. I said he would never change. She wanted to know had he ever beaten or attacked me. I told her the full story and urged her to leave. I told her about the abuse. Kathleen Mulhall was always very polite. On one occasion she told me she was pregnant and that she was calling because she knew I was also pregnant. But I later found out this was lies. She knew I was in a new relationship but I told her to leave him. I remember telling her that he would never change and that something awful would happen if she didn't.'

Farah met Kathleen Mulhall in the summer of 2001 at a nightclub in Tallaght. Kathleen abandoned her family for Noor and made her husband move out of the house in Kilclare Gardens. Her family resented her for this and John Mulhall was bitter over the break-up. At one stage, Farah and Kathleen's son John ended up getting into a fist fight over what Kathleen claimed was a row about drugs. She said the pair got into a row after taking too much heroin and that Noor became aggressive with John. The Kenyan was terrified and jumped out of a window and ran away. John had witnessed Noor punching his mam once and did not have a lot of time for him. Despite this they shook hands the next day.

In the end Kathleen and Farah decided to move to Cork to have a fresh start. Neither of them had jobs, and, apart from her family, Kathleen had no ties to Dublin. They headed off to start a new life together in Cork in September 2002.

Gardaí who investigated the gruesome murder of Farah Swaleh Noor are all in agreement that he was a sadistic rapist who took pleasure in harming himself and others. Forty-nine-year-old Kathleen undoubtedly suffered serious domestic abuse at the hands of Noor and was left hospitalised and badly injured on a number of occasions. It was common knowledge that Noor was hitting Kathleen and members of her own family had often witnessed cruel violence. Gardaí believe that it could have been the three years of sustained abuse that allegedly drove Kathleen to plead with her two children to murder the man she said she loved. Noor had no idea that the violence and brutality would eventually catch up with him – in a terrible and tragic fashion.

In the weeks following Farah's disappearance and when Kathleen was arrested and questioned by gardaí, the mother-of-six gave some disturbing evidence of just how brutal the dead Kenyan had been. The following statements were not heard in evidence during the trial of Linda and Charlotte Mulhall but were released to their defence counsel during disclosure – the right of the defence team to receive from the prosecution any information that might aid their client's case.

Kathleen said that Farah Noor often made her life hell and regularly locked her in her bedroom when they lived in

Cork, following bad beatings. He left her with serious injuries on more than one occasion but wouldn't let her out of the house to go to the hospital. She was left with 'broken ribs, two fractured hands, head injuries, cuts but never stitches'. Kathleen did sometimes manage to get medical attention. She said she was hospitalised at least three times because of the beatings but would tell staff that she had been mugged and 'never told them the truth about what happened and stayed with Farah because I loved him'.

She told gardaí: 'I had two very different relationships with Farah. When he was sober he was a beautiful person, a beautiful man, but when he was using both drink and drugs he was like the devil. He attacked me nearly every day. He was totally crazy when he was drinking. He'd beat me with his hands, his fists or with a belt. He'd mostly use a belt. He'd say, "I wouldn't beat you if I didn't love you." I believed him. He told me on a number of occasions that if I told anyone about the attacks he would kill me. I believed him when he said this. I am 100 per cent sure he was telling the truth when he said he'd kill me. That's why I got away from him. He told me on a number of occasions that he'd kill me. Farah always played the race card. He'd say, "It's because I'm black." He'd be the one fighting with people then he'd turn on people and if he started fighting he'd say, "It's because I'm black," to try to get away with it.'

She also detailed how Farah would burn himself with cigarettes as a form of relief: 'He'd light a cigarette and then put the cigarette up against his skin and let it burn his skin. It would come up in a blister. He'd burst the blister and either suck or eat the skin. The pain wouldn't bother him. He'd only burn himself with cigarettes when he was drinking. He said it was his culture and that's why he'd burn himself. He put the lit cigarette up to various parts of his body and just let the skin burn. The worst one was when we lived in Cork. He put the cigarette up to his forehead and just let it burn. I slapped his hand away because you could smell the skin burning. Only when he'd drink he'd burn himself. That was the only type of self-harm he'd do. On about five or six times I woke up with cigarette burns. I'd have been drinking and in a deep sleep and the following morning I'd see the burn marks. Farah said that I fell asleep with the cigarette but I know I didn't. After one of the beatings in Cork he left me in the house for a week. He kept the key to the front door and there was bars on the windows so I couldn't get out. I had a horrible relationship with Farah. I loved him and I still probably do, I know I do. I know Farah is a violent man with drink taken. Farah could drink three or four litre-bottles of vodka a day along with beer cans. If he had money he'd drink three or four bottles a day but not every day. With drink on him I'd say Farah is capable of anything, including killing someone. I don't even have to hesitate to answer that question. Farah is afraid of nothing and no one. The relationship we had was strange in that if I wanted a cuddle or a hug off him he wouldn't let me near him but if it was the other way round, if he wanted to touch me or have sex with me, he could.'

Kathleen claimed that Noor used to make her pretend she was pregnant 'to make other girls jealous'. He told everyone he knew that she was expecting his baby and forced her to go along with it: 'It was all lies though, it was what Farah made me tell people. I was never pregnant by Farah or any other man bar my husband. I had my tubes tied about thirteen years ago when my younger son was three years. He's sixteen years now. I think I was in the Mater Hospital for that procedure. When Farah asked me to do things, I would because I was afraid of what he'd do to me.'

Farah even forced her to phone his ex-girlfriend Paula, who was pregnant with somebody else's child, in order to make her jealous. Kathleen had to pretend she was expecting twins. A few weeks later she had to ring Paula again to say that she'd miscarried. She was regularly made to say this to people.

Charlotte also knew all about her mam's suffering at the hands of Farah. She told gardaí that the two got on well most of the time but that he hit her and that friends of Kathleen in Cork had told her this as well. She saw them have an argument once when Farah was drunk. He pushed her mother and told her to shut up. Charlotte said he was an alcoholic and was always drinking: 'He got very aggressive when he drank but when he was sober he was very quiet.' Charlotte said that Farah always carried a knife with him in his jacket pocket or trousers. He said it was to sort Irish people out because they were all racist.

Kathleen Mulhall was not the only person to bear the brunt of Farah Swaleh Noor's temper. He would lose the rag at the drop of a hat and take his anger out on whoever was closest. Although he was a bully who liked to exert power over women, Noor was also quite cowardly and could not back up his violent threats. He regularly got severe beatings or ran away from rows he'd instigated. Charlotte told detectives that she saw him start a fight with an Irishman called John Paul when he was living in Cork. Farah abused the man and pulled three knives from his pocket, threatening to stab him, but John Paul still 'battered' him, according to Charlotte.

Other people who knew Farah and Kathleen in Cork

also gave statements detailing their violent relationship. Barry Sheehan, who was the couple's landlord at 158 Lower Glanmire Road, told gardaí that Kathleen had claimed that Farah had 'kicked the baby out of her' when she was pregnant. Sheehan said that the dead man was always very abusive towards Kathleen but 'she could give as good as she got'. He did not remember Farah as a good man and said he abused everyone. He also said he was extremely violent when drinking but 'when he was sober he was the nicest fella in the world, which wasn't often'.

Kathleen also told Michael Mulrey, who lived underneath her in the same house, that she was pregnant. Mulrey believed her and found Farah Noor quite intimidating, with a stare that unnerved him. He described one incident to gardaí where Farah became very aggressive towards him. Mulrey was drinking in his local, the KLN, when Farah wanted to shake his hand as he was leaving. Michael Mulrey was getting hospital treatment at the time and didn't want to shake Noor's hand because 'he'd been coughing and spluttering all night into his hands' and he 'couldn't afford to catch anything'. Noor became very angry at this snub and shouted at Mulrey, 'It's because I'm black.' Mulrey told him that the only person that had an issue with the colour of his skin was Noor himself.

Mulrey told gardaí: 'I didn't like Farah and I never made any bones about that. I thought he had a violent streak. He had these mad bulging eyes and if he was staring at you he could be very intimidating and he had this really deep voice. He was very aggressive when he had drink on him.'

Maureen Moran was Kathleen and Farah's landlord when they lived at 105 Lower Glanmire Road for five weeks. Moran said that when she collected the rent Kathleen was covered in bruises and told her that her boyfriend had beaten her up.

Another of the couple's landlords, Michael Herlihy, who owns 13 Quaker Road, said that Noor once pulled out a butcher's knife and threatened to cut his [Herlihy's] head clean off him if Herlihy ever came back to the house to look for rent. Herlihy, who owns a shop, regularly saw Kathleen Mulhall with black eyes and other bruises.

Another man, John O'Toole, saw bruises on Kathleen's face when she moved into his house and he got the impression that her partner was responsible. He said she was very nervous and seemed afraid that this man would come looking for her.

Noor had regularly come to the attention of gardaí before his death and had amassed four previous convictions but never spent a night in jail. Although he was lucky to have less than a handful of convictions Farah was well known to gardaí, whether he was living in Dublin or Cork. They were frequently called out to deal with incidents involving him or Kathleen drinking excessively and were also well used to responding to domestic incidents.

Noor appears on the garda PULSE crime recording system twelve times. He is named as a missing person from Tallaght on a PULSE incident report recorded on 30 March 2005, the day his body was found. A second entry that day lists him as the 'injured party' in a murder. The final entry was made on 12 July 2005, when he is described as a 'found person' in response to the previous missing persons' report, which was probably made in error. His other appearances before his demise show Farah Swaleh Noor to be a man very fond of drink but with a tendency to get on the wrong side of the law when he was under the influence.

He first came to the gardaí's attention on 2 December 2000 following an ugly incident in Dublin. A bus driver was working on his normal Tallaght route, when he stopped to pick up two African men on the Harold's Cross Road, near Rathmines. The pair refused to pay the proper fare and the driver wouldn't allow them board the bus unless they had the full amount. The two men, Farah Swaleh Noor and a friend of his, became very abusive to the driver. They started cursing and shouting at him, displaying aggressive behaviour. The driver pleaded with them to calm down but they only got angrier and he had no choice but to contact the guards from his radio. A female garda from Rathmines Station attended the scene and had a word with the two offenders. She told them to calm down and go home or they would be arrested. Despite being warned by the garda, Farah Noor did not calm down and became far more agitated. He started shouting aggressively at the garda, the bus driver and members of the public. The officer called for back-up because the situation was getting more serious and a male colleague from the same station arrived minutes later. Noor then pushed and assaulted the female officer, before attacking her colleague. Yet more gardaí were summoned to the scene as Noor and his pal were out of control at this stage. The two men were threatening to attack innocent passers-by. A struggle ensued and the gardaí found it difficult to handcuff the two men, who were shouting and cursing at them in English and a foreign language. They were both eventually arrested on suspicion of assaulting a garda, obstruction of an officer and resisting arrest and were taken to Rathmines Garda Station, still mouthing abuse. Both men were bailed and were summonsed to appear before Dublin District Court on 17 September 2001.

Noor was charged with assault contrary to the Non-Fatal Offences Against the Person Act. He was convicted and sentenced to three months in jail but that was suspended. He was bound to keep the peace for twelve months and fined €190.46.

Less than a year after his first conviction, Noor was again in trouble. Gardaí Ian Pemberton and John Farmer from Kill of the Grange Station in South Dublin responded to a domestic incident in Dun Laoghaire at 2.16 a.m. on 18 August 2002. A member of the public had made a complaint that an African man with a knife was threatening a female. They arrived at the scene and observed a man they later knew to be Farah Swaleh Noor drop a knife behind a wall, close to a house. Noor had spent the day drinking and the gardaí thought he was very drunk but he denied that the knife was his. Farah claimed he had never to have seen it before. He was arrested and taken to the station where an investigation into the incident was launched. He was interviewed on suspicion of possessing an offensive weapon but still continued to maintain his innocence. Nobody was prepared to come forward and say they had seen the Kenyan with the knife in his hands so there was insufficient evidence to charge him. He was released and, although gardaí continued to investigate, he was never prosecuted. Had somebody been willing to finger Noor he could easily have found himself in jail for a minimum of three months because he was still bound to keep the peace from the incident the previous September and his sentence would likely have been re-imposed.

When Farah moved to Cork with Kathleen in September 2002 he was in the city for a matter of just weeks before the demon drink got him noticed again. On 30 November

Garda Garreth S. Kingston, who is attached to Anglesea Street Garda Station, was out on mobile patrol at 11 p.m. when he happened upon Noor in a very drunken state on North Gate Bridge. He spoke to Noor, who confirmed that he had been drinking heavily for most of the day. He was not causing anyone hassle so the garda cautioned the Kenyan and ordered him to go back to his flat, which he gave as being at 43 Heatherview Avenue.

Noor kept out of trouble until 4 March 2003, when he appeared before a judge at Cork City Court charged with intoxication in a public place contrary to Section 4 of the Criminal Justice Act (Public Order) 2004. This incident had happened at 1 a.m. on 20 February, when a garda spotted Farah in the middle of busy Leitrim Street without any top on. Garda Maurice Hickey issued a summons to Noor in the post and he appeared in person in court and pleaded guilty. He was fined €75.

On 3 November 2003 Farah Noor phoned gardaí at McCurtain Street station at 6.15 p.m. about an incident that was alleged to have taken place on the Lower Glanmire Road. Noor claimed that he was walking down the road with Kathleen when two men in their early twenties, one wearing a black jacket and black trousers, the other dressed in a white jacket and white trousers, attacked him out of the blue, punching him in the face. Kathleen was a witness to the supposed assault but neither Farah nor his partner could give a good description of what these men looked like. They could only say that they were very drunk and outside Mama Mia's restaurant when it happened. Garda Caroline O'Neill drove the patrol car around the area searching for these men but failed to find any trace. She noted that Kathleen and Farah had drink consumed.

Gardaí went to Noor's flat at 13 Quaker Road two weeks later and asked if he wanted to make an official complaint about this alleged assault. The Kenyan had sobered up at this stage and declined but thanked the guards for calling round.

After almost two years in Cork, Farah and Kathleen moved back to Dublin on 14 September 2004. They stayed in the Mountainview B&B in Firhouse while they looked for somewhere more permanent.

On 10 October Kathleen went to the manager of the B&B and confided that she wanted to leave because Farah was very violent towards her, jealous and possessive. She said she was afraid to leave him because he would come and find her wherever she went. The Health Board takes such complaints very seriously and Kathleen was moved to Lismore B&B in Drumcondra. The new accommodation was arranged for Kathleen on the understanding that she would not be in contact with Noor. Arrangements were also made for them to collect their Social Welfare money independently. As a result of the split, they were both paid unemployment benefits separately, each getting €138.80 a week. It later transpired that when Kathleen had complained about being in fear of the brutish Farah, she did it out of a desire to con more money out of the Social Welfare. The couple had most likely concocted the story because they knew that living apart they would be better off to the tune of €43.60 a week.

The couple kept seeing each other and were still very much together. Farah's violent habits, however, did not change. Gardaí Mark Dunlea, Timothy McCarthy and John O'Connell from Rathfarnham Garda Station were on patrol in a marked garda car at about 10 p.m. on 24 October, when they saw an African man repeatedly hitting a female who looked to be in her late forties. They immediately stopped the car at the Old Bawn Road, in Tallaght, and pulled the African away from the woman. The man was very drunk and told the gardaí his name was Farah Swaleh Noor. He gave his address as the Mountainview B&B, Firhouse. He was handcuffed and arrested on suspicion of assault and was taken to Rathfarnham Station. The female victim was Kathleen Mulhall and she wasn't happy that her boyfriend was being taken away in a squad car. She told the guards that he was all right and to let him go. She refused to cooperate and make a statement against Farah and he was released without charge.

Noor was abusive and violent towards Kathleen Mulhall beyond any shadow of a doubt but she always stayed with him for some reason. While she was living in Drumcondra, Farah had another of his regular run-ins with authority. He was walking on the Upper Drumcondra Road at around 7.45 p.m. on 20 November 2004, after a day's heavy boozing. He opened up his trousers and started to urinate against a car. A passer-by challenged him and asked Farah what the hell he was doing. The decent citizen was sixty-one-years old but that didn't stop the alcoholic Noor shouting obscenities at him. The man was from Ballymun and told Noor he had no business urinating on the street and said he should be ashamed of himself. The Kenyan was brave with lots of drink on board and walked up to the man and punched him in the face. Two young men, aged twenty and twenty-one, were also out walking and witnessed the assault and came to the good Samaritan's aid. They pulled Noor off him and held him down while phoning the guards from a mobile phone. Garda Anthony McCabe from

Whitehall Station responded to the 999 call and arrested Noor, who was shouting at the three men to let him go. He was arrested and taken to the garda station. Luckily, the sixty-one-year-old was not badly injured and was able to go home. Farah Swaleh Noor appeared before the Dublin District Court two days later, charged with intoxication in a public place and of threatening and abusive behaviour. He was convicted of both offences and the Probation Act was applied. He was bound to the peace for twelve months and fined €200.

A few months later Noor was quizzed by gardaí after another violent incident. He attacked Christian Silva in the Parnell Mooney pub on St Patrick's night 2005, punching him in the face with a pair of nail cutters. A uniformed officer spoke to Noor outside the pub but it's doubtful whether Farah would have been prosecuted. A witness, Michael Dunne, told gardaí that Farah wasn't at fault. Silva had also declined to make a complaint and never contacted the guards again to make a statement.

This was the final time that Farah Swaleh Noor would appear on the gardaí's radar until his dismembered body was fished out of the Royal Canal.

7

Linda's Confession

After Linda's release from garda custody on 3 August, she came under sustained pressure at home to go and confess to the guards. Her father knew that Linda had snapped and murdered Farah Noor with Charlotte, after the Kenyan had made sexual advances towards her. The two of them spoke at length about what had happened. John knew that his daughter was having trouble sleeping and was in a dark place because of the murder. Linda was haunted by what she had done.

She had initially been very cocky after being questioned and was going around the house saying, 'They've nothing on us; we're in the clear.' She had thought that surviving twelve hours of police grilling meant that it was all over, but her confidence was to be short-lived. She hit the bottle hard and wasn't looking after her kids properly. Linda's Dad was left trying to work full-time and look after a house that often had nine people staying in it. Andrew and Marie were living with their father and with Linda and her children also in the house, it was very crowded.

It got to the stage where his eldest daughter couldn't even look at her children. It was almost as if she wasn't their mother at all, she was so cold towards them. When she'd had her pregnancy scare in early April she'd realised that the last thing she wanted, at this difficult time in her life, was to have another child. When the hospital had told her it was a false alarm at least that had been one worry off her mind.

As the days passed, Linda gradually began to realise that the murder investigation wasn't going to go away. She knew that the guards would keep knocking at her door until they got to the truth. It was very tense in the house and Linda's younger sister Marie hadn't been talking to her since the arrests. When she heard that the police had searched the river at the back of the house belonging to John Mulhall's employer, Marie lost the plot completely. She tackled her sister in the kitchen at Kilclare Gardens, shouting, 'Loads of people who had nothing to do with the killing of Farah Noor are being dragged into Farah's death.' Marie warned Linda that if she didn't go to the police and tell them what she knew then she'd go to Tallaght Garda Station herself. Marie threatened to tell the guards that Charlotte had confessed to her a couple of days after they carried out the murder.

The two women had a blazing row and Linda said that she was in the clear and that the guards had no evidence. Their father was in the kitchen at the time and Marie said that if Linda didn't come clean she would leave the house for good. She went away and John told Linda that things were getting too complicated. He said it would be better for everyone if she spoke to the police. She agreed and John then phoned Marie and told her that he was going to ring the guards. He said he would get them to come to see Linda because she'd agreed to tell them everything.

John spoke to Sergeant Liam Hickey, who arranged a

meeting with Detective Inspector Christy Mangan on the morning of 17 August. John met DI Mangan in Cork Street and told him to come over to the house in Tallaght later that evening to speak with Linda. He told the inspector that she knew where the head was buried. He said she was their only hope if they ever wanted to recover it.

DI Mangan and Sgt Hickey called to 31 Kilclare Gardens at 7.30 p.m. that evening. John welcomed them in and they sat in the front room of the house, waiting for Linda to come back from Kevin Street, where she was picking up her dole cheque. John rang her mobile a few times and she told him that she was nearly home and would see the police then. At 8.45 p.m. there was still no sign of her so the two guards left and told John Mulhall that they'd rearrange the meeting for a few days later. Linda was not in town collecting her dole. She was so messed up over what she had done to Farah that she had cut her arms in what could have been a very amateurish suicide attempt. Either way she was in Tallaght Hospital getting treatment.

Two days later, on 19 August, the same gardaí again went to the house. They shook John Mulhall's hand as he invited them into the front room where they eagerly waited to meet Linda. The mother-of-four came into the room, sat on a chair and lit a cigarette.

DI Christy Mangan told Linda her father had asked them to come to speak with her about the death of Farah Swaleh Noor and asked if she had anything to tell them. She was very nervous and told him she knew nothing about Farah's murder and couldn't help them. She admitted to them that she had cut her arms on purpose and showed them her injuries but she said she was grand and had previously self-harmed. Her father served tea while she chatted with the detectives, who informed her that the investigation was not going to go away and that they were searching a stretch of river in Leixlip as part of the investigation.

Linda listened to what the men had to say but again said that she couldn't help them. DI Mangan said that he would be talking to other family members who would tell him if she was lying. John Mulhall then left the room to take a call on his mobile from his daughter Marie. While he was gone, Linda still said nothing.

After about twenty minutes of silence the guards decided to leave her for the moment. As John Mulhall walked them to their car, he asked them if Linda had told them where the head was buried. They shook their heads but Mulhall said, 'She knows where it is.' He promised to get his daughter Marie to make a full statement the following Saturday telling them what she knew, because Linda had spoken to her about the murder over the previous five months.

Less than three hours after the two detectives left Kilclare Gardens DI Mangan was on patrol in Coolock when his mobile phone rang. It was Linda Mulhall and she was in tears and sobbing. She said, 'Christopher, Christopher I need to talk to you. Will you come back at five o'clock to talk?'

DI Mangan asked her did she want to discuss the murder and when she told him she did, he arranged to see her at 4.45 p.m.

Linda Mulhall was waiting for DI Mangan and Sgt Hickey in her bedroom, which was in a specially built shed in the back garden of the Tallaght house. She was sitting at the top of her bed with John Mulhall and said she 'wanted to tell the truth of what happened with Farah'. She asked if her dad would leave the room because she wanted to be by herself when she confessed.

Over the next hour and a quarter, a tearful Linda told the two officers exactly what had happened on that fateful night of 20 March. She started from when her mother had rung the sisters and arranged to meet her and Charlotte on O'Connell Street and finished with a detailed description of how she had murdered Noor. She took a number of breaks to go to the toilet in the main house and spoke to her daughters while she was gone.

When she came back at 6.15 p.m. she agreed to make a full written statement but didn't want to go to Tallaght Station to record her confession. She was officially cautioned and read her rights and over the next ninety minutes Sergeant Liam Hickey wrote down Linda's words as she emotionally described how the murder had ruined her life and made her a nervous wreck. She signed her statement at 8 p.m.

When Linda finished her official statement she agreed to show gardaí the spot where Farah Swaleh Noor's head was buried. She hugged her father as she got into the patrol car with DI Mangan and Sgt Hickey. She directed them past the Jobstown Inn and left up a small road, past a golf course to Killinarden Hill. Linda told Sgt Hickey to stop the car as they drove past an innocuous field on the left-hand side of the road. The entrance into the field was covered with rubbish bags and was protected by thick barbed wire. DI Mangan held down the barbed wire with his foot while Linda crouched under it and entered the field, which was littered with rubbish and burnt-out cars. They walked about 300 feet to the right of the field, past a burnt-out car and towards a ditch. Linda walked into the entrance and got down the bank into the ditch. A black pipe lay covered in muck and grass and the thirty-year-old said she recognised it from when she was there the last time. The pipe was lying on the bed of a small stream.

She later stated: 'I walked into a far field and kissed the bag and told Farah I was sorry. I stayed there for ages, a long time. I had a bottle of vodka with me. I drank all of it. I took the hammer out of the bag. I left the head in the bag and hit the head loads of times to try and break it up. I fell asleep and woke up cold. It was starting to get dark. There was a mucky patch there and I turned away and pulled the head out of the bag. I put muck over it and said a prayer and told him I was sorry and said it should not be you, it should be me ma. I burned the plastic bag up there and the school bag and I ran home to bed. I am sorry for what happened. It is not my fault it happened, I'm sorry. If I could turn back time, I would. I am sorry.'

She then described how she used all her energy to throw the hammer about sixty feet into the deserted field. DI Christy Mangan took Linda by the arm and helped her out of the ditch. They then turned left and walked a short distance to an adjoining piece of land because she said she wanted to make sure she was in the right place. Finally she said 'this is it' and they continued back to the squad car. The mystery over the death of Noor was now effectively solved. Despite the extensive searches that took place in the field and Linda's full co-operation, Farah Noor's head was never recovered.

Linda was relieved that she had finally gotten the murder off her chest and now had no problem going to the local garda station to record what she had said earlier on tape. DI Mangan spoke to Sgt Mick Leahy at 9.15 p.m. and he made an interview room available.

When they were settled in the station Linda was cautioned. She was told that she could leave at any time and then Sgt Liam Hickey slowly and carefully read out her earlier statement. She cried continuously as her words were read out and DI Mangan decided that she'd had enough emotional trauma for one day.

They drove Linda home at around 10 p.m. On the short drive back to Kilclare Gardens, she told the officers that the next day she would show them where the head had originally been buried in Sean Walsh Park. She also agreed to point out where the murder weapons had been dumped.

John Mulhall came out of Number 31 when the car pulled in and he shook DI Christy Mangan's hand. Linda got out of the car and grabbed DI Mangan and embraced him, amid floods of tears. The emotions of hiding the terrible secret for nearly five months were overflowing. As the guards left, John brought his distraught daughter into the house.

Marie saw her and asked her if she told the guards the whole story.

'I've told them everything,' Linda answered. 'Me and Ma and Charlotte took his head to Sean Walsh Park but I went back and dug it up and put it in a field in Killinarden Park.'

'I don't want to know any more,' said Marie. 'Now you've told them they can leave Da alone and can deal with you and the others.'

The two women never discussed the case again after that. Although the two gardaí had made massive progress that day their work was only beginning. As they drove back to Fitzgibbon Street, they had to mobilise uniformed gardaí to seal off the field in Killinarden Hill. A full forensic examination and detailed search would take place at first light the next day for fragments of Noor's head and skull. Linda had also told the detectives that she'd stored the head in some bushes in a place called Killinarden Park the night before she buried it in Killinarden Hill. Killinarden Park is a large green area, close to the church, in the heavily populated Killinarden Estate in Tallaght. Arrangements would have to be made for this location to be searched as well.

It was late into the night when DI Christy Mangan finally got to bed and he was up early the following day, Saturday, for another visit to see Linda at her home. She had agreed to show him and Sgt Hickey where she, Charlie and Kathleen had buried Farah's head after murdering and mutilating him in the Richmond Cottages. Before they left she asked the investigators if Kathleen or Charlotte had come forward to talk to the gardaí but the officers had heard nothing from them.

Sgt Hickey drove a patrol car in the direction of the Square Shopping Centre in Tallaght to a large park, across the road from the Plaza Hotel. Locals called it Tymon Park North but it's officially known as Sean Walsh Park. The group walked into the park and the gardaí were immediately struck by the large lake in the centre.

Linda later told them: 'We walked around Tymon Park North for ages. Charlotte knows the park and we were saying we will put it here; we will put it there. We walked around for ages. We were looking for different places. Where the bench was Charlie started digging holes with the knife that me ma had in the bag. The hole was not very deep. I had the head on my back and I said to Charlie get this off me. Charlie took it out of the bag and put it in the hole. Charlie filled the hole. I could not do it. Me ma threw the knives in the water close by. We went home and I burned the bag in a fire at home in the sitting room. Me da was in bed.'

Linda showed little emotion as she returned to the scene where they had disposed of the murder weapon. DI Mangan immediately phoned Garda Niamh Coates, who worked in the Mounjoy local detective unit, and told her to preserve the area as a crime scene.

On the way back to the squad car, Mangan and Hickey asked Linda how she felt. She said she was glad to have pointed out where the head was buried and was feeling much better for having told the truth. She cheered up and told them that when she got home she was going to cook her children their favourite dinner and would make a nice trifle for them.

Linda Mulhall was not arrested during the three days when she was co-operating with the garda investigation. She had built up a rapport with DI Mangan and Sgt Hickey and there was no point in formally detaining and charging her until it was absolutely necessary.

The officers again called to her house on the Sunday morning and were kept waiting while she got changed from her pyjamas to go to Tallaght Station to clarify some issues. This was a very difficult interview for her and she was in almost continuous floods of tears. Sgt Liam Hickey struggled to take down everything she said, such was her emotional state. The recorded interview lasted about ninety minutes and Linda signed a statement afterwards. They left Tallaght at 1.55 p.m. to go and point out some more crime scenes. They were driving in the direction of the city centre when Linda asked if she could stop and get a cup of coffee because she had a headache. They were close to Fitzgibbon

Street Garda Station so they went in there and Linda made the three of them coffee and she smoked a cigarette. After twenty-five minutes in the station, the patrol car was back on the road again.

On the junction of Summerhill Parade and the North Circular Road they stopped at a red light. Linda said she recognised the Sunset House pub and told Sgt Hickey to turn left, left again and then take a right into Richmond Cottages. She pointed out a white house – Number 17 – and got out of the car to show the men the flat where the murder had happened. The front of the house was locked but one of the new residents answered the buzzer and let them in. By this stage Kathleen had left Richmond Cottages and was living in Carlow.

Linda pointed to Flat 1, on the immediate right as you enter the house, and said: 'This is it.' Then she broke down and started to sob, before becoming inconsolable and howling uncontrollably.

DI Mangan asked if she wanted to go home to Tallaght. She said she did, so the three got back into the car and headed towards the south of the city.

Linda recomposed herself as the car moved further away from Ballybough and started to talk about the murder: 'Farah was holding on to me with one hand and the other hand then went on to me, it was just a grip I could not get out of. Charlotte said, "Get your hands off Linda." I told him to get his hand off me as well. He was never like this before. Charlotte said, "Get your hands off!" It was like they were not there; it was like he could not see them. He frightened me, he did. Me ma said get his hands off me as well. It was a hold I could not get out of and then Charlie said again, "Get your fucking hands off!" and he whispered. I remember it different some days, I remember in all different ways. Because of the E we took that night I remember it in all different ways. When we were sitting in the chair, me and him before he stood up, he whispered something in my ear, that me and him were two creatures of the night and he whispered something else in my ear, I know it was something dirty he said to me. I could not really understand the language. Farah was saying, "You are so like your mammy." Charlotte said, "She is nothing like me ma. Get your hands off Linda!" Charlotte was sort of putting it up to him, you know like, she has big shoulders and me ma put her hand onto his arm and he still would not let me go and Charlie was roaring, "Get your hands off Linda!" Charlie must have seen the blade on the sink. She picked it up. Charlie opened up the blade and she cut him on the throat. The bedroom door was sort of open and me ma was like, "Get him in, get him in," and he sort of tripped. He did not fall on the floor he sort of fell onto the bunk beds. Before he fell on the floor me ma was still trying to push him into the room saying, "Get him away; get him away from me." I seen the hammer and hit him on the head. Charlotte got a knife from the kitchen. That Sean Paul CD was still playing. She stabbed him. He fell onto the floor. Charlie stabbed him. I hit him loads of times with the hammer on the head. I don't want to keep talking about this. It is driving me mental. I don't want to be alive anymore. I don't.'

As the car journey continued, Linda spoke to the two investigators about her life. She said she always seemed to be in the wrong place at the wrong time.

Linda Mulhall was born on 3 February 1975 and spent her young days at the family home in Tallaght. She met her first partner Mark Farrelly, who was three years older than her and came from Galtymore Drive, in Drimnagh, in the early 1990s. Farrelly worked as a builder's labourer and had come to the attention of the gardaí on a number of occasions. He appeared in court over twenty times and had convictions for public order offences and road traffic incidents. The couple moved into a house at 25 Bawnlea Green, in Tallaght, and Linda had her first child on 6 February 1993, a little boy. She gave birth to another son on 7 August 1994 and less than a year later, on 15 July 1995, she had her first daughter. She gave birth to her final child, another girl, on 5 December 1998. Linda and Mark Farrelly were young when they first met and were only together a couple of years when they had their first child together. Their relationship went through a number of bad patches and they eventually decided that they would be better off apart. Farrelly left the family home when they separated, around 2000.

Linda became involved in a new relationship with a man called Wayne Kinsella soon afterwards. People who know Kinsella describe him as a violent sadist who takes pleasure in hurting other people. He has over twenty-five previous convictions for crimes including manslaughter, violent disorder, assault and burglary. He had a strange and worrying hold over Linda Mulhall. She was obsessed by him and blind to his evil tendencies. Kinsella moved into Bawnlea Green with Linda and her kids in early 2003. She suffered a miscarriage in the summer of 2003, with Kinsella's baby. Around the same time there were allegations that Kinsella was physically abusing and mistreating three of Linda's children. In September 2003 the Health Board intervened and secured an order to take the minors into care.

After Linda's four children were taken into care, the

couple moved to Cork. They soon came to the attention of local gardaí, as Kinsella was suspected of breaking into houses and carrying out robberies. It is thought that Linda helped him. The couple were also said to be in regular touch with Kathleen Mulhall and Farah Swaleh Noor while in Cork and they socialised together. Linda was not happy with her mother leaving her father, but she still made an effort to meet up with her during the short time she was in the city. Her attitude seemed to be that, for good or bad, Kathleen was still her mam.

At the end of 2003, while her four children were still in care, Wayne and Linda moved to Manchester. They were thinking of permanently relocating there but they didn't settle and came back to Dublin in January 2004. Kinsella and Linda were fighting a lot during this period and in early 2004 Linda agreed to cooperate with gardaí and the Health Board in prosecuting Wayne Kinsella for the abuse of her children. Her children were then returned to her, but on 10 February 2004 she agreed to place the four youngsters into voluntary care.

Linda split up with Wayne Kinsella and really went off the rails at this point. The council threw her out of the house at 25 Bawnlea Green for anti-social behaviour and she moved around various hostels for the homeless over the following months. The mother-of-four was drinking heavily and started taking heroin. She made a number of suicide attempts by trying to cut her wrists.

On 16 May 2004 custody of her four children was returned to Linda. For a number of months they were housed at a homeless unit in the Coombe area of Dublin. They were then evicted for ongoing anti-social behaviour. When she lost the flat, she rang her dad and pleaded with him to allow them to move back to Kilclare Gardens. She was very close to her father and was extremely grateful when he agreed to intervene to look after her children, as otherwise they would have been taken back into care.

Linda, however, was still finding life difficult. On 2 June 2006 she was arrested and charged with assault, arising out of an incident involving an ex-boyfriend's new girlfriend. She also has one previous conviction for theft, going back to 1993, on her record and has ongoing charges under Section 13 of the Criminal Justice Act, with one charge under the Road Traffic Act.

In July 2004 Wayne Kinsella appeared at Dublin Circuit Criminal Court and went on trial, charged with the mistreatment of Linda's three children, aged eight, nine and ten years old. Truly shocking evidence of abuse emerged during the case. The court heard that Kinsella, who was then aged thirty-three, beat the three youngsters with a belt and electrical flex, leaving them with multiple injuries. The career criminal used to force the young children into different rooms in the house and take turns to beat them, for no other reason than to satisfy his sick blood lust. He told Linda's ten-year-old son: 'Whenever I look at you, I want to hit you.'

On one occasion he beat the boy so violently, Linda's son was left cut and bleeding, with more than twenty different injuries to all parts of his body. Vincent Heneghan, who was prosecuting the case for the State, said that Kinsella made the boy strip down to his underpants and lie face down on the bed as he beat him with a belt. He then cut the flex from a lampshade and used it to hit him all over the body. He then went to the next room where he beat the boy's nine-year-old brother. Kinsella also lifted him up, threw him to the ground and hit the boy's face off the wall. Next he went to the third room and beat Linda's eight-year-old daughter, before going back to the room where the eldest boy was now hiding, in extreme pain, under the bed. Wayne Kinsella flipped the bed over to one side, dragged the boy out from underneath and resumed beating him. The thirty-three-year-old did not stop until he was out of breath and panting from the exertion. Throughout the beatings, Kinsella shouted loudly and repeatedly: 'You made Ma lose the baby.'

After the beatings he threatened to kill them if they told Linda what he had done. Garda Damien Dempsey told the court that he received information that the children might be in danger. He found out later that when he had called to the house, Kinsella had put the two boys in a box and made them stay there until long after the guard had gone. At the time gardaí took the eight-year-old girl into protection and a few days later did the same with the other children. Linda loved her kids and was devastated when they were taken away.

Wayne Kinsella eventually pleaded guilty to three counts of cruelty, on dates between 31 August and 1 October 2003. Some detectives believe that Linda may have become desensitised after witnessing Kinsella's extreme acts of violence and depravity against her children. They think this could have driven her to carry out the barbaric murder and dismemberment of Farah Noor.

During sentencing, Judge Michael White said the children had been in a very unfortunate situation, in that they were completely at Kinsella's mercy, as Linda Mulhall had not been affording them appropriate care in such circumstances. He described Kinsella as 'a man with a predilection to violence'. In July 2004 he sentenced him to four years for beating the eldest boy, and three years to run concurrently, for each of the two other children, sentencing him to a total of seven years behind bars. Judge White told Kinsella that, as the live-in partner of their mother, he had abused his position of trust with the children.

Kinsella told the Judge: 'I am very sorry. I will make it up to them. I just snapped that day. I had just lost the baby. It was totally out of character for me.'

Judge White accepted his apology but said he did not believe the attacks had been spontaneous, as Kinsella had claimed.

These comments were proven to be well justified as just three months later, on 14 October, Kinsella was back in court, before the same judge. This time he was pleading guilty to intimidating a mother-of-five and unlawfully seizing her car. The incident had occurred on 31 May 2003, a few months before he attacked Linda Mulhall's three children.

Linda Mulhall's ex was handed a four-year sentence, after admitting to forcing Ms June Byrne and her two-year old son out of her car. Kinsella had told Ms Byrne that he had a buyer for her car, which she was trying to sell. They were driving to the purported buyer's house when he told her to pull over. He ordered them out of the vehicle saying: 'If you get the police, I'll kill you and burn your house down with your children in it.'

June Byrne, who knew Kinsella because she was friendly with his sister, told Judge Michael White she had lived in fear of Kinsella. She said she could now relax knowing he was locked up.

Judge White again described Wayne Kinsella as 'a man with a predilection to violence'. He said Kinsella's intimidation of Ms Byrne and hijacking of her car was a very serious offence. He said Kinsella had a violent history he needed to deal with. The Judge suspended the four-year sentence, on condition that Wayne Kinsella underwent an anger-management course in prison and that he not approach the victim, or her family. Kinsella was bound over to keep the peace for four years, after the date of release from his seven-year sentence.

Linda told DI Christy Mangan and Sgt Liam Hickey of how Wayne Kinsella had regularly beaten her. She also mentioned that Farah Noor was violent towards her mother. She said she couldn't get Noor's image out of her mind, so she had started to cut her arms again. All she saw when she dreamed was Farah Swaleh Noor and she wanted this to stop now: 'I'm glad I told the truth and feel much better,' she told the men as she got out of the car.

Her dad was waiting at the door and the pair embraced and held each other for a long time. She then turned to DI Mangan and hugged him and shook his hand before going into the house to have her first good night's sleep since the murder.

✂✂✂

The next twelve days were busy for gardaí. Huge searches took place in the three fields and parks in Tallaght. On 22 August Garda Eamon Bracken recovered a knife and a large hammer from the lake in Sean Walsh Park. These were the principle weapons used to murder Farah. Despite long garda hours being put into extensive searches at Killinarden Park and Killinarden Hill, nothing of any evidential value was ever recovered.

At lunchtime on 2 September, the two investigating gardaí again visited Linda at her home. She was not in good shape. The mother-of-four couldn't sleep at all now and DI Mangan suggested that she should go to see her doctor to get a prescription for sleeping tablets. She thought this was a good idea but said she couldn't go with the guards, to point out where they'd been on the day of the murder, because she couldn't organise a babysitter for her kids. She didn't want to leave them with Andrew, her eighteen-year-old brother.

DI Mangan and Sgt Hickey came back five days later and Linda was in the kitchen ironing clothes and preparing dinner for the kids, who were due home from school. She made the men coffee and told them that she'd spoken to her sister, who was going to hand herself in to them. When she finished ironing, they went back to the field in Killinarden Hill so a detective could film the scene on video. She rang her brother on the way and asked him to collect a prescription for sleeping tablets for her at the local clinic. They went back into the field and she led them to the same area where they'd been on 19 August. She said she was certain that this was where she had brought the head and smashed it up. Detective Garda Dominic Cox, a scenes of crime examiner based at Mountjoy, filmed this as evidence.

The detectives needed to know exactly where Linda and her sister and mother had been with Farah on the day he was murdered. On the way into O'Connell Street Linda started crying in the car because she couldn't stop thinking about what had happened. None of the guards had tissues so they stopped at a petrol station on the Tallaght by-pass and Linda bought tissues and cigarettes. She started to speak about how her daughter loved sports and was very good at football. Linda was sad because she knew she was going to spend a long time in jail. After showing the guards where they had drunk on the Liffey Boardwalk, they drove up O'Connell Street. She indicated where Farah and Kathleen had had the fight, after seeing the Chinese child:

'I could hear Farah and me ma fighting. We walked up O'Connell Street, where the cinema is. Some time after that we met a little Chinese boy playing with his friends. Farah started saying to the boy, "Cathy, this is my son; this is my son." My ma said, "Go away, you bleeding eejit; that is not your son." Farah said back to my ma, "It is my son, I know my own son." My ma said, "This is not your fucking son." The little boy was roaring and crying, he was really screaming. I think he was about five years old. Charlotte was still linking me at this time. I said to Charlotte, "Come on, let's walk."'

The garda car continued towards Ballybough and she pointed to the right-hand side of the bridge where they had dumped Farah's body parts: 'We got Farah into the bathroom. Myself and Charlie dragged him by the legs and me and Charlie cut him up. It was Charlie's idea. Me ma kept screaming, "Get him out; get him out." When I hit Farah with the hammer, Charlie stabbed him in the chest with the skinny knife. She cut him up with another knife with a rugged blade. She cut into his legs with the knife. She got tired. The smell was ... it won't go away, I think about it every night. I can't even look at a black person anymore. I done that to my arm [points to cuts]. I did not want to wake up. I then used the hammer and hit his legs a number of times. It took us a few hours to do it. Me ma did not cut him up. We had to put a towel over there when we were removing his legs to stop the blood rushing out. We cut him on the knees and on the elbows. Me ma had told me already that he had raped her and I said, "He won't rape my ma again." I cut his private parts off – the long piece, not the balls. We threw it in the canal with the rest. I was sitting in the shower part and Charlie was sitting on the toilet. Me ma done nothing. I had the towel over his head, over his face, and kept using the hammer. It would not come off. Both of us had to take turns with the hammer. I did not think about chopping it up but Charlotte said to do it. Me ma said, "Get it out of here." Me ma had sports bags. Charlotte started putting the heavy pieces into the sports bags but into black plastic bags first. I took the light bits and Charlotte took the heavy bits. We walked down to the canal. Me ma walked with us. You asked us to tell the truth, I am telling you the truth. We walked down to the canal a few times; it took a few times to go up and down. I see him every night in me mind before I go to sleep. I don't see him as a bad thing, just when he and Ma were happy. The smell won't go away, it just won't.'

Linda burst into tears and said she couldn't walk down to the water and could never return to the flat where they had killed a man. DI Mangan reassured her and told her she didn't have to do anything she didn't want to do, so they drove to Mountjoy Station where she made another statement.

While Linda was taking to the gardaí, Charlotte rang her on her mobile and her sister said she was with the guards. Charlotte again said she would go and see them.

Linda became upset again after this but didn't want to cut the interview short. Sgt Hickey read her final statement back to her and asked if she wanted to add anything to it.

'I'm sorry,' she whispered, as she struggled to breathe from all the crying.

Further arrangements had been made for Linda to meet with the two detectives. She spoke to Sgt Liam Hickey again on 29 August and said she had to go into hospital to get some staples removed from her stomach. They cancelled the meeting and postponed it until 7 September, when she again accompanied the two men to examine and point out the various crime scenes. The guards were looking for Charlotte at this stage but she was avoiding them, even though she had agreed to speak to them and make a full statement. Linda said that she had spoken to Charlotte the previous evening. She said Charlie had agreed again that she was also going to give herself up and tell them what had really happened. The police were also looking for Kathleen but she too was nowhere to be found.

They drove around Ballybough and over the bridge. Linda spoke about how she had gone to see Kathleen to plead with her to go back and dig up Farah's head: 'I rang me ma and said I have to go back down. I asked me ma to come with me. I went to my ma in Summerhill and asked her to come back down with me. The day I asked me ma to go with me was the day the guards were pulling Farah out of the canal. We were in the house, crying. We went down close to the bridge, close to where the guards had the tape. We walked on the side, away from Gala. We asked some people what was after happening. We went home and watched the news. We watched the news all the time.'

DI Christy Mangan was worried about Linda's mental state and rang her a few times to see how she was. She had gotten her sleeping pills but still wasn't sleeping because all she was thinking about was Farah and what she'd done to him. DI Mangan told her that if she needed anything at all to ring him or Sgt Hickey.

By 12 September Det Sgt Gerry McDonnell had tracked down Farah Noor's wife in Kenya and confirmed that Farah Noor was in fact Sheilila Salim. With the identity of the victim confirmed, Detective Superintendent John McKeown got in touch with Robert Sheehan, a professional officer at the Director of Public Prosecutions' (DPP) office. The decision was made to charge Linda Mulhall with murder.

On 13 September DI Mangan left Fitzgibbon Street Garda Station and made his way to Dublin District Court Number 44 where Judge Hugh O'Donnell was sitting. He swore information in order to get a warrant for the arrest of Linda Mulhall.

The following morning at 9.30 a.m. DI Mangan, DS Colm Fox and Garda Nichola Gleeson called to 31 Kilclare Gardens. Linda was in the kitchen and looked at Christy and the two new faces and instantly realised that the day had come when she was going to be arrested and taken away from her beloved children.

DI Christy Mangan arrested her by placing his hand on her arm and cautioning her that anything she said could be taken down and used in evidence against her. Linda said she understood and started crying. She sat down on a kitchen chair and sobbed into the table.

The inspector took a tissue from his pocket and handed it to her. 'Do you want to get a few things together, Linda?' he asked.

'I've had my bag packed since the first day I met you, Christopher,' she replied sadly. She went to her bedroom in the outside extension to change her clothes and get ready to go to jail.

Detective Inspector Mangan had purposely waited until Linda's kids had gone to school before arresting their mum. He rang Kevin Tunney, Linda's solicitor, while she was gathering her stuff together. She came back with Garda Gleeson after a minute and stopped to turn off the oven. Although it was early in the morning she was already cooking a chicken for her children's dinner that evening. She then walked out with the gardaí and got into the patrol car. DI Mangan didn't think it was necessary to handcuff her.

The gardaí arrived at Mountjoy Garda Station with the prisoner at 10.55 a.m. Garda Suzanne Carlos wrote up the custody record and was given details of Linda Mulhall's arrest. As her bag and jewellery were taken away, Linda asked that her solicitor be officially notified of her arrest. She was brought to the medical room of the station and given a full body search.

At 11.07 a.m. her solicitor, Kevin Tunney, arrived at the station and spoke to her in private. They talked for a few minutes and Linda was offered a meal by Garda Carlos but asked for a cup of coffee instead.

At 11.22 a.m. on 14 September 2005, Sergeant Shay Roche charged Linda Mulhall with the murder of Farah Swaleh Noor. The charge read: 'For what you the said accused did on or about the 20th March 2005 at Flat No. 1, 17 Richmond Cottages, Ballybough, Dublin 1 in the said Dublin Metropolitan District did murder one Sheilila Salim, otherwise known as Farah Swaleh Noor.'

Linda said 'no' as the charge was read out. She was given another cup of coffee before being quickly taken to the District Court where Judge Malone remanded her in custody to appear before him again one week later. She was released on bail the following week, to await her trial.

✂✂✂

Linda's social worker says she does not have a robust personality and is easily led. The thirty-five-year old has a strange relationship with her mother, Kathleen. She was devoted to her mam when she was young but never felt she got much in return. It was a massive blow to her when Kathleen took up with Farah Noor and the two fell out. For a few years Linda did not have much of contact with her mother but their relationship gradually improved over time and the frequent nights out in Cork helped to heal things. At the time of the murder, Kathleen had opened up to her daughter about the abuse she was suffering at Noor's hands and claimed that he had raped her. Even though they were getting on better, Linda's faith in her mother was still not great and she didn't fully believe the tales. She had never witnessed Farah being violent. She later told gardaí in a statement: 'My Ma told me she loved me better than the other kids but she never showed it to me. I was always very good to her.'

Linda's relationship with her youngest sister, Marie, was very fraught after her arrest and the two hardly spoke. She was far closer to her eldest brother, James, and regularly travelled to Wheatfield Prison to see him. After Kathleen told her son about the murder, Linda confessed to her role in it but it is hard to know whether she would have admitted it but for this. The killing was playing heavily on her mind and she asked James to look after her four children if she was jailed. He subsequently kept his promise and the youngsters are being cared for by him and his partner, Tanya.

Linda did start to get her life back on track after she confessed to killing Farah. She made sure she was in the house every day to bring the kids to school and made them dinner every afternoon when they came home. She even started to do some volunteer work at a local school. Life, however, was still difficult for Linda. She struggled with drug and alcohol addiction and was a single mother with four children. They all had to survive on the €226 in social welfare payments she collected each Thursday at Kevin Street post office. Social welfare records reveal that Linda has never worked a day in her life and has never paid tax. As her trial approached, however, she fell off the wagon and started to use drugs again and was drinking heavily. She has a history of depression and of inflicting self-harm and spent ten days in a psychiatric hospital in the days leading up to the trial. Her four children were being taken care of by relatives and were all continuing to attend school while their mother was gone.

When she was released, just before the trial was due to begin, Linda disappeared. She failed to turn up in court for the first day. She had been gone for two days and gardaí were desperately trying to contact her. They tried to ring her mobile but it was permanently turned off. At this stage Linda had moved to the Swiftbrook estate, in Tallaght, with her children and detectives feared that she had committed suicide. They went to the house and forced their way in, expecting to find her body. They nervously checked all the rooms but there was no sign of her. Meanwhile DI Christy Mangan was sending texts to her phone and was receiving delivery reports. He was sure that she was alive and getting the texts but was choosing not to respond. He sent a further text asking her to hand herself in.

After being missing for four days, Linda finally rang DI Mangan and agreed to meet him and Sgt Hickey outside her house. The detectives went to the house in Tallaght. They were waiting a few minutes when a battered taxi came up the road and pulled in. Linda was in the car, along with her two sons. She was inconsolable and had her belongings in the back of the car. She took out a sports bag, with some personal possessions and three cuddly toys. Amid floods of tears, she hugged her two boys and went with the two officers.

As the trio were about to leave, Linda's eldest son, who was aged just thirteen, went up to Detective Inspector Christy Mangan and shook his hand. He asked the garda to take good care of his mammy.

Linda was finally prepared to face her fate.

Charlotte's Confession

FOLLOWING THE MURDER of Farah Swaleh Noor, Charlotte hit the bottle in a bad way. She would start drinking as soon as she woke up each morning. When she'd had a particularly bad time, however, three or four days after it happened, and told Marie what she'd done, Charlotte knew she had to get her act together. She realised that if she didn't compose herself the guards would find her. She would then be arrested and the whole story would come out. She made a pact with herself after that that she wouldn't talk to anyone in her family about what had happened. She never mentioned her confession to Marie again and stayed away from Kilclare Gardens for the most part, only visiting the odd time.

In the weeks after the murder Charlotte spent most nights at the scene of the crime, in the flat in Ballybough. The twenty-two-year-old later said that she did go through days of feeling extreme guilt over what she had done but she still sold Farah's rings and other jewellery to some junkies she knew from the street. She also didn't seem to find it strange when her mother gave her Farah's ATM card so that she could withdraw money from the dead man's account.

After the family were taken in for questioning on 3 August 2005, Charlie's father, John, started ringing her, pleading with her to admit what she'd done. The twenty-two-year-old was having none of this. She wasn't about to sentence herself to life in prison when the police had no real evidence. After they were released, she met Linda a good few times, as she knew that her older sister was struggling to keep the secret to herself. Charlotte told her not to be stupid and tell the guards anything, because they were in the clear. She warned Linda that it would only take one word from her for the whole thing to come crumbling down and they'd then be sharing a cell together. Even though Charlotte regularly cautioned Linda not to say anything, the two of them never discussed the murder in any great detail. It had changed both of them and neither of them wanted what had happened to be dragged up again.

Sgt Liam Hickey had arrested Charlotte on 3 August and in the days following the swoop Hickey had built up a good relationship with John Mulhall. This had proved to be a very valuable link as it had led to Linda admitting to her role in the murder, effectively cracking the case for the gardaí. After he had secured Linda's admission Sgt Hickey turned his attention to Charlotte. He rang John Mulhall on 23 August and asked him if his younger daughter would be willing to talk to him about Noor. John said he would speak to Charlotte and get her to contact him.

When the Sergeant did not hear from her, he tried again the following day. John Mulhall said that Linda had spoken to Charlotte to try to convince her to talk but she still didn't ring the guard. Despite making three other attempts to contact Charlotte, Sgt Hickey heard nothing.

On 1 September he found out that Charlotte was living

with her Russian boyfriend, Dilmurat Amirov, in Artane, North Dublin. Sgt Hickey went to the house with Det Sgt Gerry McDonnell and told Charlotte that Linda had come clean about murdering Farah. He said that she had also implicated Charlie in the killing. The twenty-two-year-old knew that at this stage it was just Linda's word against hers and that the gardaí could not arrest her for questioning a second time without a warrant from a judge. As they did not have one with them when they called to see her, she presumed the evidence against her was patchy.

Charlotte said she would call them after speaking to her mother. She made an appointment to see the men at the Mountjoy Station the following day but she didn't turn up.

The detectives went back to her house in Artane but nobody was home. Sgt Hickey rang the number Charlotte had left him and it was answered by her boyfriend. He asked Dilmurat to get Charlotte to ring him but she never did.

Charlotte subsequently left the house in Artane but did not return to Kilclare Gardens. She had decided to disappear because she didn't want to talk to the gardaí about Linda's admissions.

On 5 September Charlotte rang Sergeant Liam Hickey's mobile and apologised for missing their meeting. She said: 'What Linda told you were complete lies. I will tell you all that happened tomorrow.' She agreed to meet Liam Hickey in Mountjoy the next day at 1 p.m. but again she never went to the station.

Linda was charged with Farah Noor's murder on 13 September and the courts issued an arrest warrant for Charlotte Mulhall on the same day. John Mulhall told Sgt Hickey that he'd contact him if he saw Charlie.

One month later, on Sunday 13 October, Sgt Hickey's

phone rang. It was John Mulhall and he lost no time in passing the phone over to Charlotte. She agreed to see Sgt Hickey the following Thursday, at the family home in Tallaght. Charlotte had split from her boyfriend Dilmurat at this stage and was single again.

Sgt Hickey and Detective Gardaí Kevin Keys and Adrian Murray went to the house at 11 a.m. on 17 October. The door was opened by one of Linda's children who said that Charlotte was in the 'gym' in the extension at the back of the house. Linda had been out on bail for three weeks at this stage and was still living with her dad. She came into the main house and said she was in bed with the flu. When Charlotte came in the gardaí arrested her on suspicion of murder. She did not show any emotion and asked if she could use the toilet. Then she said she wanted to see her sister. Sgt Hickey went to the extension with the two women and they hugged each other before Charlotte was taken away to Mountjoy Garda Station.

Her first interview that day took place at 12.56 p.m. with Detective Gardaí Kevin Keys and Adrian Murray asking the questions. She refused repeated offers to have a solicitor present.

Charlotte told the detectives that she and Linda had met Farah and Kathleen at 1 p.m. on the afternoon of 20 March. She said they were on the Liffey Boardwalk, drinking and taking E tablets and had then headed to Summerhill. When they were at Richmond Cottages, Kathleen started arguing with Farah, so the two girls had left the flat at about 7 or 8 p.m. She told them that they had gone back into town and stayed out drinking until five or six in the morning. She said they then went back to the flat and there was 'blood all over the bathroom and bedroom'.

Charlotte claimed: 'Me and Linda thought Farah was after hitting her [Kathleen] and they were fighting as usual. She was like, she was screaming and crying like a mental case in the flat when we went back and we said, "Mam, what's after happening?" She said she was after killing him.'

'She was screaming and crying like mental; is that what you said?' Detective Murray asked.

'Yeah. We didn't believe her and finally when we got her to sit down she said she was after killing him with a hammer and cutting his throat. We kept asking her where he was and she wouldn't tell us. She kept saying if she got locked up she was going to kill herself. Then she told us she was after putting the body in the river.'

'She said if she got locked up she'd kill herself?' Det Gda Murray queried. Charlotte's version of events was very different from what Linda had told them.

'Yeah,' Charlotte answered. 'She said if she didn't kill him he would have killed her. Then she asked us would we help. Would me and Linda help her clean up the flat. And we were cleaning up the flat, and me and Linda said that she wouldn't go to prison; we'd say we did it. We told her that we'd say that we killed him so she wouldn't go to prison. I didn't think Linda would really say it, really say that she done it, because when it came to it, I didn't.'

'But when you left the flat ... where did you go, yourself and Linda?' asked Det Gda Kevin Keys.

'All around town, drinking,' Charlie said.

'Where?' asked Keys.

'O'Connell Street, the Boardwalk,' she answered.

'About what time was this?' the detective added.

'About ten o'clock,' claimed the twenty-two-year-old.

The two detectives were totally sceptical of Charlotte's

story and knew she was lying. Det Gda Keys then asked, 'Are you suggesting that your mother, all on her own, killed him, cut him up into little pieces, all on her own, and brought him down to the canal, all on her own?'

'The only thing me and Linda done was clean up the flat,' she stated.

'So the arrangement was that you and Linda would say that youse killed him?' Det Gda Murray asked and Charlotte nodded her head. 'Whose idea was that?'

'Ours,' Charlotte claimed.

She then went on to say that Kathleen had brought her and Linda down to the canal two or three days after the murder and pointed out the spot where Farah's remains lay, under Clarke's Bridge. Linda's children were also supposedly there.

'Why did youse go down to the canal that day, two or three days later? Why did youse go down to the canal?' Detective Murray asked.

'She wanted to see if she could see anything, Charlotte replied.

'What did you see?' Detective Keys enquired.

'We didn't see anything.'

'Nothing?'

'She just pointed out to us whereabouts it was, but you couldn't see anything,' Charlotte coldly stated.

The detectives asked Charlotte to go into detail about these claims that her mother was responsible for the murder of Farah Noor. Det Gda Murray asked her, 'And what did she say she'd done to him?'

'She told us that she hit him with a hammer and cut his throat,' she claimed.

'What else?' asked Keys, pushing her for more details.

'She said when he was dead she cut him up; she panicked,' the twenty-two-year-old answered.

'Did she describe how she cut him up?' wondered Detective Keys.

'With a knife, she said,' answered Charlie.

'Did she say she used anything else?' continued Keys.

'Just a knife and a hammer.'

'Describe the scene,' Keys requested.

'There was blood everywhere'

'In what way everywhere?' he pushed.

'Pools of blood,' she said.

'Whereabouts in the flat?'

'In the bedroom, in the middle of the floor and everywhere in the bathroom, the bathroom walls, all the walls were just red,' Charlotte matter-of-factly said. She didn't seem to feel emotional, despite the horrific scene she had witnessed.

'Was there any of him left when youse got there?' asked Detective Murray.

'No,' claimed Charlie.

'Hmm,' he scoffed. 'I don't believe you.'

'Was your mother covered in blood?' asked Det Gda Keys.

'Yeah, she had blood on her clothes and on her hands,' the pregnant woman answered.

'What about her face, her hair?' Keys queried.

'Yeah there was blood in her hair.'

'Very noticeable, was it?' asked the detective garda.

'Describe it for us.'

'Just everywhere – her clothes were soaked; all her hair was soaking,' Charlotte said.

'And what about her face?' continued Keys.

'Only a little bit on her face,' she claimed.

Detective Gardaí Adrian Murray and Kevin Keys are both highly experienced detectives who have investigated numerous murders in their careers. They were all too aware that when somebody stabs a person to death and cuts up a body the murder scene would be like an abattoir, with blood absolutely everywhere, especially on the killer. They did not believe a word of Charlotte Mulhall's story.

Detective Keys then asked her: 'Are you suggesting to us that your mother killed Farah and cut him up to such an extent that there was blood on the walls, on the floors of the toilet and the bedroom and she herself was covered in blood, and that while she was covered in blood as you described, she brought the body parts down to the canal. Is that what you're suggesting to us?'

'Yeah,' Charlotte answered quietly.

'Think about it,' he pleaded with her.

'I know what I'm saying to you,' she stated, sticking to her story.

'It's lies, Charlotte, isn't it?' Detective Murray said.

'It's not lies.'

'The evidence we have doesn't support that story, simple as that. Charlotte, don't come in and make a liar of yourself,' Det Gda Keys told her.

'It's not lies,' she insisted.

'It's not the full truth. It's not the full truth, is it?" he queried, staring directly at Charlotte.

Det Gda Adrian Murray then spoke, saying: 'There is no way you'd have come into the flat with your ma covered in blood and then have to ask her, where's Farah.'

'You're not going to think something like that, are you?' the prisoner replied.

'Well you're after telling us she was covered in blood, her hair, her clothes, her hands; her hair was soaked. So why would you have to ask a stupid question, where's Farah?' Murray wondered incredulously.

'Yeah, but you're not going to think she's after killing her boyfriend,' Charlie said.

'Because it didn't happen,' Murray answered.

'It did happen,' she insisted.

'It did happen that he was killed but it's not happening the way you're saying it,' said Murray.

'It is happening,' she insisted.

'It's impossible. There's no way youse would have come in and asked her, "Hey Mam, where's Farah?"' Murray insisted.

His colleague intervened, adding, 'That story is not correct. It may be based on a true story but it's not a true story. What you've told us there is not correct.'

'It is correct,' Charlie promised.

'It can't be: that yourself and Linda arrived back, after being out in town, she's covered in blood, dripping in blood is what you're basically describing, and you have to ask her a simple question, "Where's Farah?" Where do you think he is? Don't be so ridiculous now,' Murray said.

The two detectives were now starting to put more pressure on Charlotte to see if she'd crack.

'We thought Farah was after being hitting her, as he usually does,' Charlotte responded.

'Tell us the truth about what happened,' Detective Keys ordered her.

'That is the truth,' she said.

'That's not the truth,' he replied.

'That is the truth,' Charlotte insisted.

'That's not the truth,' Keys stated.

'It is the truth,' the twenty-two-year-old said.

'So you thought Farah was after hitting her like he always did? Did Farah hit her once too often, is that what happened?' Murray asked.

'I don't know. I wasn't there,' Charlotte replied.

'Ha!' Murray guffawed. 'You were there.'

'I wasn't there when it happened and Linda wasn't there either.'

'So you're telling me you got down on your hands and your knees and you mopped and cleaned up blood and guts and bone and kidneys and any bit of his inside, you picked them up and never asked your mother, "Why did you do this?"' a disbelieving Detective Murray asked.

'Of course I asked her why,' said Charlotte.

'But you said you don't know why?' Murray queried.

'She said if she didn't do it he would have killed her,' Charlotte said.

'Why were you down cleaning up another man's blood and guts?' the detective wondered.

''Cause she's my mother,' she replied quietly.

'There wasn't just guts down there and blood, sure there wasn't? What else was there?' asked Det Gda Murray.

'Pieces of skin everywhere,' Charlie said.

'What about his head?' Det Gda Kevin Keys asked.

'She won't tell me where it is,' Charlotte claimed.

'You have to remember that we're able to prove certain things and that's what you have to remember and you're telling us a story but it doesn't add up,' said Detective Garda Keys. 'This is a huge investigation and we have a serious amount of evidence but the story you are telling us doesn't fit, it just doesn't fit, and all I'm saying to you is don't tell lies. Tell us the truth, that's all we want, the complete truth. It's not worth it to go through what you're going through 'cause you're telling us things we know for a fact are lies,' he pleaded.

The interview had been going on for nearly two hours and both detectives knew they were on the brink of a breakthrough. The evidence against Charlotte, however, was slim. All that gardaí had was Linda's word that her sister was involved. If the officers didn't manage to get her to admit it, there was little chance of charging her with Farah's murder. All the gardaí involved in the case knew they were playing for high stakes.

'She won't tell us where the head is. No, it's not the truth. We did bring the body down to the canal with her,' Charlotte said.

After sticking to her story for months, Charlotte had just admitted that she and Linda had disposed of Farah Noor's body. She had just implicated herself in the murder.

'Go on,' Keys told her.

'When we came back to the house she had it all in bags. She had all the pieces in bags. And the three of us had a bag and we just walked down and put it in the canal. Yeah, but I really don't know where she put the head,' Charlotte said, still emotionless.

'That's not the truth either,' Detective Murray said.

'It is the truth. They were sports bags,' she insisted.

'Oh, sports bags. So what was in the bag you carried?'

'I don't know; I just carried the bags. Legs and arms I think,' Charlie said, with a stony expression.

'What time of day was this?' asked Keys.

'Half-seven.'

'And how long were you in the house before you left

with the bags?' he enquired.

'I don't know; about an hour,' Charlie said.

'What were you doing for the hour?' Detective Keys wondered.

'Getting her to tell us what she'd done and trying to calm her down,' she stated.

'What did she say she was after doing?' Murray asked.

'She said they were fighting and she hit him with a hammer and she cut his throat.'

'Charlotte, will you tell us the whole truth now and don't be skirting around it? You're coming and going, just tell the whole truth,' Detective Adrian Murray requested.

'It is the whole truth I'm telling you.'

'Your mother didn't cut up that body on her own,' asserted Keys.

'She did.'

Murray tried a different approach, gently saying, 'Does it hurt you to go through it over again? Is that the problem? It can't be easy talking about it.'

'It's not easy talking about it,' she agreed.

'But we are gonna have to get to the bottom of it, Charlotte. Do you understand that you're gonna have to explain it some time?'

Charlotte again insisted that she was telling the truth, but the two detectives pointed out that she had been saying that ten minutes before and she had now changed her story. She then told them that she was lying about Farah's head. 'She had it in the house,' Charlotte admitted.

'Whereabouts?' asked Keys.

'In the back garden,'

'Did you see it?' the detective asked.

'No. I can't tell you anything else,' she maintained.

The pregnant woman then went back into her shell and swore that she and Linda had arrived back at the flat to find Farah's body packed in bags beside the bedroom door.

The two detectives decided to change topics and quizzed her about what she and Linda had done in town when they'd left Kathleen and Farah alone at Richmond Cottages.

She said that she and Linda were walking around the streets and met 'loads of people' and got a bag of heroin from a Chinese man for €20 and started smoking it. She told them that they went up Marlborough Street, where she usually hangs around, and then to O'Connell Street.

Detective Kevin Keys reminded her that they would know that she wasn't telling the truth. 'All over town, you know, we have hundreds of CCTV tapes, thousands and thousands of hours of tapes, all relating to that period of time and you're on some of them. You're aware of that, you know that?'

Charlotte still maintained she was giving them the full story. She repeated that when they got back to her mother's flat: 'She had all the pieces in bags. And the three of us had a bag and we just walked down and put it in the canal.'

Detective Murray then asked her about the bags and if there were: 'bits of legs sticking out or bits of arm sticking out. It's not nice, sure its not? Fingers, they're all real living parts. There had to be feet sticking out or fingers. Bits of body just don't fit neatly into a bag and you can zip it up.'

The two skilled detectives worked together to try to get Charlotte to tell the truth. Detective Keys said that he understood that she had gone through a difficult ordeal because: 'We saw the parts as they were coming out of the canal. We were there; we can only imagine what it was like. I know what it was like myself and I can only imagine and understand what it was like when you were there.'

Charlotte ignored his sympathetic approach and said that after dumping the body the three women spent five or six hours cleaning the flat and 'there was a disgusting smell'. She told them the head was in the back garden and was stored there for a few days after the murder, before the bin men took it away along with the sports bags used to transport the limbs to the water.

The guards knew that she was holding the full truth back. Detective Keys asked her how were they expected to believe her: 'Here you are saying you came back to a flat that was covered in blood – walls, floors, pools of blood, bits of bone, skin, everything – everywhere. A man has been murdered, obviously. You help, you say, to carry his body or bits of his body down to a canal and you tip it into the canal and you don't bother to find out why the man has died?'

She maintained that she was telling them the truth and said that it was Linda who was lying to them: 'She's crazy, really, saying that she done things and she didn't. What thanks is she getting for it anyway off me ma. Why should she take the blame for something that she didn't do?'

Detectives Murray and Keys said it didn't make any sense that Linda would confess to a gruesome murder if she hadn't done it.

Charlotte told them: 'I think she's fucking mental to be honest with you because she's saying she done things that she didn't do, just to protect me mam.'

She said that her relationship with Kathleen was now fraught. 'Things are after changing now. Sure the woman hasn't rang me, hasn't done nothing … I've tried to get through to the woman so many times. No one ever knows where she is; well, I don't.'

Just as the interview was about to be completed, Charlie became emotional for the first time. She got upset when she was asked about her mother supposedly cutting up Farah. The two men asked her why she was crying and she replied, 'It's not a very nice thing,' before adding, when they asked what the dead man had meant to her, 'I just knew him.'

After the interview ended senior officers in the investigation met to review the progress of the last few hours. Detectives Keys and Murray were confident that it was only a matter of time before Charlotte cracked because her original story had now been turned on its head. Their colleagues agreed and it was decided to re-interview Charlotte after she'd had a rest and some food.

Charlotte Mulhall sat in a lonely cell in Mountjoy Garda Station and must have wondered how she had got herself into this almighty mess. She was twenty-two years old, single and had just found out she was pregnant. She was possibly wondering what chance her child would have in life. She had gone to the station with the intention of saying nothing to implicate herself and had practised her story long and hard over the last few weeks, but she'd messed that up. She was now in serious trouble. She'd admitted to the detectives that she'd carried the body to the canal, tipped it in and then cleaned up the house. She wasn't a legal expert but she knew that surely that was a crime of some sort. She would probably be charged and might even go to jail. What would happen to her baby then?

Life for Charlotte Mulhall had never been simple. She was well used to getting arrested and spending time in police cells but a murder investigation was a new departure. She had first come to the attention of the gardaí on 28 July 2000, aged seventeen. She was arrested after stealing money from Bewley's Café in the Square, Tallaght, but she wasn't prosecuted. A few months later, she was detained by gardaí from Sundrive Road on after a public order incident on the Long Mile Road, but again was released without charge. Officers from the same station arrested her on 27 March 2003 after she was caught throwing cans at a house belonging to the new partner of one of Linda's ex-boyfriends. She was charged with this offence and given the benefit of the Probation Act in court on 2 October 2005, just two weeks before she was arrested on suspicion of murdering Farah Noor. She was arrested for assault on Grafton Street on 20 June 2003 but that charge was later thrown out of court. Three months later she was held again after being found in an intoxicated state on O'Connell Street and was also given the benefit of the Probation Act. Charlotte was picked up again on 3 September 2004, following a public order incident at the Mespil Road in Dublin and was taken to Donnybrook Garda Station.

In total Charlotte had been arrested eleven times and charged on fourteen occasions for a variety of offences, including intoxication in a public place, refusing to give her name and address, threatening behaviour, assault, damaging property, failing to appear in court, and loitering for the purposes of prostitution. Despite this record, she only had two actual convictions at the time of the Farah Swaleh Noor murder. Gardaí at Donnybrook are familiar with Charlotte and she is a well-known prostitute, operating around the Baggot Street area. She has never had a job and is believed to have turned to prostitution in her late teens, to earn some extra cash. She worked regularly in Lad Lane, on the Grand Canal near Baggot Street Bridge. Gardaí say she was a popular prostitute who was always kept busy.

Kathleen Mulhall had claimed in her interview that it was Charlotte who introduced her to prostitution because she wanted to earn some money to send back home to Farah's family in Kenya. They had got drunk one night and Charlotte supposedly brought her mother up to Lad Lane and showed her how things operated. Charlotte was a heavy girl and was good with her fists and many other prostitutes were afraid of her. They wouldn't dare to work her patch for fear of Charlie losing her temper, which she did quite often.

She got through boyfriend after boyfriend and seemed to have a particular fondness for African and Eastern European men. In 2003, she had moved to Cork for a while to live with an African, although this relationship broke up. She was not involved in a relationship with the father of her child. His identity is unknown but she was seeing a man from Kazakhstan for a short time before she got pregnant. When she was finally re-arrested, she told the detectives that the reason she didn't keep her appointment with Sgt Hickey was because she was in the Coombe Maternity Hospital, having a scan.

It later emerged that Charlotte had been involved in a bizarre incident in the Coombe the week before her arrest when she went in seeking a pregnancy test. She presented herself to emergency room staff at around 8 p.m. on Thursday, 6 October. She was quite drunk and asked a nurse for a test. She was told that the hospital didn't carry out pregnancy tests and she should go and see her GP. Charlotte became very upset and started crying. The nurse asked her if she'd been drinking and she admitted she had, just as a bottle of Southern Comfort fell out of her bag. She then said she was very upset and needed to speak to the nurse in confidence. Charlotte said she was involved in a murder case because her mother had killed her boyfriend, a black man who used to beat her up. She said she'd been drinking with the pair in town on the day of the killing and had gone back to her mam's flat to find it covered in blood. She claimed her mother had told detectives that Charlotte and her sister had killed her boyfriend but she told the nurse that she had nothing to do with it. She also told the nurse that her father was 'wonderful' and the 'light of her life'. She then said that she made her money working on Baggot Street and Leeson Street and got €2,500 for a 'few good shags'. She boasted that it was the best money she ever made and said prostitution paid far better than nursing. The twenty-two-year-old said she'd had an alcohol problem since she was fifteen-years-old and the nurse gave her the phone number of Alcoholics Anonymous in Tallaght. After giving her advice on how to check whether she was pregnant and tips on how to stay healthy while expecting, the nurse sent Charlotte on her way. The mother-to-be said she was going outside for a fag and the nurse told her it was a bad idea and could harm any child she was carrying. Charlotte told the nurse to 'get a life' and left the hospital.

Although Charlotte had a cold demeanour and certainly appeared harder than her older sister, the murder affected her. She went to see a doctor and was prescribed with anti-depressants because she couldn't sleep at night. She used a cocktail of vodka and sleeping pills to try to get rest and was also a user of many drugs, including ecstasy, cannabis, cocaine and heroin. Charlotte did not have many friends growing up and was absolutely devoted to her family and got on best with Linda and her brother James. She found it hard when her parents separated and made an effort not to take sides and still saw her mother, even though many of her siblings ostracised Kathleen. She was awarded €42,000 compensation in late 2004 as a result of a road accident a couple of years previously and shared it among her family. She bought her father a new motorbike, gave her mother over €5,000, gave Farah €1,500 and bought him a new mobile phone and also looked after her brothers and sisters. Such generosity towards her family was typical of Charlie, but she had squandered the cash in a matter of months. She bought drink and drugs and by her own admission, 'just wasted it really'. She didn't even have a bank account and lodged the money in Linda's account and took it out as she needed it. People who knew Charlotte say they were not surprised when she was arrested for Farah's murder. If somebody pushed her far enough, she had the habit of snapping; if her family were at risk, then doubly so. Such was her devotion to them that she would go to any length to protect them – even murder.

Charlotte's thoughts were disturbed at 4.21 p.m. when Detective Sergeant Gerry McDonnell and Detective Garda Mike Smyth came into the cell to bring her back into the interview room. Again, Charlotte Mulhall refused to see a solicitor.

The younger sister's few hours of head time did not prompt her to start telling the guards about what really happened in her mother's flat that night. She stuck to her story, repeating that she and Linda had left the flat at about 10 p.m. and drank around town until 5 or 6 a.m. the following morning.

Det Gda Mike Smyth told her that Linda had told them a different tale. He commented: 'If she's not telling the truth she is very, very specific, whereas can I just say your interview earlier on was very, very watery. Linda has told us exactly what happened in the flat that night. Now nobody, not even a great novelist would be able to think up the stuff she has told us, she has been so specific in the detail,' Detective Smyth declared.

Charlotte said that nobody rang John Mulhall after they dumped the body. She denied that she had discussed the fact that her mother had murdered somebody with him afterwards, and said that the subject hadn't come up in conversation with Linda either.

She continued to insist that she and Linda left the flat at Richmond Cottages because her mother and Farah Noor were fighting in the front room. 'I don't know what the row was about. I think it was about the Chinese guy, I think, or the Chinese child,' she said.

Det Sgt Gerry McDonnell asked her, 'Are you trying to say that yourself and Linda up and went at that stage? Is that what you're trying to say?'

'Yeah,' she replied.

'That's the portion of your story we don't believe,' the detective sergeant told her.

'That's what happened,' declared Charlie.

'It's not what happened though, sure it's not?' said Det Gda Mike Smyth. 'If you can tell me one place in town where I'll see you on video that night, I will tell you what I will do. I'll give you a million euro and I will let you out of the station here and now.'

'We were all around town.'

'Just you name one place, at one time, where I can find you on video that night?' Smyth pushed her.

'I don't know the times,' was her weak reply.

'You're home and free; you're gone Charlotte; you are

laughing,' added the detective.

'On the Boardwalk,' Charlotte eventually said.

'On the Boardwalk? So if I check the garda videos on the Boardwalk that night I'll find you? That night between 10 p.m. and 6 a.m. in the morning, I'll find you? Do you want to have that bet with me? Do you think I'm going to go up now and ask someone to look at eight hours of video, so they can't see you on the Boardwalk that night?' Detective Smyth said dismissively.

'Charlotte, you know what you have told us from there on is a pack of lies,' said DS Gerry McDonnell.

Charlotte, however, stuck to her guns. She was proving more difficult to crack than they'd anticipated. She had been in custody for over four hours at this stage and nobody had expected her to stick to a story that was obviously made up for so long. Charlotte did not want a solicitor and obviously believed that she could maintain the lie alone.

'Are you aware that Farah had your mother on the game?' asked McDonnell.

'No, I can't say I ever heard that,' she replied.

'No? Did he ever threaten her? Did he ever threaten your mother? Are you aware of that?' DS McDonnell queried.

'Yeah, I did. I worried about her a few times. I know he broke her ribs,' she answered.

'Did she tell you that he threatened to kill her?' Det Sgt McDonnell continued.

'Yeah, that night when me and Linda came back, like,' Charlie said.

'Before that, no?' McDonnell said. 'You're saying that you're aware of it, before that night, that Farah had threatened your mother or he had beaten up your mother. Is that right?'

'Yeah.'

'Several times, broken her ribs even?'

'Yeah,' Charlie said.

'And yet you tell us that a row erupted between them and in order to protect your mother you left with your sister Linda. Is that what you said?' Gerry McDonnell asked incredulously.

'You were there that night and you were involved in it, up to your neck in it. You were covered from head to toe in that fella's blood from where you chopped him up with a hammer and a knife,' Detective Mike Smyth interrupted, taking on the role of bad cop in the interview. 'Do you remember all the blood, do you? Hard to clean up, was it?' he asked.

'Yeah, it was,' Charlotte answered.

'I'd say it was. Did he struggle much when you were killing him?' Smyth said.

'I didn't kill anyone,' insisted Charlie.

'Yes you did. Cut his throat, didn't you?' Detective Smyth was getting animated now.

'No, I didn't,' she responded.

'Do you remember the expression on his face?' asked DS McDonnell

'Did he say anything while he was dying?' Detective Smyth interjected.

'I told you I wasn't there,' Charlotte insisted, rattled by the tough line of questioning.

'Yes, you were,' Smyth said accusingly.

'I told you; I wasn't,' she declared.

Det Gda Mike Smyth looked Charlotte in the eyes and said quietly: 'You were there and you know you were. I'd say you've had nightmares about it every night since. I'd say the only reason you ever get a night's sleep is because you drink so much and take so much drugs to go to sleep. You know and I know that's the truth. I'd say you've demons coming, crawling out of the wall.'

Det Sgt Gerry McDonnell intervened and asked Charlie if she'd like to see a solicitor but she declined.

Det Gda Smyth then summed up the case against Charlotte: 'There's nowhere on the videos where you are that night, apart from 17 Richmond Cottages, all right? You're not on the Boardwalk and you're not on O'Connell Street, so that's just a complete and utter crock. If you were going to come in with an alibi, you had plenty of time to think about it; you most certainly could have come in with a better one. But your only alibi is Linda, who puts herself in the flat. Your mother puts you in the flat when the murder happens, your brothers unfortunately do as well. Now you have to say your whole family are a bunch of liars. Now that leaves you with a very sticky wicket at the moment, Charlotte.'

The interview then changed direction again as the detectives started to go over what happened after Farah was murdered and dumped in the canal.

Detective Sergeant McDonnell asked Charlotte, 'Did you stay in 17 Richmond Cottages? Did you stay there for a period of time?'

'Yeah,' she admitted.

'In the month of March, you were staying there then?'

'I stayed there all the time,' Charlotte confirmed.

'What happened to Farah's phone and his ATM card?' the Detective Sergeant next asked. The police believed that Charlotte had taken Farah's mobile and his bank card.

'Me mammy gave me the card to go down and get money out of it,' she said.

'Did you get money out?' asked DS McDonnell.

'Yeah.'

'How much?' he asked.

'I don't remember,' Charlie claimed.

'A couple of hundred?' the Detective speculated.

'Sixty euro,' was the response.

'So this fella … is dead and you're off down the bank machine taking money out of his account,' said a disbelieving Mike Smyth.

Charlotte repeated to the two detectives that she and Linda were out when Farah was murdered. She again said they were drinking around town and smoking heroin into the early morning and returned to find him cut-up in plastic bags.

'When you start telling lies you have to be a very, very good liar because one lie leads to another lie. But it's the small lies that catch you out, and you're catching yourself out with all these lies,' McDonnell told her.

'You do everything liars do – you cross your legs, put your arms in front of you and look down all the time. You see, every attribute of a person telling lies, you currently have it Charlotte, and you have had since you walked into the station,' his partner added.

'Charlotte we don't want to upset you. We are not here to judge you or punish you, we are here to try and find out the truth and come to the bottom of it,' DS McDonnell said understandingly. 'You told us you went down to the canal with those bags. How were you feeling when you were down there that time?'

'Sick,' she responded.

'You were sick,' he said, nodding his head. 'Have you been sick since in relation to thinking about it?'

'Yeah,' Charlie confirmed.

'All the time?' Det Gda Smyth wondered.

'Yeah.'

'Did you ever think you were capable of such a thing?'

'No,' she said, as she slowly shook her head.

'Do you feel like you're some kind of a monster? Well you're not,' DS Gerry McDonnell said compassionately.

'Who's the closest person to you? Charlotte who's the closest person to you alive?' the Detective Sergeant continued.

'Linda,' she responded.

'You've a lot of time for Linda, haven't you?' he stated.

'Yeah.'

'I would go as far as to say you love your sister,' McDonnell said.

'Yeah,' Charlotte nodded, saying she did love Linda.

'But telling lies is neither going to help you or Linda. Do you understand that? Do you understand that?' asked McDonnell. 'But the truth is what you came here to tell us and you haven't told us the truth. Charlotte, we will listen to the truth, we don't want to be giving you a hard time or upsetting you. Are you all right?' he asked.

Charlotte nodded that she was all right but she was starting to lose her composure. The twenty-two-year-old had spent the day being grilled by four skilled investigators and it was catching up on her. They were beginning to wear her down. 'Do you want anything?' Det Gda Smyth asked her, 'A glass of water or something?'

She shook her head and Det Sgt Gerry McDonnell pleaded with her, 'Will you tell us the truth, Charlotte?'

She nodded her head.

'OK, you're OK,' he said reassuringly. 'Are you all right?'

'Yeah,' she said.

'OK Charlotte, what happened?' DS McDonnell asked, gently trying to push her over the line to an admission.

'Everything that Linda said,' Charlotte finally whispered and started crying, the relief of finally getting the murder off her conscience now clearly on show.

'We will have to go through it in stages. We don't mean to be painful with you or anything like that. What do you want to say about what you told us earlier?' McDonnell asked.

'Sorry,' Charlotte sobbed.

'Were you doing it to try to protect Linda, were you?' he asked.

Charlotte started crying again and nodded that she was. She then talked the two detectives through what happened, starting with Kathleen Mulhall spiking Farah Noor's drink with ecstasy: 'She said he would be on the same buzz as us. He was drinking for ages and everything was grand and the two of them started arguing as usual, and Farah started saying shit to Linda and he wouldn't let her arm go.'

'Yeah? Do you remember anything, when you say shit? Was there any phrase?' queried DS McDonnell.

'Yeah, something like "we're two creatures", something similar,' Charlotte elaborated. 'Everyone was just arguing. Me mam kept saying to me and Linda, "Just please kill him for me. Kill him for me."'

'She kept saying that, your ma? OK,' McDonnell nodded.

'Then she got the hammer and the knife she gave to me and Linda, but he wouldn't let Linda go, and I cut him,' she admitted.

'You cut him. Where did you cut him?'

'On the neck,' she said, pointing to the side of her neck.

She didn't remember what kind of knife it was but after she stabbed Farah, she said Linda hit him with a hammer in the bedroom. 'I don't remember how he died in the bedroom. Then we didn't know what to do with him.'

'When he was dead, yeah?' asked the DS McDonnell.

'Yeah. Me Mammy said just cut him up,' Charlotte claimed.

'How did you cut him up?'

'With the knife and hammer,' she said.

The detective sergeant asked, 'What's your recollection of cutting him up?'

'I just remember cutting. I cut him up with the knife,' she told the guards.

'Right. Did you use anything else?'

'Yeah, the hammer.'

'You cut his skin with the knife ... and then what would you do with the hammer?' DS McDonnell asked.

'Linda used the hammer. I don't know,' she claimed.

'Do you strip him naked though, while you're cutting him up?'

The detectives were trying to get a clear picture of exactly what happened on the night of the murder.

Charlotte agreed that they did and said: 'We just cut him up and brought him down to the river.'

'The river – you mean the canal?' Det Gda Mike Smyth asked.

'Yeah. We cleaned up. We went back and just started cleaning up, just cleaning up for hours.'

'Are you OK? Do you want time to compose yourself?' asked McDonnell.

Charlotte was still upset at this stage. She had bottled the secret up for so long that it was a relief to finally get it off her chest, but it still distressed her.

'No. We had everything in the flat cleaned up. Then we went up to the Watergate Park and buried the head. After we done that we went back and started cleaning the flat again,' Charlotte told them.

Gerry McDonnell asked: 'Who decided to cut his head off?'

'I can't remember,' she claimed.

'What about his penis?'

'I can't remember who cut it,' she replied.

'And what happened the head?'

'Linda put it somewhere. At first the three of us went to the park and put it there but Linda moved it,' Charlie explained.

At 5.53 p.m., one hour and thirty-two minutes after the second interview commenced, the detectives decided to take a break to allow Charlotte to compose herself. She had confessed to the murder but they still needed her to fill in the blanks about who decided to dismember Farah Noor's body and who actually took part in the process of chopping him up into eight pieces.

At 7.57 p.m. Det Sgt Gerry McDonnell and Det Gda Mike Smyth interviewed Charlotte again. Gda Karl Murray was also present for a time. They showed the twenty-two-year-old exhibits that gardaí had recovered. Detective Superintendent John McKeown had granted a six-hour extension to her detention period at 5.10 p.m. During her rest period Charlotte was fed and had a lie down in her cell. She did not contact anybody or ask for a solicitor.

Garda Murray showed her the knife that had been recovered from the lake at Sean Walsh Park. Charlotte said she didn't recognise it and that it didn't look like the one she

The ‘Scissor Sisters’ get into a prison van on their way back to Mountjoy Women’s Prison.

Above: Linda Mulhall standing outside the court during a break in the trial.
© *Collins Photo Agency*

Right: Charlotte Mulhall on her way into the Central Criminal Court in Dublin.
© *Courtpix*

Detective Garda Kevin Keys and Sergeant (now Detective Sergeant) Liam Hickey.
© *Sunday Tribune*

Detective Inspector Christy Mangan arriving at the Coroner's Court for Farah Noor's inquest.
© *Liam Mulcahy/Independent Newspapers*

Raonaid Murray, the seventeen-year-old murdered in Dun Laoghaire in September 1999. Farah Noor bragged that he was responsible for her killing.

Linda Mulhall crying outside the Central Criminal Court during a break in proceedings.
© Collins Photo Agency

Linda and Charlotte Mulhall, accompanied by a prison officer, outside the Four Courts complex in central Dublin.

The controversial photograph of Charlotte Mulhall joking with a fellow Mountjoy inmate as she holds a knife to his throat.
© *Evening Herald*

Kathleen Mulhall fled to the UK and managed to avoid detection until December 2007.
© *Mark Condren/Sunday Tribune*

Farah Noor with the family he left behind in Kenya.

Farah Noor's nineteen-year-old son, Mohamed Said, wants to confront the Mulhalls about why they butchered his father.

Farah Noor's Kenyan wife, Husna, and their eldest daughter, Somoe, who died shortly after hearing of her father's murder.

had used to murder Farah. She was also shown the hammer but again said she didn't recognise it because she said that she hadn't used it.

The detectives then showed her a series of photographs from the flat at 17 Richmond Cottages. She said that the bedroom looked different because the bunk beds were now in a different place and there was different wallpaper and carpets in the bedroom.

She was shown a photo of the bunk bed and Det Gda Mike Smyth asked, 'Did he bleed on the bunk bed?'

'I don't know if he did,' she answered.

'Did he put up any struggle?' queried DS McDonnell

'I really can't remember any,' Charlie said.

The Detective Sergeant queried her about Farah's consciousness after he was stabbed and hit with the hammer in the bedroom: 'How did you know he was dead and he wasn't just seriously injured?'

'He wasn't breathing,' she explained.

'Why? Did somebody check on him?'

'Don't know; might have been scared to,' Charlotte told him.

The detectives then moved on to the bathroom where the dismemberment had taken place and showed Charlotte pictures of the shower. Detective Smyth said to her, 'I've been in that. That's a very small shower. You didn't do all the cutting up in the shower?'

'It wasn't in the shower, it was on the floor,' Charlotte answered.

'On the floor. And how, when you were doing the cutting up, how was he, how did you position him?' Smyth asked.

'Just on the ground,' she said vaguely.

DS Gerry McDonnell then moved on to the issue about the number of wounds that Farah Noor received, saying, 'Now the pathologist, his report I think indicates that he [Farah Noor] was stabbed over twenty times. Would you accept that?'

'I really … I really can't remember.'

Charlotte seemed shocked at hearing about the extent of Farah's injuries. Linda was also surprised when she was told of Farah's shocking injuries. The women did not realise just how far they had gone when they attacked Noor.

'I'm just saying that's what the pathologist has said. Would you accept that you had stabbed him?'

'No,' Charlie answered.

'How many times did you stab him?' Detective Sergeant McDonnell queried again.

'I don't know, a couple. It was nothing like that.'

'Is there any situation there where your mother would have stabbed him or anything like that?' McDonnell continued.

'No,' she said, emphatically.

'When he was dead, then what happened? Were you panicked? What did you do after that?' the detective wondered.

'I don't know. Me ma said the only way it's going to get rid of this is you're gonna have to cut it up now,' she claimed.

'What's your view on what happened that night, Charlotte? Are you annoyed with your mother over it?' asked DS McDonnell.

'I can't be annoyed with her. We're the stupid ones that done it,' Charlotte said.

Detective Garda Mike Smyth wanted to understand what had driven two seemingly ordinary women to carry out such an extraordinary act. He asked Charlotte: 'Would you say there was a point in the night that made you go from just arguing to killing him? What made you?'

'The way she kept going on, just telling us, "He's going to kill me; he's going to kill me. Youse have to kill him."'

'Right, but what specific thing happened? Was it him grabbing Linda?' Det Gda Smyth pushed.

'Yeah, I think so,' she said.

'That turned youse?' he wondered.

'Yeah.'

'Are you saying the decision to kill him really came from your mother?' DS Gerry McDonnell asked.

'Yeah,' Charlie answered.

'She made the decision in relation to that?' asked the detective sergeant.

'Yeah,' was her response.

'What are your thoughts on all of it now? I mean how do you feel? Do you feel sorry for him? How would you describe how you feel?' asked Mike Smyth.

'I feel sick,' Charlotte responded.

'When the decision came to cut him up, are you saying that decision again was made by your mother?' DS McDonnell wondered.

'Yeah.'

'Did she make it there and then or did she have to consult with somebody?' he continued.

'I don't know. She just kept telling us she'd think of something, she would think of something to do,' Charlotte claimed.

'And whose decision was it to drag him into the shower room or bathroom?' McDonnell queried.

'She told us to bring him in,' she responded

'Whose decision was it to cut off his head?'

'I don't know,' Charlie again answered.

Now that Charlotte had confessed, the detectives needed to get a clear picture in their own heads about the exact events of the night of the murder and deliberately revisited earlier questions.

'You don't know? Or [whose decision it was] to cut his penis off?' DS McDonnell queried.

Charlotte shook her head, to say she didn't know.

'Was that done for any reason?'

'I don't know,' she insisted.

'Or was his head cut for any reason?'

She shook her head again.

'Was there any reason why he was chopped up?'

'We didn't know what else to do,' Charlie claimed.

'Yeah, but was it to make it look like something else?' asked Gerry McDonnell. Det Gda Mike Smyth intervened and told Charlotte: 'It was just when this happened – I am sure you read all the newspapers – most people thought it was something else altogether.'

'You've heard of ritual killings, have ya?' Det Sgt Gerry McDonnell queried.

'No,' Charlie stated.

The two detectives had got Charlotte to admit that she had murdered Farah Noor. She had been questioned for over five hours and they decided there was no point in pushing her in the circumstances.

They were almost finished with Charlotte, when Gerry McDonnell asked her, 'How do you feel now, after you told us?'

'Better,' she muttered.

'Sorry?' Gerry McDonnell couldn't hear the mumble.

'A lot better,' Charlie stated.

'You feel better. Why do you? What way do you feel better after you told us? Do you feel like it's a load off your chest, do you? Do you?' he asked.

She nodded in agreement.

Mike Smyth asked her, 'Did people ever ask you about it, after Linda was arrested?'

'Yeah, a few people around town,' she said.

'What did they ask?' Det Gda Smyth wanted to know.

'Just what all this was about,' she replied.

'Is it hard to keep this type of thing secret?' Detective Sergeant Mc Donnell wondered.

'Yeah,' Charlie agreed.

The two officers were trying to understand how somebody could keep such a secret and wanted to know how it had affected Charlotte and her family.

'Is it? What way will it affect the family? Will it eat into the family?' DS McDonnell asked.

'I've hardly seen them, my family,' Charlotte confessed to the detectives.

'You've obviously discussed it with your sister Linda?' Gerry McDonnell enquired.

'Yeah,' she answered.

'And your father?'

'After we were all ... after we were all arrested, yeah,' Charlotte confirmed.

'What are you expecting now, Charlotte?' Mike Smyth asked.

'I don't know,' she said.

'What do you think will happen?'

'I'll be locked up for a long time, I suppose,' the twenty-two-year-old said sadly.

'Do you want to ask us any questions, Charlotte?' Det Sgt Gerry McDonnell asked.

'What's going to happen?' she wondered.

'Well basically I suppose the Director of Public Prosecutions will be contacted and it's going to be for him to decide what charge will be laid. He will be contacted tonight. If he gives a decision you could be charged tonight. Does that upset you?' the Detective Sergeant asked.

'Yeah,' she told him, staring at the floor.

The interview then ended.

Charlotte had been interviewed for a total of five hours and thirty-one minutes during her ten hours and thirty-five minutes in garda custody. She was asked on nine separate occasions if she wanted a solicitor present but declined each time. Linda had received legal representation but Charlotte was confident that the guards wouldn't realise that she was not telling the truth and didn't feel like she needed a solicitor.

At 9.40 p.m. on 17 October 2005 Charlotte Mulhall was charged with the murder of Farah Swaleh Noor, after Detective Inspector Christy Mangan had consulted with Pat Godfrey, a professional officer at the DPP's office. She was formally charged by Sergeant Declan Healy, the member in charge of Mountjoy Station. She replied 'nothing to say' when the charge was read out to her.

Charlotte Mulhall appeared before Dublin District Court the following morning at 10.15 a.m. Judge O'Donnell remanded her in custody for one week, to allow for the book of evidence to be served. Charlotte did not apply for bail until the next court sitting.

Farah and Kathleen

KATHLEEN WAS GENUINELY shocked when they were all taken in for questioning about Farah Noor's murder, on 3 August. She had stressed to Linda and Charlotte that there was no evidence against them and they'd be fine if they sat tight and said nothing. She went to Kilclare Gardens the day after the arrests and Linda told her that Charlotte was in Mountjoy over outstanding warrants. When they spoke about the previous day, Kathleen shook her head sadly and said: 'It was James; it was James. There were things being said that were only said to James.' She could not believe that her first-born child had betrayed her.

Two days after she was released, she went into Fitzgibbon Street Garda Station and asked to speak with Garda Sheelagh Sheehan. She wanted her passport and social welfare card returned and was carrying a photograph of Farah. She started crying and said that the photo was all she had left of her boyfriend. Kathleen claimed she slept with it under her pillow at night. She said she'd been involved in a brief relationship with a Russian man named Alex but he'd left her when she told him that her ex-boyfriend had been murdered.

Over the next few weeks Kathleen cut-off all contact with her family and moved to Carlow without telling anybody. She had no friends or family there but it obviously felt far enough away from Dublin. She lost contact with her two daughters during this time and didn't return any of Charlotte's many phone calls. Charlotte only heard that Kathleen was in Carlow from somebody she knew who had seen her mother down there.

On 2 September Kathleen was back in Dublin, collecting her dole money at North King Street Social Welfare Office. She had just left when she saw DS Gerry McDonnell coming towards her. She warmly greeted the sergeant and asked him was there any chance she could get a lift with him to the post office in Dorset Street. The detective sergeant agreed to take her and during the short journey he told her that Linda had confessed to them. He said that Linda had told them that Kathleen had asked her two daughters to murder Farah Noor in her flat at Richmond Cottages on 20 March. The Detective said that Linda had made an official statement and that Kathleen would have to respond to the allegations in some way. She agreed to ring DS McDonnell after she'd had a chance to speak to her two girls. She got out of the car, saying she would talk to him later.

Kathleen Mulhall never made any contact, however, and the guards spent a week trying to get in touch with her, without any success.

Kathleen had a lot of time for Garda Sheelagh Sheehan who had interviewed her a couple of times on 3 August. On 13 September Gda Sheehan found out that Kathleen had secretly moved to Carlow. Detective Superintendent John McKeown travelled down to Carlow District Court that afternoon and made an application for the re-arrest of

Kathleen Mulhall for the murder of Farah Swaleh Noor. The application for a warrant was granted.

The following morning Det Sgt Gerry McDonnell, Det Gda Pat Keegan and Gda Cliona O'Brien drove to Carlow, arriving at 84A St Mary's Park at 12.35 p.m. When Kathleen opened the front door she was officially arrested and taken to Mountjoy Garda Station for questioning. Kathleen said she needed cigarettes and they stopped at a garage just outside Carlow. She tried to talk to DS Gerry McDonnell about the case during the car journey but he said they couldn't discuss it until they got to the station.

They arrived at Mountjoy Garda Station at 2.05 p.m. and the forty-nine-year-old was processed and told that Linda had been charged with Farah's murder. Kathleen said she wanted to talk to her solicitor. Daragh Robinson spoke to her by telephone at 3.07 p.m. and made plans to go to the station to see his client.

Kathleen was then interviewed from 4 p.m. to 6.26 p.m. by NBCI Detectives Malachy Dunne and Pat Flood. Detective Superintendent John McKeown granted a six-hour extension to her detention period after this.

Det Sgt Gerry McDonnell and Det Gda Pat Keegan went into the interview room at 6.50 p.m. and asked her to tell them the truth about what had happened in her flat at 17 Richmond Cottages on 20 March. Kathleen agreed to tell the men exactly what had occurred and she had just started to open up when there was a knock at the door. The detectives were informed that Peter Mullen, a colleague of Daragh Robinson's from Garret Sheehan's office, had arrived at the station and wanted to speak to their client. Kathleen initially indicated that she didn't want to see the solicitor but then changed her mind and said she'd see him for five minutes.

The interview was suspended at 7.04 p.m. and before Peter Mullen went off to a private room to advise Kathleen, DS Gerry McDonnell told him that she was just about to tell them what had happened when he arrived. During her session with the solicitor, Kathleen also consulted with Daragh Robinson. She spoke to him two more times by phone, at 7.05 p.m. and 7.25 p.m. respectively.

The interview resumed at 7.38 p.m. and, between that time and her eventual release at 12.15 a.m., Kathleen stuck to the story she had told the gardaí when she was detained on 3 August. She denied any knowledge of her boyfriend's murder. She also claimed she didn't know anything about Linda admitting to carrying out the killing and pointing the finger of blame at her. She was asked how she felt about Farah Noor's death and replied: 'If you loved someone and they were found chopped to bits, how would you feel?' She wouldn't concede that Farah had been murdered in her flat and denied that he lived with her because he 'never spent a full week there'.

Det Sgt McDonnell and Det Gda Keegan asked her if she spent every night at the flat.

Kathleen replied, 'Actually, no, I didn't. The nights I didn't stay there I was out selling myself for money.' She told the detectives that she had turned to prostitution to earn money to send back home to Farah's family in Kenya. She claimed: 'I started going up to Baggot Street to get money for Farah to send to his family, but he didn't know I was going up there.' She said that she had only started working the streets around the south city in the weeks before the murder because she was worried that Farah was claiming social welfare cheques he wasn't eligible for as he was working.

When questioned, she couldn't remember how many nights she had worked in and around St Patrick's Day because she was drinking a lot, but thought it was probably 'a good few'. She claimed that it was Charlotte who had introduced her to prostitution when she was short of cash. She said her daughter had brought her to an area called Lad Lane, just off Baggot Street, and showed her what to do to sell herself for sex, for fifty or sixty euro a go. Kathleen hadn't even known that the notorious red-light area had existed until her daughter brought her down. After that she regularly worked the streets for extra cash. She was never arrested by the guards and said she used to spend nights in clients' houses, before getting a taxi home the next morning.

She claimed that on the day of her boyfriend's murder she spent the early afternoon drinking with him and her two daughters and stopped at an off-licence on the way home for some cans and vodka. After buying the drink she said: 'I went off on my own, maybe down the street. I didn't go home that night. Farah said he was going to see an ex-girlfriend. I was going my own way.'

She denied seeing Mohammed Ali Abubakaar on O'Connell Street when she was with the group, commenting, 'That man did not even know my daughters.'

She also denied that Farah and she had an argument and even lied about them having a relationship: 'No, me and Farah weren't a couple. We didn't have a relationship. He was my friend.'

The detectives could not believe what they were hearing. They knew for certain that Kathleen was involved in a relationship with Farah Noor but she was openly telling them lies – lies that she would obviously not be able to get away with.

Kathleen claimed that when Farah left her on O'Connell Street he promised to phone, but she never heard anything from him again. She said she walked down O'Connell Street, across the quays in the direction of Baggot Street, where she spent the night on the game. She drank the vodka as she went, to give her the courage to put herself in the potentially dangerous situation of selling herself for sex in a dark alleyway. After finishing her stint on the streets, Kathleen said she got a taxi home. It had started to get bright and there was nobody in the flat when she arrived. Something had happened though, because when she got into the flat, Kathleen stated: 'All my clothes were pulled out of the dressers, pulled out everywhere. I went to the toilet and then I slept on the couch. I got up and started to fix my stuff. I noticed Farah's clothes were gone except for a white jacket and a couple of T-shirts. All his other stuff was gone.'

She said she didn't notice anything else strange about the flat and certainly didn't see any blood there. After tidying her stuff she went back to sleep and was woken by Linda and Charlotte who had come in the open door.

She told the detectives that she never spoke to the girls about Farah. She said she'd tried to ring him a few times since but his phone was off. She had just assumed that he had gone off to live with his ex-girlfriend in Kilkenny, who had a sick child.

Again, the gardaí knew that she was lying and that her story made no sense. You don't just let a man with whom you've had a long-term relationship walk out the door and not check where he has gone. The detectives were used to people telling them lies but Kathleen was excelling herself.

Farah's wallet was gone as well, but Kathleen explained

that she had his ATM card. She said he had given it to her a long time ago, to look after, because he wasn't great at managing money. She said she'd used his card loads of times before because he owed her money but she didn't have any information on the bank card being used after his murder. When the detectives questioned her about the card, she said she didn't have it now and didn't know where it was. Kathleen said she didn't know anything about using the card after Farah died. She claimed that she had not taken any money out, even though bank records showed that his account had been accessed after he died.

'As far as the government here are concerned Farah doesn't know where any of his family are but he did know because he sent them money,' she said. She claimed that she gave Farah €1,500 to send to his mother in Africa. She paid €63 to wire it to Kenya and that a woman called Lulu signed for it on 6 December 2004. Kathleen said she was always lending him cash to send back home. She told them that Charlotte had given Farah €1,000 out of a compensation claim pay-off she'd received as a result of a road traffic accident, to send to Kenya. The €1,500 Kathleen had lent him was also part of a gift from Charlotte. When pressed, Kathleen estimated that in the three years they were together she'd lent him another €6,000, which came from her dole money.

The guards were surprised to hear this. Kathleen had been telling them a few minutes before that she was not even in a relationship with Farah. She insisted she was telling the truth, however. Kathleen also told the gardaí that she'd survive on less cash each week so Farah's family could have food back in Africa.

Kathleen was interviewed for more than three hours

and kept her composure, even though the gardaí asked her some very tough questions. They formed the impression that she was a very cold woman and was also very hard. She didn't seem to be nervous, despite the fact that she was being questioned as part of a murder investigation.

Kathleen declared that after Noor had left her to go back to his ex, she had started re-decorating the whole flat. She told them she took up the carpet in the bedroom because it was infested with cockroaches. She said she bought the new carpet from Carpet Mills and put the infested carpet in black bags and the bin men took it away. She swore that there was no blood on the carpet and said: 'I don't know if Farah was killed in that flat, I wasn't there.'

When she was questioned about her ex-husband, John Mulhall's, involvement, Kathleen said that John never had any contact with Farah. She claimed she knew nothing about John threatening him. She told the gardaí that she had not been in touch with her husband for years. The gardaí knew this was a lie and had phone records to prove it. Kathleen, however, continued with her story, which was flying in the face of all the evidence.

She claimed the only time she had rung him was when her daughters started visiting her in Cork. The mother-of-six said that Linda had told her she was having a problem with her father. Kathleen said she rang him to talk about it but she would not elaborate on the details of the conversation.

The last time Kathleen said she'd seen John was the previous Christmas Eve when she was at the family home in Tallaght. She said she'd also spoken to him a couple of times since then, about how their two sons were getting on in prison. Since Farah had disappeared she admitted speaking to her husband a few times but denied that he came to the flat and removed the bloody bedclothes after they murdered Farah.

'John was never in my flat. I never had a conversation with him. John removed nothing from my house,' she declared.

The gardaí knew she was lying and were all too aware that John Mulhall had helped to clear items from the murder scene. Kathleen vehemently disputed this.

Kathleen pretended that she was shocked about Linda confessing to the murder. She said that her daughter was lying to them when she said that her mother had urged her to do it, or was in anyway involved: 'I don't know if Linda or Charlotte harmed Farah. I don't believe Linda killed Farah.'

She described Linda to the detectives as: 'A mentally disturbed sick girl. She's very unstable. She uses drugs. She's bulimic. It relates to her dad. If she wants to talk to you about it she can, but it's not my business. She didn't have a good life.'

The guards were surprised to hear Kathleen talk about her daughter with such frankness. Most mothers try to protect their children and paint them in a good light but she was different. The officers were beginning to realise that Kathleen Mulhall was not going to volunteer much helpful, or honest, information.

Kathleen also spoke about how Farah Noor was violent and had a fascination with knives: 'He had knives in his bag, a big Nike bag, a shoulder bag, grey blue. I don't know where the bag is now. He mostly had kitchen knives; he threatened people with them.'

She said that the most violent thing Farah ever did was tell her that he was responsible for the murder of Raonaid Murray. Kathleen told them: 'He told me he stabbed her

[Raonaid Murray]. She was a friend of an ex-girlfriend. He told me I would end up the same way. He said he was too good to be caught. He told me it was somewhere down a laneway he killed her with a knife.'

She said that Farah was very drunk when he first confessed about the murder but a week before his death he had brought it up again during an argument.

After Kathleen Mulhall told gardaí about Noor's confession, investigators still working the case at the Dun Laoghaire headquarters were immediately informed. They accepted that Farah was 'a nasty piece of work' but were satisfied that he was not the killer.

At this stage Kathleen admitted she lived 'in big fear' of Farah. She said he had threatened to kill her and her family on numerous occasions but that he had never raped her or boasted about raping anyone else either. She claimed that just a week before the murder she'd had a massive row with the Kenyan and he'd threatened to kill her.

As the interview finally ended Kathleen signed a statement saying: 'I was getting my social money for Farah and myself. I said to Farah, "I can't keep collecting as you are working and if the Social find out my money will be stopped." So I went to the Social Welfare and I told them I was not with Farah anymore and I told them to stop his money. I asked them for a letter and they gave me a letter. Farah rang me up that night and he told me I was a fucking liar and that I had his money. I told him I had a letter to say I wasn't getting his money. I gave him the letter. He looked at it, read it and said all I was was a fucking cunt and said I wouldn't get away with this. He said, "I am going to fucking kill you just like I did with the whore in Dun Laoghaire, Raonaid Murray." I asked Farah not to kill me, as I didn't do anything on him. He started beating me. Then he threw me in the bedroom in my flat. Then he tried to smother me with pillows and I couldn't breathe. Then he jumped on top of me. I don't know where I got the strength from but I kicked him in the stomach and he came off me. Then when he got up I made a 999 call and I said I would ring the police. He ran out to the kitchen and got a knife.

'He said, "I am going to chop you up into little pieces and eat you."

'I said, "You can't. If Charlotte rings and I don't answer, she will know there is a problem and come to the house."

'He said, "Cathy I am going to chop you up into little pieces, put you in the fridge and eat you piece by piece." He said, "No one will ever find you 'cause I will tell them you fucked off."

'So then he sits down and started thinking and he calms down. He said if I ever told the police he would kill me and my family. I told him to leave my flat and there would be no problem. So he took some stuff and he went. I said, "Farah can I have the keys of the house, please?" He said no he was keeping the keys. I told him to keep the keys and to fuck off. He then said, "You will never get away from me," and he started saying things about James and John being fucked in prison every day. I said, "You don't know my sons. Don't say that about them." He went.'

Kathleen Mulhall broke down crying three or four times during the course of the day, saying she could not believe that Farah was dead. Detectives were certain that she had played a central role in the killing but had to release her for the second time. There was not enough concrete evidence to hold her, despite what Linda had said.

Before Kathleen left the garda station she said, 'I would

love to help you. If I could help you I would, but I am sorry, I can't. One day the truth will come out what happened Farah. Then I want an apology. I would help you 100 per cent if I could.'

Kathleen Mulhall met Farah Swaleh Noor in Coco's nightclub in Tallaght in the summer of 2001. Ironically, Kathleen's daughter Marie had already met Farah before they got together. At the time Marie was going out with Robert Steward from Kiltalawn, in Tallaght, and was in his house when Farah came in with Robert's brother, Trevor. Marie went to the local shop and bought the so-called Somalian cigarettes, not realising that he would later be the cause of her family breaking-up. To complicate things further, Linda was seeing Trevor Steward around the time that Farah and Kathleen first met.

The mother-of-six and the 'refugee' immediately began having an affair, even though Kathleen had been married for twenty-nine years. She fell for Farah in a big way and early the following year separated from her husband, John. She took a barring order out against him, alleging that he was beating her up. She forced her husband to leave the family home in Kilclare Gardens but her children sided with John and went to live with him. She was snubbed by many of her family and friends when her marriage ended. After a hard few months living with Noor in Tallaght, they decided to move to Cork in the summer of 2002. They had been having problems with some neighbours from around Jobstown and Kathleen wanted to start a new life away from the messy situation in Dublin.

The couple moved to Cork City and lived at seven different addresses over the next two years. Farah had a lot of friends in Cork, as he had previously lived there and knew the city well. Kathleen did not have a job and spent her days drinking and pottering around, living on the €148.80 she was paid from the State, plus her rent allowance. Farah showed a bit more initiative than Kathleen. Noor worked at various odd jobs around the city to earn extra cash. As well as signing on, he got a job on a building site across from City Hall, which is now the site of the Clarion Hotel. Noor could not drive and did not have a licence so he was a familiar figure around Glanmire and Cork City, cycling his black mountain bike. The couple spent most of their days drinking and going to house parties thrown by other Africans living around the city. People remember that Farah used to refer to Kathleen as 'The Boss'.

Linda and her then-new boyfriend Wayne Kinsella moved to Cork for a short time and the two couples would meet in pubs a few nights each week and drink together. McCurtain Street was a favourite hangout for them but Farah was a regular in a fair few pubs throughout the city.

During the summer of 2003 Farah and Kathleen were living in Flat 2, 9 Wellington Terrace, Grattan Hill. Noor was friendly with the man who lived in Flat 1, Ahmed Ahmed, and Ahmed's friend Hamed Salim Miran. Hamed went to live in Flat 2 when the couple left Wellington Terrace in September 2003.

Farah and Kathleen moved to a flat at 105 Lower Glanmire Road. The new flat was in Kathleen's name only and Farah was not supposed to be staying there. The owner of the three-storey terraced house, Maureen Moran, met Farah once when he was helping to move Kathleen's clothes in. Maureen got a call two weeks after Kathleen arrived to tell her that there had been a row at the flat and that the guards were called and an ambulance had come as well. She went to see the mother-of-six the following day and noticed splashes of blood in the living room and hallway. It looked like some sort of weapon had been used during the fight the previous night. Kathleen promised to clean the blood from the walls and said she would do a good job. The owner wasn't happy that gardaí were being called to disturbances on her property, however, and asked Kathleen to find somewhere else to live.

The following week when Maureen called around to collect the rent, she noticed that this time Kathleen was covered in bruises. She said Noor had beaten her but another tenant told Maureen that it was Kathleen's son. Although Kathleen was on rent allowance she was slow to pay her percentage towards the rent. In the end the landlady asked Kathleen to leave the flat after about five weeks.

After being evicted from the flat at 105 Lower Glanmire Road, Farah and Kathleen found another flat just down the road at number 158. They moved into Flat 5 around 20 October 2003, paying a €300 deposit to the owner, Barry Sheehan, and signing a letting agreement. Sixty-year-old Gerard Finn worked collecting rent for Barry Sheehan and often had dealings with the couple. Finn used to call to collect rent from Farah and Kathleen each Friday but he often had to return again during the week because the two were always slow to pay. Kathleen told Gerard that she was pregnant and often wore a loose dress to hide her 'bump'. He subsequently heard that she had lost the baby, supposedly due around June or July 2004, but he never spoke with Kathleen about it. When he visited the flat Farah was often drunk and Kathleen was a few times as well. Local people used to say that the pair enjoyed drinking too much and were well known in pubs around Glanmire.

Mr Finn later stated: 'Farah would be quite abusive at times to me when I'd collect the rent, he could be quite contentious. Kathleen would be the pacifier, always telling Farah to leave me alone, that I was only doing my job. Farah I believe thought he was regularly the victim of racism. I think he could provoke people and got into fights. That's what I heard anyway.'

Apart from Farah drunkenly abusing him, Mr Finn didn't have any real trouble with the couple and was never called to the house for any disturbances.

Other tenants had complained about noise and fights at night and often rang the guards or Barry Sheehan. One such tenant who was not impressed with Farah Noor was Michael Mulrey who lived in Flat 4, directly under Farah and Kathleen. He felt that Noor was a violent man when he had been drinking. Mulrey had had a run-in with Farah in the pub after he refused to shake Noor's hand. The Kenyan also wrongly thought that Mulrey was responsible for cutting the wheel on his bicycle. Michael Mulrey did have time for Kathleen 'when she wasn't drinking'. He later said she knew that he was getting hospital treatment for an illness and made an effort to be extra quiet at night so he could rest. The forty-eight-year-old also remembered that Kathleen was very heavily pregnant when she came into the house 'and then very suddenly she wasn't'. He heard that the landlord had to get a lot of blood cleaned from the flat because she'd lost her child.

Around this time Charlotte was a frequent visitor to the city and was going out with an African man for a while. She used to stay with her mother and Farah told a few people that they were not getting on. He said he was unhappy that Charlotte was with them. He complained that she drank far too much vodka and used to go through bottles each day.

Linda and Charlotte also visited Cork together on at least one occasion and stayed with their mother in the flat. Michael Mulrey remembered seeing the two girls with Kathleen but took them to be her sisters: 'They were rough and in my opinion they were hookers. There used to be fierce rows between them all. I remember one occasion when Farah was shouting at them, as he came down the stairs, that they were all tramps and prostitutes and they responded in equally colourful language. The girls would roar at each other and when Farah was there, roar at him. I thought they were well-matched.'

When Michael Mulrey heard on the news that it was Farah Noor's body that had been cut up and pulled from the Royal Canal in Dublin, he 'straight away thought of the three women: Kathleen and her two sisters. I think they would be well able to do that. They were very rough.'

At one stage, the fire brigade had to be called to the flat to free Kathleen after she got stuck in the bathroom. Farah and Kathleen would also often ring Gerard Finn about a leak in the skylight and this once caused their TV to blow up. In addition they also had regular problems with their shower, which was often clogged up, and they were angry about this. They didn't make any effort to do up the flat while they were there, however.

Barry Sheehan was annoyed because they were so bad about paying him and he threatened to evict them several times. The last time he went to collect rent was 10 September 2004. Farah gave him €66 and Kathleen handed over €20. One night soon afterwards the couple left the house, still owing rent, and didn't return their keys.

Hamed Salim Miran used to bump into Farah and

Kathleen on Patrick Street in the city and would often go out drinking in pubs with them. Miran was from Somalia and knew Farah Noor from back home. They regularly spoke about Africa in Swahili, a language Farah also spoke, and spent a bit of time together. They had given Farah the nickname 'America' because when he first arrived in Ireland he rang his wife and said: 'I'm in America; I'm not coming home.' Although Farah was from Kenya he was such a skilled liar that he even managed to convince his close friends that he was Somalian. They never suspected his true identity.

When Hamed first came to Cork in late 2003, Farah had told him that Kathleen was pregnant but she didn't look like she'd much of a bump. He remembered, however, that Kathleen regularly used to complain that she was having stomach pains. Miran didn't like Kathleen and said she had a 'devilish' look about her and he 'didn't like the look of her'. He used to notice that Farah often had cuts and bruises on his face.

Farah invited Ahmed and Hamed over for Christmas Day in 2003 and they all had dinner together. A few days later, just after the New Year, Farah rang Ahmed Ahmed on his mobile and told him that he had had a fight with Kathleen. The following morning he turned up at his old flat at Wellington Terrace, with all his bags. He said that Kathleen had had a miscarriage four months into her pregnancy, and he was going to stay with someone in Kilkenny. He told the two men that he'd had a big row with Kathleen the night before and that one of her sons had pulled a knife on him because he saw Farah hitting his mother. Farah panicked and jumped from the second floor window and hurt his leg but wouldn't go to hospital, but Kathleen was brought there by ambulance.

Farah wouldn't stay with his two friends and supposedly left for Kilkenny, but Hamed ran into him in the city two or three days later. His friend told him that the two were back together. Hamed thought that Farah used to drink a lot and would 'become a different person' with drink on him. He thought that Farah also used soft drugs. Hamed met Charlotte Mulhall a few times and later remembered that she was regularly down from Dublin, visiting her mother.

In the run-up to Christmas 2003 Farah registered for FÁS courses in computers and retail sales. He started the six-month computer course in December. It was taught by a woman named Breda Murphy and took place at the National Software Centre in Mahon. Classes were on in the afternoon and Farah often came in with cement on his clothes after he had spent the morning working on building sites. Breda Murphy remembers Farah as being very likeable. She said: 'He was very quiet but would take a slagging and give one.' He didn't have great English but got on well with all his classmates and rarely missed days. He also always phoned when he wasn't going to be in. Farah never smelled of drink during the computer course but would sometimes look at the screen blankly. Breda Murphy said he wasn't very good with the computer 'and appeared to be of low intelligence' but that he enjoyed playing Solitaire.

Farah told people on the course that he had three children in Somalia, two in Dublin and that Kathleen Mulhall was pregnant with his sixth child. The tutor got the impression that Farah was involved in a custody battle over his children in Dublin and remembers that in March or April 2004 Farah came back from Dublin with cuts and bruises to his face. He said he had been beaten up because of his colour.

Breda Murphy was only ever out once with Farah socially and that was on the final day of the course. Farah attended the afternoon course and a separate group met in the morning. Both groups came together for the first time at a pub called the Cloverhill House, in Mahon. They had had lunch and a few drinks when Noor became involved in a scuffle with another student. People said they were fighting because the African claimed he was overcharged for some drugs. Some of the group seemed to get drunk very quickly and were knocking back whiskey outside the pub. Breda Murphy intervened to break up what could have developed into a fist fight. Farah then told her that if anyone upset her he would kill them for her. She laughed it off and joked that she'd keep his number close in case she ever needed it. A few people laughed and Farah got insulted because he was being serious. Breda Murphy remembers thinking that Farah wasn't very pleasant when he had been drinking. She didn't see him again after that last day.

Breda met Kathleen two or three times during the course and found her to be very polite. She thought she looked like a 'reformed alcoholic – kinda shook, but tidied up'. Kathleen always wore smocks and spoke to Breda about her baby.

After he completed the computer-training course, Farah started his second FÁS training scheme, attending a ten-week retail sales course at the end of June 2004. This also took place in Mahon and there were eighteen other people in his class.

Farah sat beside forty-four-year-old Carolyn Murphy, who lived with her three children in Mahon. Carolyn found Farah to be quiet but 'a very humble sort of fella'. She gave him a spare highlighter one day and told him to keep it and 'it was like the best thing ever to him'. Farah had poor English, she said, 'except when he spoke about money – it seemed perfect when he spoke about that'. He told Carolyn that his wife had been murdered in the genocide in Somalia and that his father was looking after his children. He said he couldn't re-enter the country and his kids couldn't get out. He bragged that he could have six wives because he was a Muslim and already had gone through three. Carolyn used to have a good laugh with him and joked that she wouldn't be number four. Farah once confided in Carolyn that he had no money and got food vouchers through St Patrick's Church after going there late at night looking for food. He also claimed that he got a lot of hassle because of his colour and said that his colleagues on the building sites used to refer to him as 'Al Qaeda' after the September 11 terrorist attacks. Noor claimed that when George W Bush was due to come on an official trip to Ireland, gardaí arrested him in Cork one night as a terror suspect because he was Muslim and black.

Fifty-year-old Carol Elliot was also in the class and later told gardaí that Farah 'knew how to work the system' and was able to get away with not turning up every day. Noor told his colleagues that his partner 'was on her last legs' and that he had seven kids by two different women in Dublin. He used to complain that he was getting a raw deal in Ireland and said he was going to quit the course because the government had agreed to give him €2,000 to go to New Zealand. This was total rubbish but Farah liked to tell stories and regularly made things up. Noor also said he had another girlfriend in Cork who was pregnant but he wasn't bringing her to New Zealand with him because it was too cold for the child there but once he had settled he would send for them. Carol said: 'Every day he turned up in class he had the same story to tell us. You wouldn't believe half of it. He was a con artist.' His classmates all noticed that he fancied a young girl who was doing the same course. Farah could hardly keep his eyes off her.

The last time Carol saw Noor was when he was at FÁS collecting his cheque. All students participating in FÁS courses are paid a weekly wage to supplement their social welfare payments. The courses are designed to help to prepare people to get back into the workplace. He had a boy of about eight with him and said the lad was his son. 'Farah's eyes were rolling around in his head. He used drugs, definitely, I'd say.'

Michael Foran was also on Noor's FÁS course. The two men used to get the bus together every day and spent the journeys chatting. The pair became quite friendly and used to socialise together as well. Foran liked Farah and said he got on with everyone in the class but found it a little daunting. Noor spoke very good English but had difficulty understanding accents and struggled in Cork where the local accent is very pronounced. Michael remembered that Farah liked women and had said that he had two children in Dublin, 'His plan was to have a child on every continent.' Noor used to reminisce about his life in Somalia and talked about how he was a 'gigolo on the beaches'. He bragged that he and his friend used to go onto boats with older Italian women. Noor also confided in his Irish friend that he had a UN passport because he was a war refugee and said he planned to leave Ireland for Canada. He said that his wife had been shot dead back home in Somalia.

Michael Foran met up with Farah and Kathleen in August 2004 at the Oval Bar in the city. They met at around

10 p.m. and Farah was 'fairly well on'. Foran thought that Kathleen looked about eight months pregnant. She sat by herself all night and didn't say one word, not even hello. She was drinking minerals all evening and Foran didn't stay long. He remembered that Farah was a heavy drinker who used to go to the KLM bar down by the docks each evening and 'drink himself into oblivion'. He said his friend smoked hash but he didn't think he used any other drugs.

In early September 2004 Foran met Noor in Fitzgerald's Park and he bragged that he had been arrested the previous night. He said he had only been released from custody that morning. Foran got the impression that he might have been very drunk and was detained for his own protection. He was with two young children, aged about five and seven, and said they were his sons. Both of the kids were totally white, however, and did not resemble the African. The guards do not know who they were but there is a possibility that they were Linda's children.

Michael Foran and Farah kept in contact and had exchanged telephone numbers. Foran also had Kathleen's number because there was a problem with their FÁS cheques one week and Farah wanted to be contacted when Michael found out what had happened.

Farah was frequently absent from his course and eventually decided to drop out. On his last day he told Carolyn Murphy that he got a job in construction in Dublin and was leaving. He said he needed to earn money for his baby.

✂✂✂

The couple moved back to Dublin on 14 September 2004. They told people they'd left Cork because they had been targeted by an IRA man who didn't like Farah because he was black, but there is absolutely no evidence of this. When they arrived they got off the Dublin bus and headed straight for the Asylum Seeker Unit at 77 Upper Gardiner Street, seeking assistance to find accommodation. They were interviewed by Community Welfare Officer Derek O'Connor who arranged a room for them at the Mountainview Bed and Breakfast at 2 Killakee Way, in Firhouse. The couple were told that this accommodation was only temporary, for a maximum of two weeks and the onus was on them to find a permanent home. Mountainview guesthouse was exclusively for foreign nationals who were referred there by the Northern Area Health Board. It is not a long-term residence and most people housed there only remain for a few days.

Kathleen was already in receipt of unemployment benefit and Farah also requested funds from Officer O'Connor but as Farah had left the FÁS course by his own choice he was not entitled to full dole payments. This was explained to him and he was given cash from an Emergency Need Fund instead. It was agreed that he would sign-on as a dependent of Kathleen. From October the Health Board started paying Kathleen €234 each week, on the basis that she was married to Farah. Noor wasn't very happy with this situation. He was always anxious to get his cash quickly and wanted to be paid his money independently of Kathleen. There was nothing he could do, however, and the couple went to Tallaght to the B&B run by Mary Andrews and owned by Niall Hade. Mountainview has eight bedrooms and there were fourteen people living there when Farah and Kathleen arrived. The couple were placed in Room 3.

When Kathleen went to Mary Andrews on 10 October, requesting a transfer because she was afraid of Farah, the manager contacted Officer O'Connor. Arrangements were made to move Kathleen to Lismore B&B in Drumcondra, which is run by Hanji Bob and her husband Catalin.

Two or three days later Kathleen called in to the Health Board offices because they wanted to speak to her about her claim. Officer O'Connor noticed that she was shaken and appeared to be very nervous. She was not nearly as confident as she had appeared when she was there with Farah. The community welfare officer assured her that Noor would not be able to get her new address and she seemed to relax on hearing this. While Kathleen was still living in Drumcondra, she met Derek O'Connor again. She told him that she had bumped into her boyfriend on the street one day and that Farah now knew where she was living. Kathleen's claims that she lived in fear of Noor were clearly lies, however, as she had told Hanji Bob that she had a Somalian boyfriend named Farah. On one occasion Bob had also heard Noor and Kathleen having an argument in her bedroom.

Farah Noor also left the Mountainview B&B in early October, at around the same time as Kathleen. He frequently returned to the guesthouse to collect his post and called out around St Patrick's Day, just before the murder. Mary Andrews remembers that Farah was often dressed in his Ireland-away jersey and during one visit to collect his post she said 'fair play to you' because he was supporting the Irish soccer team. When she heard that the body found in the canal had the same jersey on, she thought about Farah and hoped it wasn't him.

After leaving the guesthouse Farah re-registered with Adecco Recruitment. He returned to work at Excell Sydney Coopers again on 7 October 2004. He stayed there until

28 January 2005, when his temporary contract expired.

On 25 February he started another job with Schmitt ECS, who are based on the Hewlett Packard site in Leixlip, Co. Kildare, and was still employed there when he died. Farah last attended work on 16 March and didn't bother turning up on the final few days he was alive. He didn't ring in sick, to either the company or Adecco, and this was noted on his permanent record at the recruitment agency.

Farah's pay was lodged into his AIB account in Cork and his payslips were sent to the Mountainview B&B. He seemed to use it as a semi-permanent postal address, even though he no longer lived there. His wages for the week ending 20 March 2005 were paid into his account five days later. They amounted to €157.42 for the three days he had worked that week. The staff at Adecco remember Noor as being of medium height and build, with 'watery eyes and a runny nose'. He always wore 'casual gear, but trendy and he was always clean'. He wore a gold band on his wedding finger and always had a Manchester United ring on his middle finger. He wore two or three other rings on his right hand.

Adecco sent Noor's P45 to Mountainview on 22 March but he never received it. Mary Andrews wrote 'return, gone away' on the letter but forgot to put it back in the post. Community Welfare Officer Derek O'Connor liased with Adecco about Noor's work record and all the reports he received back were satisfactory. Mr O'Connor always thought that Noor looked scruffy, as if he was homeless. He said he had been in his office between four and eight times, from September 2004 until February 2005, and was never clean.

The last time Farah Swaleh Noor made contact with the Health Board was on 11 March 2005. His payments had risen to €148.80 a week from 24 February and he was also given Supplementary Social Welfare Allowance. This was pending a claim he was making for Unemployment Assistance, as he had filled out a provision for Unemployment Assistance form on 24 February. He used to collect his money every Thursday in Gardiner Street.

With their money sorted out, all Farah and Kathleeen had to do now was find somewhere to live and they'd be set up. Kathleen Mulhall answered an advert looking for tenants and moved into Flat 1, 17 Richmond Cottages in Ballybough on 1 December 2004. The landlord, John Tobin, later said that he often saw Charlotte around as well and thought she lived there for a while. Kathleen told him that her daughter was interested in one of the flats but later rang him to say that she changed her mind.

Farah and Kathleen quickly settled back into life in Dublin and Kathleen started to rebuild her relationship with her family. She frequently saw Linda and Charlotte and regularly went to visit her sons, John and James, in prison. Farah also reacquainted himself with other Africans living in Dublin. After a few weeks it was almost like they had never left the capital.

The couple invited Farah's friend Ali Suleiman Abdulaziz over to Richmond Cottages on Christmas Eve 2004. Ali had been one of the first people to greet the couple when they came back from Cork. Charlotte was also there that evening and they had a good night, enjoying some food and a few drinks. Ali later told gardaí how Farah used to jokingly refer to Kathleen as his mother and how 'he used to make a joke of it but I think he used to love that woman and she used to love him'. Farah made sure that Ali, Kathleen and Charlotte had enough food and drink before he went off to work as a security guard that evening. He produced a small bottle of Hennessy Brandy and some cigarettes and gave them to the women to have while he was gone. Ali said that this type of thing was typical of Farah and that he was generous.

Farah Noor's mind, however, was troubled in the weeks before his death. He would confide in Ali that he was scared but he wouldn't go into details about why. His friend said he 'used to give him advice not too drink too much; he drank too much, to be honest. And I said to stay away from people who take drugs'.

The couple had not been getting on and Noor had asked several people to keep their eyes open for any free accommodation because he was thinking of leaving Kathleen and moving out of Richmond Cottages. Some residents at Richmond Cottages reported more shouting and fighting than usual. It was clear that the couple were not getting on well and were coming to the end of their violent and tempestuous relationship. Farah undoubtedly beat Kathleen and, if her story can be believed, which is doubtful, had threatened to kill her and cut her up into pieces not long before he died. Kathleen told the gardaí that she was afraid of Farah but there is evidence that he was equally scared of her. In the months before he was murdered Farah had phoned his mother, Somoe Bakari Shigoo, and told her that he would have to get a knife for his own protection because Kathleen had threatened to kill him. A lot of people also came forward to say that they had seen Farah with bruises on his face and that Kathleen was no shrinking violet. She was well able to fight back and give as good as she got.

Farah's mother was very concerned and sent her son a gift a parcel of clothes. Farah rang her four days later to make sure that she had posted it. On 10 March Farah's cousin, rang Kathleen to see if the package had arrived but she said that Farah had walked out on her.

The last call that Farah made to his mother was some time around the middle of March. Somoe said it was a very strange call and her son was upset, confused and rambling, which was not like him. She felt that it was as if he was saying a final goodbye to her and was apologising for all the mistakes that he had made in his life.

Farah was in a dark place and kept referring to the son he'd had with the Chinese woman 'Lynn'.

St. Patrick's Day 2005, like many others in the lives of Kathleen and Farah, was spent on the beer. They started drinking early in the Parnell Mooney pub, on Parnell Street, with Farah in his ever-present Ireland-away jersey. There was a ballad session taking place to mark the day and all the customers were in good spirits. Christian Silva was in the same pub with his friends, 'Kenyan' Ali and Sam. They all moved to the downstairs bar because it was so packed in the main upstairs lounge. Silva had gone to the bar and ordered a pint of Guinness when he heard a woman call his name. He didn't recognise her but she came over and said, 'You remember me.' She said she had met him upstairs in the bar before. The woman was Kathleen Mulhall.

A black man came in after her and Christian thought he was from Nigeria. Farah Noor started being aggressive and shouted at him: 'Why do you talk to my girlfriend?'

Christian didn't want any trouble and replied: 'You ask her.'

Farah pulled a pair of nail cutters from his trouser pocket and punched Silva under the left eye with them. He went to hit him again but Silva caught his hand and Noor got a cut to the head in the ensuing struggle.

Christian went back to his two friends and they brought him to the toilet because his eye was bleeding.

A bouncer saw what had happened and rushed over and threw Noor out. Kathleen, however, stayed in the pub.

After Christian had cleaned his eye up, the bouncer asked him if he wanted the guards called. Silva said no and went down to the small garda office on O'Connell Street instead and told Garda David O'Leary that he had been assaulted. Garda Patrick Buckley from Store Street Station was on mobile patrol in a van when he received a call to go to the garda office. Christian Silva agreed to go back to the Parnell Mooney with the gardaí and point out the man that had assaulted him.

Silva and Garda Buckley drove the short distance to Parnell Street and saw two men standing outside the pub having a cigarette. Silva said that the man wearing the long-sleeved Ireland jersey had attacked him and the black man identified himself as Farah Swaleh Noor. The other smoker was an Irish man, Michael Dunne from Ballymun, who had joined Farah for a cigarette. Dunne had witnessed the row and asked Farah if he was OK and they had got talking.

Garda Buckley explained to Noor that an allegation had been made that he had assaulted a man but Farah said nothing.

Michael Dunne then identified himself and gave the officer his mobile number. He told the garda that the row wasn't Farah's fault.

At this stage, Farah Noor said he didn't know his own phone number but that his girlfriend was still in the pub and she had it. Garda Buckley decided not to go looking for Noor's partner and took Christian Silva back to O'Connell Street as he did not have to go to hospital and was not badly injured. He dropped him off and went back to the garda office and gave the details to Garda O'Leary for further investigation.

Meanwhile Michael Dunne went back inside the Parnell Mooney and told Kathleen that she had better go outside because her husband had nearly been arrested. She left and joined Noor who was still waiting. Kathleen wasn't happy that her night had been ruined and started for home in a huff. Farah followed her and barely spoke for the rest of the night.

Between 8 p.m. and 9 p.m. that same night, Farah's friend Ibrahim Mohamed met the couple. They were both extremely drunk and Farah was bleeding heavily from a nasty gash to his head. Kathleen was trying to get her boyfriend home and they only stopped and spoke briefly. Ibrahim vaguely knew the couple from Cork because they had lived in a flat next door to his friend and had been to a few of the same parties. He subsequently told gardaí: 'Farah would talk too much with drink. He would fight. Farah wouldn't say much when he was sober but he would talk a lot when he was drunk. I didn't really listen to him when he was drunk.'

Relations between Farah and Kathleen were very strained. The couple had spent the previous night drinking in the same pub at a reggae night and according to witnesses were also quite drunk that night. Farah continued drinking for the next two days and didn't turn up for work as scheduled. He was on an almighty bender and immediately started drinking cans when he woke up on 20 March.

Kathleen told him she was meeting her two daughters in town and asked if he wanted to come. He said he would. It could be a good opportunity to make up for the last few days and the fight on Paddy's night. He got dressed and headed towards O'Connell Street, hand-in-hand with Kathleen. Maybe they could work through their problems after all.

10

Tragic John Mulhall

WHILE FIFTY-THREE-YEAR-OLD John Mulhall initially told gardaí that he had nothing to do with the murder of Farah Swaleh Noor, he later admitted that he was in 17 Richmond Cottages just a couple of hours after the murder was committed. Some detectives privately believe that it could have been John Mulhall who cut up Noor and not his two daughters.

John Mulhall was an honest man and a hard worker who was devoted to his family. He seemed to be the one element of normality in the topsy-turvy world of the Mulhall family. He was devoted to his six children but did not seem to do a good job raising them. His two eldest sons, John and James, had a long history of run-ins with the law and were both behind bars when Linda and Charlotte murdered Noor.

John married Kathleen Mulhall in 1972 and she gave birth to their first child, James, in December of that year. Linda followed in February 1975 and the second son, John Junior, was born in 1977. Charlotte was the fourth addition to the family, after a gap of six years and Kathleen had another girl, Marie, the following year. The final Mulhall child, Andrew, was born in 1988.

John was involved in a bit of trouble when he was a teenager and had a number of minor convictions but when he met Kathleen he settled down and cleaned up his act. He didn't come to the attention of the gardaí again until January 2004, when he was stopped on suspicion of drink driving on James's Street in Dublin but he wasn't charged. He was also involved in a traffic incident on the Nass Road on 15 May 2005 and was being investigated for dangerous driving, but apart from these incidents he never had any dealings with the law.

The father-of-six had worked on and off for the previous twenty-five years as a fitter in a company called City Glass, in Donore Avenue, Dublin 8. He drove a white 97 D Berlingo van belonging to the company and brought it home from work most nights. He effectively treated it like his own car, even though it was registered to the company. He also drove a motorbike in his spare time. John's brothers Andrew and Eric worked as fitters with him in City Glass.

John and Kathleen's marriage was healthy and happy for many years but in the mid-1990s he had an affair. When she found out, things between them were never the same again. Kathleen subsequently made allegations of domestic abuse against her husband. Gardaí believe there was some element of truth to this but he was never prosecuted. In late 2001, after meeting Farah Swaleh Noor, Kathleen said the marriage was over but she didn't walk out on him. Instead Kathleen demanded that she be allowed to remain living in Kilclare Gardens. John Mulhall wasn't a confrontational man so he reluctantly agreed. This led to the bizarre situation where Kathleen moved Farah Noor into Kilclare Gardens while John, Marie and Andrew moved out. They went to stay with Linda at her house in Bawnlea Green for about a month. The father-of-six was then forced to leave Linda's overcrowded house and go and live with his son John Junior, taking Marie and Andrew with him. They stayed there for about two months.

The marriage break-up tore the family apart. John did not have any contact with his wife after she left him. He was very angry and bitter that she had turned her back on nearly thirty years of marriage. He was also furious with Farah Noor. Marie rarely spoke to her mother again. Linda also took her dad's side, as did John Junior and Andrew, who stayed living with his father. Charlotte was more neutral and made an effort to get to know Farah Noor, while James also remained relatively impartial.

Shortly afterwards John received a compensation payment of nearly €80,000 from an accident he'd had in 1997 while working in Carlow. With money in his pocket, he rented a house in Rathmintin Court, in Tallaght, and lived there with his two youngest children for about six months. It was during this period that Kathleen decided to move to Cork with her boyfriend. She agreed to allow John back into the house, and in July 2002 he moved back into 31 Kilclare Gardens with Marie and Andrew. Charlotte occasionally came to stay as well and would sometimes live there for months at a time. In the summer of 2004 Linda and her four children also went to live with John after Wayne Kinsella's court case. At the time of the murder there were nine people living in the three-bedroom house. A large extension that had been built in the back garden provided some much-needed extra accommodation.

Following Farah's murder, a number of people came forward to say that John Mulhall had made threats against the Kenyan. Mohammed Ali Abubakaar was the last person to see Farah Noor alive. When he gave a statement to gardaí on 16 May, reporting that his friend was missing, he also detailed a dispute between John Mulhall and Farah Noor. He said: 'Farah's girlfriend, Catherine, is older than him and she is separated from her husband in Tallaght. She has blonde hair. About two years ago, before Farah moved to Cork, he told me that Catherine's ex-husband had threatened to kill him. He told me that the ex-husband said to him, "I will kill you and nobody will be able to identify you." Catherine at this time was in dispute with her ex-husband because she wanted the family home to be sold and she wanted half the money. I advised Farah to leave the country or to move down the country. Farah was concerned at the time about the threats. At this time Farah and Catherine went to live in Cork.'

During the investigation, John was asked whether he had made threats, either directly or indirectly to Farah Noor, and answered no to both questions. Even so there is little doubt that there was little love lost between the pair.

The relationship didn't improve after the couple separated and Kathleen didn't help as she liked to wind her husband up. In one set of incidents, a few months after she moved to Cork, she started texting her daughter Marie's phone, telling her that somebody was sick in the family and asking to talk to John. Her ex-husband would obviously be concerned and ring his wife but she would then play dumb and pretend not to know what he was talking about. This really upset Marie and she cut off all contact with her mother at this time. When she bumped into Kathleen a few times over the years in Tallaght, she ignored her.

John tried to get on with life as a single man, although it was difficult at times. The fact that he had the support of his family, however, kept him going. On the night of the murder, he was sitting in the front room of his house when his mobile phone rang at 11.41 p.m. He checked and realised that Linda was ringing him. He wondered what she wanted at this hour of the night. 'Hiya, love,' he answered, but the voice that replied at the other end of the line was not Linda's. He instantly recognised the deep husky voice of his estranged wife.

'What do you want?' he asked Kathleen.

Kathleen wouldn't tell John what was going on and he was furious that his wife was still playing games with him after all this time. She would only tell him that there was a problem and that she couldn't talk about it over the phone. His ex-wife said she wanted him to go over to her flat at Richmond Cottages, but he wasn't falling for that. He had no intention of going unless he knew exactly what the problem was. He hung up the phone after 134 seconds and sat down, cursing his wife.

John Mulhall was raging but his love for Linda and Charlotte was far stronger than his hatred of Kathleen. He sat down and thought for a few minutes and decided that if his girls were in trouble he needed to make sure they were OK. At 11.51 p.m. he reluctantly rang Kathleen's mobile and demanded to know what was going on. She still wouldn't give him any information and said he'd have to come to her flat to see for himself. She sounded normal but wouldn't tell him if Linda and Charlotte were all right. Instead she insisted that he drive over to Ballybough. The conversation lasted two minutes and fifteen seconds.

The father-of-six didn't have a choice. He wouldn't be able to sleep, wondering if his girls were in trouble and if they needed his help. After thinking about it for a few more minutes, he rang Kathleen again and told her he was on his way. He barked down the phone at her, as he was in no mood to be nice to the woman who'd ruined his life. All he cared about was Linda and Charlotte. She could go to hell as far as he was concerned. He hung up within twenty seconds.

John got the keys for his van and drove from Tallaght to Ballybough. He had previously been to Richmond Cottages to collect Charlotte on New Year's Eve 2004 and knew where it was. The journey took him no more than twenty minutes and he pulled up outside 17 Richmond Cottages at about 1 a.m. He knocked on the door and Kathleen answered after a couple of seconds. His ex-wife looked at him and said, 'Farah is dead. The girls killed him,' John Mulhall must have thought his world was ending. Kathleen wouldn't go into details when he shouted, 'What the fuck happened?' All she said was Farah had attacked Linda and was now dead. The father-of-six must not have been able to believe his eyes when his daughters then came in and told him they had killed Farah and cut him up.

In the subsequent investigation it emerged that John didn't notice any blood on the floor or on the women. Neither did he remember a vile smell, even thought it would have been the type of stink you would expect when a body has just been cut up. Their father shook his head and whispered to the women, 'This is too serious for me to be involved in. I can't help. You're own your own.'

As soon as he got out onto the street John got physically sick on the pavement. He then jumped in his van and sped away from Ballybough, as fast as he could. On the way home he later claimed he contemplated contacting the police but decided not to. He was in a state of shock.

The fifty-three-year-old couldn't sleep a wink that night

and got up soon after 5 a.m. on 21 March. It was Charlotte's twenty-second birthday and her father was thinking about that as he drank a cup of coffee in the kitchen.

John loved his family but he was not used to breaking the law. He now found himself in an impossible situation. Either he helped his two girls to sort out the monumental mess they were in, or they would be arrested and spend the next twenty years behind bars. He'd long since stopped caring about the woman who was still legally his wife, but he felt it was his duty to help his own flesh and blood.

Finally reaching a decision, John Mulhall got back into his van and drove to Ballybough again. He picked up three black bags containing clothes, duvets, towels and other items that had been used, or got sprayed with blood, during the murder. He put the bags in the back of his van and drove home to Tallaght.

As soon as he re-entered the flat in Richmond Cottages, in the eyes of the law, John Mulhall became an accessory to murder. As he did not contact the gardaí and tell them that a man had been killed in the flat, he became part of the conspiracy to cover-up Farah's death. He was now in serious trouble. The father-of-six was facing the possibility of ten years or more in jail, if the police came knocking at his door. He was all too aware of this as he went through the early morning traffic, but he'd made his choice.

In the weeks after his daughters killed Farah, John spent his days working and attempting to put his life back together. He was also trying to convince Linda and Charlotte to come clean. Then one incident, a few weeks later, highlighted the mess they were all in. During May 2005 a work colleague of John Mulhall's, Florian Williams, was having problems with his mobile phone. He was looking for a new one and mentioned it in passing to Mulhall. John told him that he'd see if he could get his hands on one for him. A few weeks later, he came back with a silver Sagem phone and sold it to Florian for €50. The phone was in fact Farah Swaleh Noor's and Charlotte had given it to her father. John Mulhall had just sold his work pal a mobile phone that had belonged to the murder victim.

Williams innocently used Farah Noor's SIM card a total of eight times from 3 June 2005. In late June, Florian was out working in the house of family friend Marc Millea in Clondalkin when Marc said in passing that his phone was out of action. Florian said he had an old phone he could give him and brought it over the following Sunday. Mark Millea put his own SIM card into the Sagem V-55 and used the phone up until August, when he was contacted by gardaí.

Both Williams and Millea used the phone and SIM card in good faith and didn't for a minute know where it had come from. When detectives subsequently interviewed John Mulhall, enquiring as to how he had happened upon the mobile of a murder victim, he pleaded ignorance. He said he must have got it from Charlotte or Linda. He claimed he didn't know that Farah had owned it, but detectives very much doubt this and believe that he was lying. It is likely that Charlotte gave him the phone but whether or not John knew Farah was the previous owner is open to speculation.

John Mulhall had stored the items he removed from the murder scene in the shed in his back garden. He was waiting for the chance to dispose of them. An opportunity finally arose in mid-July.

On Wednesday 13 July Vincent Mahon was sitting in the back garden of his house at Mill Lane, in Leixlip, Co. Kildare. He was enjoying the evening sun, resting on a bench he often sat on, overlooking the River Liffey. This time, however, he noticed something unusual out of the corner of his eye. It was about 7.30 p.m. and a big white duvet was floating on top of the water. Mahon got up to take a closer look and immediately noticed a man in his neighbour's garden, two doors up in Castle Park. The man looked like he was aged around fifty and was about 5 ft 8"to 5 ft 10" in height, of stocky build, with a tight haircut. He was tanned and wore jeans and a T-shirt. Vincent knew that his neighbour, Harry Byrne, was on holidays so he kept a close eye on the man. The stranger continued to throw black bags into the Liffey from Harry's back garden. Whatever the mystery man was throwing in seemed to be quite light, as the bags floated the 180 feet between the two houses in a matter of seconds.

Vincent sat and observed the man and saw that he threw about seven or eight bags into the river. He didn't even bother throwing the last one in but just emptied its contents into the water. This bag contained cans and bottles and, by the sound of them hitting off each other, there were a good few in the bag. Vincent didn't say anything but he went out the front of his house and headed towards Harry's. He saw the man walk up the garden, away from the river and noticed a white or cream van parked outside Harry Byrne's. Vincent Mahon had never seen either the van or the driver there before. It was a small car-van and didn't look like it had any writing on the side. Vincent decided not to get involved and went back into his house without confronting the litterbug.

John Mulhall got into his van unchallenged and drove away from Leixlip, having finally got rid of a problem that had been sitting in his shed since March.

The following Thursday forty-nine-year-old Vincent Mahon finished work again and went outside to relax when he spotted a wheelie bin, with the number thirty-one painted on the side of it. It was standing diagonally up in the water between his house and his neighbour's, Val Lenane. Val is Harry Byrne's next-door neighbour and Vincent assumed that the man who had dumped the rubbish from Harry's back garden was also responsible for the bin. He was annoyed and decided to ring his neighbour to tell him what was going on.

The following day he rang Niamh Byrne, Harry's daughter who sometimes babysat for him. He left a message and Harry's wife, Roisin, called him back, saying she didn't have a clue who was using her property as a rubbish dump. Roisin said she had organised somebody to come and do some work in the garden on the Tuesday they were away but nobody should have been there on the Wednesday.

It later emerged that John Mulhall was at the house in Leixlip on 13 July to do some odd jobs around the garden. He was there because Harry Byrne owned City Glass and was John Mulhall's employer.

The following Sunday, Vincent's neighbour, Martin Murray, waded into the Liffey and walked across to where the bin lay. It was lying diagonally in the water, was open slightly and was full of water. He opened it up to check what was inside and a plastic bag and some soggy paper fell out. The paper broke apart and sank and the other bits floated quickly downstream. Martin emptied the water out of the bin and took it to the bank just as Vincent arrived. The two neighbours left it at the Mill Centre, which is a small light-engineering industrial centre beside Vincent's house on the opposite side of the riverbank. As they were heading back to their houses, Martin Murray bumped into his friend Paul Murray and told him the story of the bin in the river. Paul was interested and decided to take the abandoned bin home because it would come in useful for some work he had planned doing on his nearby house. Little did he realise that the abandoned number thirty-one wheelie bin would be a potentially crucial piece of evidence in a murder investigation and would prompt a massive search of the river when gardaí learned of its existence just a few weeks later.

John Mulhall was very close to his two brothers and his sister. When he was first brought in for questioning on 3 August 2005 and was released from custody without charge, his brother Andrew went to Store Street Garda Station to collect him. John's other brother, Eric, travelled with him, as did his sister, Eileen. The Mulhall brothers also picked up Linda, who had been released from the same station, and forty-one-year-old Andy drove the car in silence to his house in Drimnagh.

When they got home Andrew and John had a word in private together. He asked John why he had been arrested for murdering his ex-wife's boyfriend. His brother denied that he had anything to do with the killing. He admitted that on the night of the murder he had got a phone call from one of the girls telling him they were in trouble and asking if he'd go to Kathleen's flat in Ballybough. He told Andy that he drove over and looked in and when he saw what they had done he'd said. 'Ye have done it now; ye are on your own,' and left the flat. John didn't say directly that he saw the dead body but he knew Noor was dead and that his wife and two daughters were in the house. He thought that his family had committed the terrible murder because Noor had tried to have sex with one of the girls, but he didn't tell his brother this. Andrew did not question him further because he knew John was upset.

Three or four weeks after John's release, Eric Mulhall was out working with him and asked his brother a question that he'd wanted to get off his chest for a while – why had he been arrested? John repeated the same story he'd told Andy and was vague in details. He said he didn't want to talk about it any more but when the brothers were travelling together in the van and Farah Noor's murder was mentioned, John broke down crying each time.

After Charlotte and Linda were charged, he always cried when he saw his daughters on the television or read one of the frequent newspaper articles about them. He was obviously struggling to come to terms with what had taken place. After his release, John Mulhall rarely spoke to his extended family about his arrest. Apart from conversations with Andy he never mentioned the death of Farah Swaleh Noor again. Linda and Charlotte never spoke to their uncles either.

John might have got away with avoiding the subject when he was with his brothers but after the arrests, the murder of Farah Noor was the talk of the house in Kilclare Gardens and little else was mentioned. Marie had spent the day of the arrests minding Linda's children and had been told by her uncles that her dad was also in custody. When John arrived back to the house the two of them sat in the front room and Marie asked him why he had been taken away by the guards. He said the police thought he had moved Noor's body after he was murdered but her father promised that he'd had nothing whatsoever to do with the killing and said he wouldn't do anything to get himself into trouble. On 30 March John and Marie had been watching the evening news on TV3 when Farah's body was removed from the canal. The father-of-six had said it was a terrible thing to happen. He hadn't given Marie any idea that her two sisters were behind the ruthless murder, and Marie, filled with dread, had not said anything about the drunken confession Charlotte had made to her a few days before the body was discovered. After his release from custody in August, Marie believed that her father wasn't involved and decided to tell him about Charlotte's confession but he seemed to already know about it.

After the arrests, life in Kilclare Gardens was very difficult. John struggled to hold things together as his children fought. Marie wouldn't talk to Linda. She later said her sister 'thought that the killing of Farah Noor was finished with when she was released. She was sure she got away with it.'

Meanwhile John was putting Linda under a lot of pressure to talk to the guards about the murder and to clear her conscience. When he was arrested John hadn't given the gardaí any information, but Sergeant Liam Hickey's instincts had told him that John Mulhall knew more than he was telling. The experienced officer got the impression that whatever had taken place at Ballybough had sickened John and was eating away at him. He decided to keep in touch with the fitter and regularly called on him after he was released.

Sergeant Hickey had seized John's work van for forensic examinations on the day he was arrested. When all tests had been completed three days later on 5 August, he asked Garda Karl Murray to pick the white Berlingo up from the garda compound at Santry Garda Station and drive it to Mountjoy Station. Garda Murray found a licence in the vehicle and after examining it, he realised that it belonged to Mulhall. On closer scrutiny the garda also discovered that the licence was a forgery and after making inquiries, this was confirmed by Dublin City Council. Nothing was said, however, and the vehicle was returned to John Mulhall.

On 10 August at about 5.30 p.m., Sergeant Liam Hickey and Garda Karl Murray stopped John Mulhall at Sundrive Road, in Crumlin. The father-of-six was driving his work van and Sergeant Hickey asked him for his licence and insurance details. Mulhall said he did not have them with him but said he'd produce them at Tallaght Garda Station. Garda Murray then produced the forged licence and John confirmed that it was his. The two gardaí told him that the licence was a fake, but the fifty-three-year-old insisted it was genuine. He said he had given Kathleen Mulhall his documentation and the money to renew his licence a number of years previously and she had given the licence back to him. Mulhall claimed that the Carriage Office in Harcourt Square had previously examined the licence in order to give him access to Dublin Airport for the purposes of a job he was doing there. He continued to insist his licence was real.

Sergeant Hickey told him that they were investigating a murder and were very thorough in all their lines of inquiry and there was no doubt that they were correct. Hickey then asked him if he could help the guards with their investigation into Farah Noor's death and John Mulhall replied: 'It had nothing to do with me.'

The Sergeant again asked if he could assist them and

Mulhall answered, 'Not really.' He agreed to go with the men to Sundrive Road Garda Station and parked his van on the footpath outside. Once inside the station, he repeated that he could be of no assistance and undertook to produce his documentation in Tallaght.

One week later, on 17 August, Liam Hickey received a call on his mobile from John Mulhall at about 9.30 a.m. He asked to meet the sergeant in a side street off Cork Street, Dublin 8, an hour later. When they met up, John showed Sergeant Hickey his Dublin airport ramp pass, demonstrating that his licence had previously been checked.

Liam Hickey replied that everything had been checked and that 'we are not barking up the wrong tree'.

John Mulhall said, 'I know that but it had nothing to do with me. Go talk to Linda; tell her I have been arrested and you have found the head in Leixlip or something like that.'

Coincidentally it was that same day, 17 August, that the Noor murder investigation team had got to hear about the dumping incident at the Leixlip home of John Mulhall's boss. As a result of the link between Harry Byrne and John, gardaí were certain that the fitter had taken advantage of Byrne being away to dump evidence from Richmond Cottages in the river. It was decided that a full search of the water should be carried out to see if the dumped material was connected to the Noor murder.

Sergeant Hickey was surprised when John mentioned it and asked if the head was in Leixlip. John replied: 'No but I heard the gardaí were digging up Harry's place. Someone told them I dumped stuff up there.' The garda asked him had he dumped anything and he admitted that he'd 'dumped a couple of barrels in Harry's place,' but he said the head wasn't there.

The meeting ended but John Mulhall agreed to meet Sergeant Hickey and Detective Inspector Christy Mangan later on that day, at the same place.

During the second meeting John Mulhall made a number of sensational revelations – Sgt Hickey's clever persistence had paid off. Linda's father told the gardaí that his eldest daughter knew where Farah Noor's head was buried and that she was the gardaí's only hope of ever recovering it. He said he'd had many long conversations with his daughter about the brutal killing and that he thought she would tell them where she had stashed the head. He denied any knowledge of what had happened in the flat, however, and said he had played no part in the murder but he agreed that he would help them to get his daughters to confess. This was a massive development in the case and it was brought about by a combination of good solid police work and John Mulhall doing the right thing.

Meanwhile Sergeant John Bruton and his crew from the Garda Water Unit arrived in Leixlip and were briefed by DS Colm Fox. They were requested to search the River Liffey from a short distance downstream of Leixlip Bridge. Sgt Bruton, along with Gardaí Eoin Ferriter, Glen Brady and Dave Morris, spent two days searching the river, using a Zodiac MK3 boat for transport. Among the items they recovered were a green plastic rubbish bin, an Aldi bag with a weighing scale, a white plastic bag with a newspaper dated 2 July 2005, a white plastic bag containing rubbish and a second Aldi bag containing beer bottles and crisp packets. A TV aerial, an oven mitt and two plastic bags were also recovered in another Aldi bag. Two old shirts and jumpers were taken from the river, in addition to a red single duvet cover, pillows and another old duvet orange cover.

The following day, the Divisional Search Unit attached to the Dublin North Central Division went to Harry Byrne's house in Castle Park to dig up the river embankment at the end of the house. The embankment consisted mainly of earth, on top of two or three layers of sand and rubble, on top of plastic sheeting. At the edge where the river and the embankment meet, there are layers of plastic sheeting, metal strips and sand. Garda Gavin Dunphy recovered a number of items of potential evidence during the dig. A Dublin Corporation envelope, dated 10 June 2005, was recovered along with a Scooby Doo picture frame with a picture of Adolf Hitler inside. A Meteor mobile phone receipt from the Esso garage on Richmond Road was found, along with a brown degradable bag containing hair and maggots. A blue plastic bag was also dug up, containing a pair of gloves, a cigarette lighter from Gala stores in Ballybough, a bathroom towel and a chain. A large knife with a black handle was also found. Detectives were sure that the Liffey find was linked to the murder. They believed that John Mulhall had stored the duvets and other items he'd removed from the Ballybough murder scene in his shed for a few months before deciding what to do with them. When Harry Byrne went on holidays, they were sure that Mulhall had decided that the river at the back of his house would be the perfect place to dispose of the bags of evidence. He wasn't very clever in getting rid of the evidence, however, and hadn't realised that he was spotted carrying out the early evening dumping exercise. Allowing the wheelie bin to fall into the water was a particularly amateur error, considering his house number was on the side of it. It wouldn't take much investigation to lead gardaí straight to him.

John Mulhall was questioned in his house in September

2005 about the Leixlip dumping and admitted that he had thrown bags into the river. He told Sgt Liam Hickey that he did casual work for his boss Harry Byrne at his Castle Park house. He'd often cut the grass, trim the hedges and do general maintenance at the house. He said he'd been cutting the grass and watering the plants in Harry's garden. He admitted he had brought a green wheelie bin, with the number thirty-one on the side, from his house in Tallaght, with him. There was normal domestic rubbish at the end of the bin but his son Andrew had partially filled the top of it with gravel. John claimed he had been tipping the bin over the riverbank, to put some hedge cuttings in it, when he'd lost his balance and let it drop into the water. It had floated downstream, too far away from where he was standing, and he couldn't recover it. He added that there was an old duvet cover from his house, which had been left out in the rain, and that this was also in the bin. Four separate strips of carpet, about 4 feet by 2 feet long, in a black plastic bag, John said were also probably in the bin. John denied that anything that had ended up in the river came from the murder scene in Ballybough.

Gardaí were never able to definitively link what was found in the river to material taken from 17 Richmond Cottages but there is no doubt, in the investigators' minds, that these items came from the flat. One senior detective estimated that gardaí only know about 70 per cent of what really happened on the night of Farah Noor's murder. It is possible that half a dozen knifes were used to kill him but were disposed of elsewhere.

With the help of pressure from John Mulhall, Linda finally

rang Detective Inspector Christy Mangan on 19 August and told him that she wanted to meet. She did this because John had wanted her to tell the truth and face up to the consequences of her actions. Linda had confided in her dad over the previous few months and he knew that she wanted to clear her conscience, but the pressure Kathleen and Charlotte put on her to say nothing was making it difficult for her. The pair had discussed the horror of the events at 17 Richmond Cottages in detail and John knew exactly what had happened, even if he wasn't telling the gardaí. When he had met DI Mangan and Sgt Hickey on 17 August Linda had failed to keep the appointment. During the following forty-eight hours, John put a lot of pressure on Linda to meet with the detectives.

That evening it was John who answered the door to the two gardaí and brought them to Linda's room in the extension at the back of the house. After she had opened her heart, confessed and agreed to drive with the two officers to the crime scenes, John was there waiting at the door to hug his tearful daughter and tell her that everything would be OK. He was waiting at the door of the house again, hours later, when the unmarked garda car pulled up with Linda inside, and he shook the two gardaí's hands.

During the first few difficult weeks after she had come forward to try to atone for what she had done, John looked after Linda. He took an unfailing interest in the case. For example, in one instance after the gardaí had spent a full day searching for the head at Killinarden Hill, he asked Sgt Liam Hickey, 'Have you found it?' He urged the Sergeant to keep searching the field, because, he said, 'I'm 100 per cent accurate that's where it is.'

John Mulhall continued to have regular contact with

the police. He was interviewed again on 10 November at Kilmainham Garda Station by DI Christy Mangan and Sgt Liam Hickey. He admitted that he called to the murder scene at around 1 a.m. and stayed there a couple of minutes, but he said that he had left in disgust and gone back home to Tallaght. He swore that he wasn't in Richmond Cottages the morning after the murder but conceded that he did remove Kathleen's TV, video, CD player and dishes later on. He said that 'to my knowledge' these didn't end up in the Liffey at Harry Byrne's house.

After Linda and Charlotte were charged with Noor's murder, it was John Mulhall who picked up the pieces and took over looking after Linda's four children. He tried to give them as normal a life as possible during the very traumatic period in their young lives. When his two daughters were brought before the courts it was a very awkward time for John and his other kids. Friends and neighbours were constantly asking them about what had happened and the case was the talk of Jobstown. Linda's children also had to put up with the stigma of having a murderer for a mum. From August onwards, everyone was under a lot of pressure, especially John, who started to withdraw into himself, struggling to comprehend the events that had led up to his family being ripped apart.

John Mulhall was working with his brother Eric on the Castle Park Construction site in Cork Street in the south inner-city. The two men had worked for City Glass for nearly sixteen years and were very close. They were happy when they were given the same jobs because they could catch up and spend some time together. It was Thursday, 8 December 2005, three months since Linda had been charged with Farah Swaleh Noor's murder and nearly seven weeks after

Charlotte had been charged. John had been depressed and in bad form at times since Linda and Charlotte had admitted killing Noor. Those close to him understood. He was devoted to his family and blamed himself for what had happened. He had urged Linda to confess as he knew that ringing Detective Inspector Christy Mangan was the right thing to do. She probably would have said nothing but for that and now his two girls were facing the prospect of life behind bars. This ate him up inside. He also couldn't live with the guilt of knowing that they had killed a man.

John and Eric finished work at about 5 p.m. that night and John drove his van back to Tallaght, while thirty-two-year-old Eric went to his house in Kimmage.

Marie Mulhall rang Eric at about 7 p.m. that night and asked him to go with her to the vet on the Old Kilmainham Road because her dog was sick. John drove Marie and the dog there and Eric met them outside. When the vet had treated the dog and given it a clean bill of health, the three decided to go for a drink. They headed to Ryan's pub on James's Street and had a few pints together. John was in great form. He met a couple of old friends he hadn't seen in years and was laughing and joking with them. It was as though he'd finally managed to put the hell of the last few months firmly behind him.

The group left the pub at about 10 p.m. and John and his daughter drove to the Texas Fried Chicken takeaway in Crumlin. Eric followed behind them in his car. They were all hungry, as they hadn't had dinner, and they bought some food to take back to Tallaght. John also bought snack boxes for Linda and his four grandkids and they all went back to Kilclare Gardens to have a meal.

When they arrived, Linda was there with her kids but

she was very drunk. She had obviously spent the evening drinking vodka and was in a shocking mood. It was obvious that she was going to take it out on somebody. Sure enough she turned on John and started laying into her father: 'It's your fucking fault that we're in the trouble we're in. You've never fucking done anything for us.' As she shouted at her father, they all looked on in shock. John was used to such displays from his wayward daughter and knew that it wasn't wise to respond. Instead he put his arm on her shoulder and tried to calm her down but she just got worse and started calling him every name under the sun. She stormed from room to room, turning the place upside down, saying that Charlotte had stolen her Christmas money for the kids. Christmas was less than three weeks away and she said that she'd planned to go down to the Square to get Santa presents. Her dad told her to calm down and promised he'd get the money back from Charlotte. Linda said it must have been Charlotte who had taken the money because she was the only one who knew where it was hidden.

Eric and Marie had gone upstairs during the fight but they could still hear all the screaming. Linda eventually relaxed a bit and seemed happy enough that she'd get her cash back. 'I only want to get Christmas toys for the kids, Da,' she said.

'I know you do, love. You'll get your toys; don't worry,' he told her and she went outside to the garden extension to have a rest and calm down.

John sat in the front room for a few minutes and then he walked upstairs to his bedroom. Eric went out to the landing and asked him if everything was okay. John said he was going to go out and find Charlotte and get Linda's money back. Eric asked if he wanted a lift but John refused and said he wanted to go by himself. He took the keys for the van and went out the door with a vacant look in his eyes.

Eric decided to stay in Tallaght that night to make sure that things were all right and no more trouble kicked off. When he woke up the next morning, he went to wake up John but his bed was empty. His heart sank. It wasn't like his brother to not come home. He was a devoted family man who was always up early to go to work and get Linda's kids off to school. Eric immediately felt that something wasn't right but hoped that his brother had found Charlotte and stayed with her. He thought John might be trying to talk some sense into her about stealing money from the family.

When John hadn't turned up after a few hours, Eric rang Tallaght and Rathfarnham Garda Stations to see if his brother had been arrested but they had no record of coming across John Mulhall at all. Eric also contacted the Mater and St Vincent's hospitals in case his brother had had an accident in the van and had been brought there by ambulance, but they had no information either. In the end Eric drove to work with a sick feeling in the pit of his stomach. He spoke to Marie a few times during the day but John still hadn't come home or made contact with anyone.

After work Eric went back to Kilclare Gardens but there was still no sign of his missing brother. He finally drove up to Tallaght Garda Station and officially reported his older brother missing. When a plainclothes detective knocked on the door later that night, Eric knew that he'd never see his brother again.

✂✂✂

The row with Linda had been the last straw for John. All he wanted to do was look after his family and he'd failed.

His two daughters were facing a murder trial after admitting they had killed and cut up their mam's boyfriend; two of his three sons were in prison for serious crimes. What had he done wrong? He drove the van around Tallaght looking for Charlotte but didn't have a clue where she might be. They'd hardly seen her since the charge and it was like trying to find a needle in a haystack. As he drove aimlessly around the city, he thought about his life. He had been wild in his younger days and got in trouble with the law but he had tried to steer his children onto the right path. What hope did they have though? His own wife had up and left him for a refugee after twenty-nine years of marriage. He was hopeless, worthless and had let everyone he knew and loved down. The thoughts went round and round in his head until he had finally made up his mind.

John Mulhall steered the Berlingo van in the direction of the Phoenix Park. He was familiar with most areas of Dublin and had played there as a lad. He knew where he would be able to find a good spot to do what he was about to do. He drove through the park gate at St James's Gate and went up to the first roundabout and turned left. He would have ended up at Garda Headquarters if he'd taken the right-hand turn. He got onto Wellington Road and could see the imposing presence of the Wellington Monument, through the van's spotlights. He parked the van at the side of the road and turned off the ignition.

He got out and walked to the back of the small white van and opened up the rear door. After he left Kilclare Gardens, through the front door, John had climbed into the back garden and taken the rope from the washing line down. He rooted around among his tools and found the rope that he'd thrown in the back. The street lights did not do a great job at illuminating the area and John must have struggled to make anything out as he walked towards the forest, opposite the monument.

John Mulhall must have been wishing to God that things could have turned out differently. But he knew that he couldn't turn back time. He might have wished that he had done something twenty years ago when the kids were smaller and possibly that he had treated Kathleen differently. Maybe he was thinking that he should have looked after her and made more of an effort to be around the house, staying away from other women and being a better person. The demons had taken over John Mulhall's mind – the same demons that had made Linda's life hell after she murdered Farah Noor. Once the mist descends it is difficult to raise it and John Mulhall was doomed.

The fifty-three-year-old father-of-six took the rope and threw it over the thickest branch of a nearby oak tree.

He then took out his wallet from his pocket and got a €50 note. Using a pen, he wrote a short suicide note, leaving all his possessions to Marie. He put the note back in his pocket. He then scaled the tree and skilfully tied a double-knot that would easily carry the weight of a man, even one as stocky as he was. He put the end of the rope around his neck. His family believe he would have blessed himself. Then he jumped. It was all over in seconds.

The following morning, just before 11 a.m., a thirty-six-year-old local woman was out enjoying a morning stroll when she saw what looked to be somebody lying asleep under a tree, just inside a wooded area beside the memorial to Wellington. She went over for a closer look and was horrified to see a middle-aged man with a rope around his neck. It looked like the rope had snapped and broken a branch above. She knew instantly that the poor unfortunate man was dead and dialled 999 on her mobile.

Garda James Buckley from Cabra Station arrived at the scene and an investigation was immediately launched. Senior officers from the station, Detective Inspector John Kelly and Sergeant Paul McCarville, took charge. Photographs were taken of the scene in case foul play was suspected but it was obvious that the victim had taken his own life. The deceased's wallet was in his trouser pocket and he was identified as John Mulhall from Tallaght.

A doctor pronounced John Mulhall dead at 3.25 p.m. and his body was taken by Stafford's Undertakers to the City Morgue.

John's estranged wife, Kathleen, was due to celebrate her fiftieth birthday two days after his death.

✂✂✂

At around 7 p.m. Detective Garda John Stack was knocking on the Mulhalls' door, with the news that all gardaí dread giving families. It is never a pleasant experience informing anybody that their loved one has been prematurely taken away, but at least it is easier to understand if somebody has been killed in an accident or dies suddenly from a medical condition. That is fate. How can you explain that somebody has willingly taken their own life and left a loving and heartbroken family behind, looking for explanations and wondering if they could have done anything differently to prevent it? Garda John Stack broke the news to Eric, who had been dreading that something like this might have happened ever since John had failed to come home. He rang his brother Andy and sister, Eileen, telling them that John was dead.

To say that things were tense in the Mulhall house after John's suicide was an understatement. John's funeral in his native Tallaght was a big event, attended by his many friends and work colleagues. Members of the Clondalkin Motorbike Club, of which John was an old and dedicated member, formed a guard of honour in memory of his passing. Sergeant Liam Hickey and Detective Inspector Christy Mangan also attended and members of the extended Mulhall family came up to thank them for how they had treated John, Linda and Charlotte while they were in custody. Linda was very upset and cried when she saw the two officers and thanked them for coming. It was a very difficult time for his children who were obviously stuck in the blame game. If Linda hadn't attacked him that night would their father have still taken his own life? Nobody will ever be able to answer that question but the tension between some of his children was clear. Marie and Andrew Mulhall took their father's death especially hard. At the ages of twenty-one and seventeen, they now had to face a life effectively without any parents. His other four children also took the loss of their father badly. The Mulhalls were a dysfunctional family but they were close and loved each other, through thick and thin.

While there is no doubt that John Mulhall was the foundation on which the Mulhall family was built, his role in the murder of Farah Swaleh Noor has never been satisfactorily explained. Some detectives privately say that he played a far bigger part in events than has been acknowledged. Linda, Charlotte and Kathleen Mulhall have always refused to acknowledge that John Mulhall was at Richmond Cottages on the night of the murder, even though John himself volunteered that information.

During the trial of Linda and Charlotte it did not emerge that traffic cameras in Ballybough had captured a white Berlingo van heading for Ballybough Bridge at 6.14 a.m. on 21 March, the morning after the murder occurred. The registration plates were not captured but when John Mulhall was asked about this incident, he admitted to gardaí that this was his van, although he was confused about dates. He said that he had dropped his daughters to their mother's flat on the morning of the murder, 20 March. None of the three women ever told gardaí this and John's story does not make sense.

There are two possibilities about what could have occurred at Richmond Cottages. The first possibility is that John Mulhall got the call from Kathleen, as he later admitted, and went to her flat at 1 a.m. but went home in disgust after he found out about the murder. When he got back to Tallaght he couldn't sleep and finally decided that he had to help his daughters and drove back to Ballybough at around 6 a.m. and picked up the bloody clothes and duvets so they could be dumped later on. John had always claimed that this never happened but forensics linked the items pulled from the River Liffey to Richmond Cottages, so he certainly did remove evidence at some stage that day. There is also evidence that he then rang Kathleen briefly, at 7.15 a.m., as he was driving home with the bags to Tallaght. Many gardaí believe that this is the most credible scenario.

Other officers, however, favour the second possibility, which is that it was John Mulhall, and not his daughters, who cut up Farah's body. They think that when Kathleen rang him before midnight, she told him what Linda and Charlotte had done and asked him to come over to the flat to help them to dispose of the body. John Mulhall was a law abiding man but what father would not do anything to stop his little girls going to jail for life? The theory goes that when John got to the flat, Farah was lying in the bedroom, after being bludgeoned and stabbed to death. The women were in shock after carrying out the murder and it was John who dismembered the body and packed it in bags for them to dump in the canal. He then drove home and rang Kathleen at 7.15 a.m., asking if they'd put Farah in the water yet. A witness had told gardaí that John Mulhall had previously threatened to kill Farah and said he wouldn't be identifiable. Was this a case of a jealous, spurned ex-husband taking the ultimate act of revenge on the man who had broken up his marriage?

At various times John, Kathleen, Linda and Charlotte have all told the police that John and Kathleen rarely, if ever, talked. They all agreed that since the collapse of their marriage the couple had a mutual dislike for each other and had spoken less than a handful of times in three and a half years. However mobile phone traffic between their two mobiles tells a very different story. John phoned Kathleen four times the day after the murder, at 7.15 a.m., 8.57 a.m., 10.19 a.m. and 4.35 p.m. from his mobile. During the investigation he couldn't explain why he had suddenly become friendly with his ex. He said he mightn't have got through and was probably ringing to see if the girls were OK and if they were coming home.

Kathleen was also busy on the day after the murder, making calls of her own. She rang John on six occasions from 11.11 p.m. until midnight.

John again claimed that she didn't get through, but the duration times of three of the phone calls were one minute twenty-eight seconds, one minute twenty-nine seconds and two minutes eighteen seconds, disproving his claims. Two people who hated each other were hardly off the phone to each other the day after their daughters had committed murder, but the question is, why? Maybe they were fighting about how Kathleen had got their daughters into a situation where they had ended up as killers, or perhaps they were getting their stories straight.

Unless Linda and Charlotte volunteer more information it will never be known what was said in those phone calls. It is highly unlikely, however, that they will shed light on the unanswered questions surrounding their father's involvement. They have both steadfastly denied that John Mulhall played any part at all in the murder of Farah Swaleh Noor. They have been consistent with this story since the day they were arrested. Both girls were extremely loyal to John, even though they had regular and often explosive rows with him.

When Charlotte admitted her role in the murder she told officers that she had never told her father about what had happened and that Linda never rang him after the murder had taken place, despite phone records proving the contrary. Charlotte played dumb about the frequent calls between her parents and said that the only reason John would ever ring Kathleen would be if he needed to contact her.

'So if something were to happen, would it be unusual for your father to make phone calls to your mother?' a detective asked.

'Yeah, unless he was ringing looking for me,' she replied.

'Looking for you? So would he ring your mother looking for you? You're pretty close to your father?' Charlotte said she was and was asked, 'Did you tell him about this?'

'No,' she claimed.

'Kept it all from him, yeah?'

'I didn't tell him,' she insisted to the incredulous officers.

She was shown the evidence of Linda's phone call to John immediately after they had carried out the brutal murder. She claimed she didn't have a clue about this but the detectives interviewing her had their own ideas and told her: 'Well you know if she was ringing your father to tell him about this major crisis in the family, now all the family were involved in this horrific murder.'

The twenty-two-year-old prostitute told the gardaí that she didn't know what her dad thought of Farah but the two of them had never had a row or an argument. She told them that her parents didn't get on anymore and commented: 'Me father doesn't visit me mammy.'

She totally denied that her dad had driven over to Ballybough in his work van and collected evidence to dump: 'Me da doesn't be near me ma's house. They don't exactly get along.'

Linda denied that her father even knew about the murder and claimed she hadn't told him anything about it whatsoever.

During her interview Kathleen also denied that John was involved in the murder, although she denied that it had taken place at Richmond Cottages at all. After she left him for Farah, the husband and wife didn't speak for over three years but had had some brief conversations in the year or so before the murder. She admitted that she and John had several conversations after the murder but said: 'If I rang him it was because there was a problem with one of his children. My son James was having a problem. I visited him in jail and he asked me if I could pass on a message to John. I passed it on. I don't have a good relationship with John.'

Following John Mulhall's tragic death his family, which he had worked so hard at trying to keep together, fell apart. It had a huge effect on Linda and Charlotte, who were both out on bail. They went totally wild and started drinking heavily and using hard drugs.

One garda detective who knew the glass fitter said: 'John was the rock that the family was built on. He urged his two girls to do what was right and admit that they killed Farah Noor. A lot of credit has to go to him for that. He was a loving family man but obviously couldn't cope with the horror of all that had happened. He was the one bit of stability that his kids had and it was inevitable that when he died the whole thing would crumble down. That's exactly what happened. It's a tragic story.'

11

Life Behind Bars

One of the most eagerly awaited criminal trials in years got underway at the Central Criminal Court on 12 October 2006. The nine-day trial would be one of the most gruesome and fascinating cases ever heard in an Irish court.

Charlotte Mulhall was a mother by the time her trial started. She had given birth to a baby boy at the Coombe Hospital on 28 May 2006 and was looking after the infant in a flat on Grosvenor Road in Rathmines. The council had taken back the house at 31 Kilclare Gardens following John Mulhall's death and Linda was now living with her children in the Swiftbrook estate, in Tallaght. She had originally failed to turn up for the court case, causing an adjournment. She had disappeared on her release from hospital, following her suicide attempt, and she was also abusing heroin and drinking heavily at the time. She appeared to be in good condition when she did arrive, however, and listened intently to the evidence, as the trial got under way.

Linda and Charlotte Mulhall had pleaded not guilty to the murder of Farah Swaleh Noor, otherwise known as Sheilila Salim, at 17 Richmond Cottages, Ballybough, Dublin, on 20 March 2005. A jury of six men and six women were sworn in to hear the case, which was presided over by one of Ireland's most experienced judges, Mr Justice Paul Carney. The small Courtroom Number 2 was packed to capacity, with throngs of media eager to hear the gruesome evidence that was expected to emerge.

Linda and Charlotte sat in the body of the court and stared impassively as Senior Counsel George Birmingham stated the case for the prosecution and alleged that the two defendants had murdered thirty-nine-year-old Noor. The remains of Farah Swaleh Noor had been recovered from the Royal Canal at Ballybough and a post-mortem revealed that the victim had been stabbed twenty-two times and had injuries to 'pretty well all' of his internal organs. The victim died from stab wounds and it seemed he had been dismembered after death. Mr Noor's soft tissue had been cut through with a knife, while the bones had been severed by being repeatedly chipped with a cleaver or an axe. The victim's head and penis were missing and had never been found. Mr Birmingham told the jury they would hear evidence given to gardaí by the Mulhall sisters where both women admitted their involvement in the murder and subsequent disposal of Farah Swaleh Noor's body.

Mr Birmingham stated, 'Charlotte Mulhall had a knife and Linda Mulhall wielded a hammer with which she struck him a significant number of times on or about the head.' He told the court that the women's mother, Kathleen Mulhall, had been involved in a stormy relationship with the victim, who appeared to be violent towards her from time to time.

Ali Abubakaar gave evidence of seeing Farah Noor in the company of Kathleen, Linda and Charlotte Mulhall on the night he died. He said that his friend appeared to be drunk and they were talking when Kathleen came up and said: 'Just leave him alone, he's OK.' He remembered that Farah had been wearing his Ireland-away soccer jersey. When he then read an article in the *Metro Éireann* newspaper a few months later, which said that the body found in the canal had a similar jersey, he said: 'I just thought Farah used to wear this T-shirt and I ring people to see if they had any contact with him.'

Brendan Grehan, Linda Mulhall's Senior Counsel asked Abubakaar if he knew whether Farah Noor's personality changed when he was drinking.

The witness replied: 'I never lasted the whole night with him. I only heard, but I don't know that.'

Dr Bríd McBride, a forensic scientist at the State Laboratory told of how she visited Flat 1 at 17 Richmond Cottages on two occasions and found the presence of a number of blood stains in the bedroom which were later found to match the victim's. She said that the blood splattering discovered was consistent with a serious assault having taken place in the bedroom, at a low-down location, such as the floor. There was also evidence of bloodstains in the grooves of the pine planks on the wardrobe but not on the surface of the wood. She commented that this was consistent with a clean-up having taken place to remove the blood.

Dr McBride agreed with Charlotte's Senior Counsel, Isobel Kennedy, that the use of the chemical luminol to show up blood stains could give a false positive reaction to certain chemicals found in cleaning products. However, the witness said she had based her findings on conventional evidence as well.

Scientist Claire Timms told the court she had carried out a toxicology test on a blood sample taken from the blood that was later identified as Farah Swaleh Noor's. It revealed the presence of ecstasy in the blood, at a level of 0.14 microgrammes per millilitre. This was a result of Kathleen spiking his drink when they got back to the flat.

The youngest Mulhall daughter, Marie, spoke of how Charlotte had confessed to her about her involvement in the murder: 'Charlotte was very upset. I'd just come in from work and she came to my room crying. I asked what was wrong with her. She appeared to be drunk. She told me she was upset because they were after killing Farah. She told me it was herself and Linda. She didn't say too much about my mother but I knew my mother had been there. I just let her tell me what she was saying.'

The apprentice mechanic told the court that she didn't believe what her sister told her but that she'd started to have second thoughts when she heard on the radio that a body had been taken from the canal.

Linda and Charlotte did not give evidence at their trial and the jury had to rely on the statements they'd given to gardaí to decide on their guilt or innocence. They were present in court for the whole trial and read books, newspapers and celebrity magazines during breaks in evidence.

Lawrence Keegan, who had seen Farah Noor's head in Sean Walsh Park, in Tallaght, at the end of March, was another witness. He spoke of noticing the object in the ground and kicking it with his foot to try to dislodge it. He said: 'I knew it was something else but part of me thought: "It's nothing to do with me," if you understand me.' He was asked if he told the park ranger that it could be a human head belonging to the body pulled out of the canal, and said: 'I'm an alcoholic. I could have seen pink elephants in the park if you understand where I'm coming from.'

Detective Inspector Christy Mangan took to the stand on day five and told of how Linda Mulhall had contacted him saying she wanted to talk to him about the murder. DI Mangan spoke about how Linda had talked to him and Sergeant Liam Hickey about what had happened on the day of the murder. The statement she made to gardaí, detailing her exact role in the murder, was read out to the court. The Detective Inspector agreed under cross-examination by Linda's counsel, Brendan Grehan, that the garda investigation had made only limited progress until she contacted him and co-operated. He agreed that she had often cried and been emotional during his dealings with her and seemed like a very different person to the type who would be involved in a murder like this one. Mr Justice Paul Carney told the jury that Linda's statement was only admissible in relation to her case, and could not be used as evidence either in favour, or against, Charlotte.

Detective Sergeant Gerry McDonnell gave evidence on day six and spoke about Charlotte's statements in relation to the murder. He read over the statement he had taken on 17 October 2005, in which Charlotte described bringing Farah's body down to the canal and tipping it in. Detective Garda Kevin Keys was present when the statement was taken from Charlotte and agreed with Charlotte's counsel, Isobel Kennedy, that she had become increasingly upset as her interview went on and it was often very difficult to hear what she was saying. He also agreed that she was very protective of Linda.

As Charlotte sat through the reading of her statement in court, she began to lose her composure. The gardaí had put it to her that Noor had been stabbed over twenty times and asked her if she remembered how many times she had stabbed him: 'I don't know, a couple. It was nothing like that,' she had replied. Charlotte had spent the first five days of the trial displaying few emotions and was almost like a disinterested observer. However, this changed when her words about cutting up the body were entered into record and Isobel Kennedy told Judge Carney: 'Ms Charlotte Mulhall feels she's going to be ill.' The trial was adjourned for the day at that point.

By the following day Charlotte had regained her composure as her mother's alleged role in the murder was discussed. Charlotte's claim that it was Kathleen Mulhall who had asked her and Linda to kill Farah Noor was read out: 'She just kept telling us, "Will you do it? Will you hurry up, quick, kill him?" Me mammy said just cut him up. I just remember cutting. I cut him with the knife.'

Farah Noor's violent history was discussed. 'Lynn', the Chinese girl who'd had a son with Farah in the late 1990s, took to the stand and spoke of meeting the dead man at Dr Quirkey's amusement arcade on O'Connell Street. She said she played two games of pool there with Farah before going back to his flat where: 'He tried to do something on me. He tried to do something, make sex with me.' When asked if she wanted to have sex with Farah, Lynn answered, 'No, he forced me to do it' and said she had become pregnant following the intercourse.

'Paula' was also called as a witness and gave testimony about her three years with the violent murder victim. She told the court how he raped her on an almost daily basis and how she'd feared that he would kill her some day before she left him.

Evidence was also heard that Kathleen had sought medical treatment in Cork because of injuries Noor inflicted on her. Det Sgt Gerry McDonnell was asked if Charlotte might have witnessed her mother being assaulted. 'She could well have,' he said. Farah had assaulted Kathleen in front of plenty of people and didn't attempt to hide what he was doing.

The trial concluded on the ninth day with the closing speeches. Una Ní Raifeartaigh BL, who was part of the prosecuting team, told the jury that they'd heard some 'distressing, disturbing and shocking' evidence and the prosecution believed a verdict of murder was appropriate in both cases. She did remind the six men and six women, however, that they must also consider the defences of provocation and self-defence.

Linda Mulhall's lead counsel, Brendan Grehan, said that although both women had been tried together the cases against them had to be considered separately. He said that the jury could not be satisfied beyond all reasonable doubt that his client was guilty of murder. He argued that it had not been proven that Linda Mulhall striking Farah Noor with the hammer had caused his death. He also stressed that she had been frightened when Farah Noor grabbed her and would not let her go. This had all the hallmarks of a sexual motive on the dead man's part, Senior Counsel Grehan said. He reminded the jury that the investigating gardaí had described his client as a 'genuine' person. He concluded by telling the jury that it was possible for them to return a verdict of accessory after the fact of the murder.

Isobel Kennedy SC said that Charlotte Mulhall had initially denied all involvement in the killing to protect her sister Linda, the one person she was 'utterly devoted' to. She said that the finding of self-defence was an option to the jury, as was a defence of provocation, which would reduce the offence of murder to manslaughter. Senior Counsel Isobel Kennedy echoed Brendan Grehan in pointing out the accessory after the fact verdict was also available to the jury.

Mr Justice Paul Carney briefed the jury on the legal complexities surrounding verdicts of murder and manslaughter. They rose to consider their verdicts at 12.30 p.m. on Wednesday, 25 October.

Most of the gardaí and press reporters who were present each day of the trial were in agreement that it would not take the jury very long to come back with guilty verdicts on both women. Seasoned court reporters were speculating that the verdict would be in within three or four hours. This didn't prove to be the case however.

Wednesday dragged into Thursday and there was still no word from Linda and Charlotte's twelve peers, who were obviously locked in deep discussion in the jury room.

After lunch on Thursday, Judge Carney informed the jury that a unanimous verdict was no longer required and that a minimum of 10–2 majority would be permitted. Observers got a hint of what the jury were thinking, when they came back that afternoon seeking clarification on the definitions of self-defence and provocation.

The investigating detectives had done a thoroughly professional job at preparing the case and were fully expecting guilty verdicts but even they were beginning to get nervous as Thursday wore on. They were feeling even edgier when the jury were sent to a hotel for the second night on Thursday evening.

While the jury was out deliberating, the detectives involved in the investigation had lots of time to go back over the case for anything they might have overlooked but they were satisfied that they had prepared a rock-solid file for the Director of Public Prosecutions (DPP). The only possible weakness was the lack of response from the Kenyan authorities to their requests for assistance. The DPP, James Hamilton, had written a letter on 30 January 2006 to The Competent Judicial Authorities of the Republic of Kenya. He had outlined the facts of the murder of Farah Swaleh Noor and emphasised that the matter was urgent because two people were before the courts, charged with Farah's murder. He had requested that the Kenyans:

A. Liaise with the family of the deceased to update them on the investigation.
B. To obtain an official birth certificate for Sheilila Said Salim, born 07 July 1965.
C. To obtain a witness statement and a sample of DNA from the mother of the deceased, Somoe Bakari Said.
D. To obtain a witness statement from Mrs Husna Mohamed, the former wife of the deceased.
E. To obtain a witness statement from Lulu (cousin of the deceased) and Mustapha (step-brother of the deceased) and any other per son that has information to offer that could establish the identity of the deceased.
F. To obtain a full background report on the deceased.

Mr Hamilton had also requested that Detective Sergeant Gerry McDonnell and Detective Garda Malachy Dunne be allowed travel to Kenya to advise the Kenyan police on how to collect evidence so it is admissible in an Irish trial. He had further asked for an interpreter to be provided. Gardaí believed that their direct presence in Kenya would be crucial in building a case against the Mulhalls, but the lack of response by the Kenyans to the Mutual Assistance Request made this impossible. It meant that gardaí had to rely on telephone and fax contact with Farah's relatives, via interpreters.

In February 2006 DS Gerry McDonnell forwarded a request for mutual legal assistance in the investigation via the Department of Justice. It is common practice that countries would cooperate with each other in investigations involving their nationals but the Kenyan authorities again failed to respond, even though a number of reminders were sent to them reiterating the urgency of the case because the trial of the Mulhalls was due to commence on 3 October 2006.

A separate request to Interpol Kenya for a check on Noor's previous convictions, if any, had also been sent. The gardaí received an acknowledgment on 16 June 2005, saying, 'Your above quoted message refers. Please be informed that we are still waiting for clearance from the Attorney General's office. You will be informed whether the subject has any criminal record.'

The required clearance obviously never materialised because nothing was ever heard back from Interpol Kenya, even though lots of reminders were sent, one as late as 25 September 2006. Interpol Dublin had also made direct contact with their Kenyan counterparts but with the same result.

When Friday dawned and the jury continued to try to reach a verdict for the third day, the paucity of information from Kenya may not have been the only aspect of the case weighing on some of the detectives' minds. The jury returned on Friday afternoon, after deliberating for a mammoth fourteen hours and thirty-seven minutes. The foreperson did not have a verdict, however, and told Judge Paul Carney that they had reached a deadlock.

The Judge told them: 'You're not the only jury in the building deliberating for this time. There are five children who have a vital interest in this, as you know, and we're anxious to reach a conclusion. If you're in any doubt as to the evidence you should resolve it in favour of the accused and if there's any further help I can give you I'll be delighted to do so.'

The jury did not require any other information and went back to try to iron out whatever disagreements they had over the verdicts.

The twelve men and women came back at 6.30 p.m. that evening and the foreperson said: 'We've come to a deadlock. We have a majority but not the one brought forward by the court.'

The judge asked them to give it another half an hour, and when they had left, George Birmingham stood up and told Mr Justice Carney: 'You have unbalanced what up to now has been a balanced trial.' Mr Birmingham was unhappy because he felt that the judge's comments could lead to the jury acquitting the women if they didn't feel the evidence was strong enough. Judge Carney obviously did not agree with him and told the senior counsel: 'Let's get real, Mr Birmingham.'

At 7 p.m. the female foreperson came back and told Judge Carney: 'We're talked out. The air upstairs is blue and we wish to come back to this tomorrow.' For the third night in a row they were sent back to the hotel for some rest. Nobody in the courtroom had seen this in the script.

The jury returned the following morning, Saturday,

28 October, and dozens of reporters from the Sunday newspapers were in court, praying for a verdict to splash across the front pages the following day. Their prayers were answered at 2.30 p.m., when, after eighteen hours and one minute of deliberations, the jury finally came back with a decision.

Linda, who was wearing a chocolate-brown leather jacket over a white blouse and navy jeans, glanced at the twelve men and women as they prepared to determine her fate. She clutched a copy of the *Irish Times*.

Charlotte, dressed in black trousers and a black vest top, carried a copy of *A Million Little Pieces*, a novel by James Frey about drug and alcohol addiction.

John and James Mulhall had been released from Wheatfield Prison at this stage and were present in court for most of the trial, as was Marie Mulhall. The three sat together in the public gallery as the verdicts were about to be delivered.

Charlotte was the first to be sentenced and sat stone-faced as she was found guilty of the murder of Farah Swaleh Noor by a 10–2 majority. She did not even flinch, even though the verdict meant that she would automatically be jailed for the rest of her life.

Linda stared straight ahead and showed little emotion as she was found guilty of Noor's manslaughter by an 11–1 majority.

There were gasps from the public gallery as the verdicts were read and Judge Carney remanded the women in custody for sentencing on 4 December 2006. As the Mulhall sisters were about to be led to the cells below the court, they finally allowed their masks to slip. James and John Mulhall, their two brothers who had made the phone call that led detectives to Linda and Charlotte, walked across the courtroom and hugged and kissed both girls. Linda started crying and said, 'Thank God it's over,' while Charlotte also allowed herself to shed a tear.

James Mulhall made his way out of the courtroom, past the assembled media, who were informing their newsrooms of the verdicts, and thanked the group of investigating gardaí as he left. Detectives told the press corps that they were satisfied with the verdicts.

Linda and Charlotte Mulhall were christened the 'Scissor Sisters' by the media immediately after the guilty verdicts and became publicly associated with this nickname. The American band the Scissor Sisters have spoken of their astonishment that two Irish killers have been named after them. Frontman, Jake Shears, joked: 'You know you've made it in this business when they name killers after you.'

Linda and Charlotte were immediately taken to a prison van and transported the short distance to Mountjoy Women's Prison, on the North Circular Road. The two convicted women were placed on suicide watch during their first night in prison, as is standard practice. Prison sources later said that the sisters quickly adapted to life in Mountjoy Women's Prison, but the Dóchas (Irish for hope) Centre isn't exactly a tough institution.

The Dóchas Centre is a progressive prison that focuses on trying to rehabilitate the women there. It is a medium-security prison built at a cost of €16 million in 1999 and houses about eighty women at one time. It is like a five-star hotel compared to the men's equivalent next door, which is a decrepit building from the Victorian era that should have closed down decades ago. Instead of cells, each woman has her own single room in one of seven separate 'houses', all named after trees. An additional house is provided for mothers who are looking after their babies while serving sentences. There are no bars on the windows and the prisoners have their own key to their house and bedroom. They can effectively come and go as they please during the day. Prisoners aren't even called prisoners and are instead referred to by the more politically correct title, 'women'.

When Linda and Charlotte were taken from the Central Criminal Court to the Dóchas Centre they would have been brought through to the reception area, where all new prisoners immediately have a shower. They are then routinely searched by a reception officer who takes a prisoner's personal details, such as name and address. If a new arrival has any cash, it is handed over and lodged into a personal bank account. All personal property has to be signed for and mobile phones have to be handed over and are stored away until the sentence is completed. Prisoners are then given fresh bed linen, underwear, a tracksuit and runners, if they want them, as well as toiletries. They are also handed the Dóchas Centre's Information booklet, which contains all that the prisoners need to know to get them through their sentence.

The Centre's 'Vision Statement' states: 'We are a community which embraces people with respect and dignity. We encourage personal growth in a caring and safe environment. We are committed to addressing the needs of each person in a healing and holistic way. We actively promote close interaction with the wider community.'

When a prisoner has being processed, she is taken to see a nurse, who should be told about any medical conditions or if the prisoner has any forthcoming hospital appointments. The Health Care Unit in the Centre is quite impressive. As well as having a nurse available twenty-four hours a day, a dentist regularly visits and an optician or chiropodist is available on request. A psychiatrist also comes in twice a week, although a GP referral is needed for this service. Prisoners struggling with addictions can consult with alcohol and drugs counsellors. The probation and welfare officer is based in the Health Care Unit and can assist with 'family/child care matters, accommodation difficulties or other personal problems'.

As the notion of 'prisoner' does not exist in the Dóchas Centre, neither does a 'prison officer'. Their equivalents are 'house officers' who escort new arrivals to their room and hand them their key. These officers don't even wear uniforms, in an effort to 'break down barriers' with the women and communicate on a more equal level. An intercom system is installed in each room in case the women need to summon a house officer. Each room contains a TV, locker, dresser, wardrobe, bed, bin, cutlery, toilet, toilet brush and a bathroom bin. The women are not allowed to visit other houses without the permission of the governor. The governor is available to meet every day except Sundays and also regularly calls to each house. Any special requests, such as enquiring about particular visits, temporary release or extra phone calls, are made through the governor and the decision will be based on how a prisoner is progressing in their prison job or schooling. If a member of staff feels that any woman is behaving inappropriately, they are brought before the governor and may be punished. Punishments for prisoners can include losing shop privileges or time earned off their sentences for good behaviour. It is at the discretion of the governor what punishment to impose after she hears evidence from her staff and an explanation from the offender.

The daily routine for the women is the same from Monday to Friday but varies at weekends. Each room is unlocked at 8 a.m. and the next ninety minutes are spent getting dressed, collecting medication, having showers, cleaning up the house, preparing for school or work and eating breakfast. Each of the four daily meals varies from day to day and there is a menu available for dinner and the women help themselves to a variety of foods from a buffet table.

The Dóchas Centre has its own hair and beauty salon where prisoners can go to have their roots done. The salon is mainly staffed by fellow prisoners doing a FÁS course in hairdressing, one of many available in the Centre. From 9.30 a.m. to 12.30 p.m. the women's time is taken up by schooling or work. Prisoners are able to take courses in a range of subjects, including computers, music, cookery, soft toy making, speedwriting, photography, stained glass, drug awareness and meditation. Women can study for their Junior and Leaving Certificate English and Maths papers and can do computer courses to help prepare them for jobs when they leave the prison environment. Jobs are also available across the Centre, with the opportunity of working in the kitchen, the garden and the library. Each woman is paid €2 per day, regardless of whether they work or not, and the cash is put into their bank account. If the cash is not spent in the prison tuck shop a lump sum is handed over at the end of the sentence. The Dóchas Centre does not have its own tuck shop and all orders are sent over from the men's prison. Newspapers, magazines, sweets and phone cards can be purchased. Items can only be ordered on Wednesday and Sunday evenings and aren't delivered until the following morning because of logistical difficulties. The Centre information booklet advises: 'So remember, patience is a virtue, girls!'

Lunch is served in the dining room at 12.30 p.m. and the women are free for leisure time until 2.15 p.m. They can go for a walk in the yard, head to the well-equipped gym or head for the library to listen to music, watch a video, access legal information or borrow a book. As many of the women in the Dóchas Centre are non-nationals, books and other materials are available in Russian, French, Albanian, Serbian, Croatian, Polish, Chinese and Arabic.

They go back to school or work until 4.30 p.m., which is when dinner, the main meal of the day at the Centre, is served. Prisoners can relax and go to the gym or watch TV from 5.30 to 7.15 p.m. and must go back to their room after supper is finished at 7.45 p.m. Quizzes take place most weekends and Mass is celebrated each Sunday but a chaplain is available every day to offer religious support.

Phone cards can be bought and used in the Centre but only four pre-designated numbers are allowed and one of these has to be the prisoner's solicitor. Before the card is first issued a house officer contacts the numbers to see if they will take phone calls from the prisoners. Each prisoner can contact the Samaritans free of charge. The cards can only be used from 5 to 7 p.m.

Visits are allowed each Saturday and Sunday from 10 a.m. to 12 noon and 2 to 4 p.m., although each prisoner is only allowed one thirty-minute visit per week, from preapproved individuals. A maximum of three adults are allowed per visit but there is no restriction on the number of children who may visit. Visitors can bring money and other treats for prisoners, which are left at reception for inspection. Linda's four children visit their mum in prison each week, while Charlotte is said not to have many visitors. Linda's kids were taken into the care of her brother James and his partner after she was convicted. They have continued to go to the same schools they attended before their mother became an infamous national celebrity.

After they were found guilty of the murder and manslaughter of Farah Swaleh Noor, Charlotte and Linda were inundated with interview requests from members of the media. In one case a journalist attempted to gain access to Linda by applying to visit one of her housemates but eagle-eyed prison service staff spotted the scam and refused him access. Psychologists and academics also tried to interview the women, in an attempt to understand what drove them to carry out a crime of such unspeakable horror. There were even reports that the sisters were receiving fan mail from across the country, with several men regularly sending letters wanting to be their pen pals. One street trader was also said to be planning to produce T-shirts bearing the girls' faces.

After their convictions Linda and Charlotte were kept together and assigned to the Hazel House complex of the Dóchas Centre. Their bedrooms are on the same corridor, only a few feet apart, and they spend a lot of time socialising together. Charlotte is said to be friendlier than her older sister and mixes freely with staff and her fellow prisoners. Linda was involved in an ugly incident as she waited to be sentenced when she made a death threat against a fellow inmate. Linda accused a prisoner who was a member of the travelling community of stealing her bedroom key and taking clothes from her wardrobe. A number of officers were alleged to have heard the elder Mulhall sister promise that she would kill the young traveller and say when she was challenged: 'I'm going down for one – another one isn't going to make any difference.' It is believed that an internal inquiry was carried out about the threat and Linda was formally disciplined.

Charlotte was back in court in November 2007 in relation to a charge of soliciting on Lad Lane the previous September. She had been out on bail at the time, awaiting her trial for murder, but was still selling sex on the streets of Dublin. She pleaded guilty to the offence and was given seven days to pay the €200 fine.

The Mulhall sisters have been behind bars in Hazel House with some of the country's most notorious female offenders. Among them is fellow Tallaght native, Martina O'Connor, who clocked up her seventy-third conviction in early 2006, despite the fact that she's only eighteen years old. She was involved in a vicious street assault in which a woman's hair was set alight. O'Connor's two-year prison sentence was subsequently increased to three years by the Court of Criminal Appeal. Delivering judgement on O'Connor, of Birchview Heights, Tallaght, Judge Brian McCracken said she had 'an appalling record' that suggested she was 'clearly a teenager out of control'. In the assault on the woman on O'Connell Street, when she was just sixteen, O'Connor had removed the woman's cap before setting her hair alight. The fire was quickly extinguished but then clumps of the victim's hair were pulled out and she was dragged to the ground. The court heard that 'when she [O'Connor] drinks she goes into an animal like rage'.

Another Hazel House resident was mum-of-four, Lisa Moran, who brought her children on shoplifting sprees. A judge told her that her kids would be 'better off without her' while she served a two-year sentence. The thirty-seven-year-old frequently attacked and threatened shop workers during her trips. Originally from Cork, Moran has pleaded guilty to over one hundred offences in just four years. Gardaí have told court hearings that she has hidden behind her children, aged from seven to thirteen, to avoid jail. She had also used them to commit the shoplifting offences and they had witnessed her violent reaction when challenged by shop staff. She has been convicted of driving without insurance on over twenty occasions and is banned from the road for twenty-five years. She's also been found guilty of assaulting gardaí, security staff and other members of the public, theft from more than twenty shops, using forged or stolen cheques, and theft of handbags, mobile phones and wallets.

Another long-term resident of Hazel House is drugs mule Breda Maguire, a thirty-three-year-old single mother-of-two, who was born in Ireland but had lived most of her life in London. She is serving a six-year term after being arrested in May 2001 transporting €500,000 worth of heroin into Dublin Port. She fled the country when she was given bail but was later extradited back to Ireland and sent to the Dóchas Centre.

One woman who was said to be very unhappy at the Scissor Sisters' emergence as the big fish in the Dóchas Centre pond was the so-called 'Black Widow', Catherine Nevin. Nevin was convicted in April 2000 of the murder of her husband, Tom, a well-known publican. He was gunned down in Jack White's Pub in March 1996 and his former wife is serving a life sentence. She was also convicted on three counts of soliciting three different men to murder Tom Nevin in 1989 and 1990 and was sentenced to three seven-year sentences on those charges. Nevin had claimed that she was in the pub counting the takings with her husband when armed and masked raiders burst in, tied her up and shot Tom dead at point blank range. Gardaí had doubts about her story and she was convicted after one of the most sensational trials in Irish legal history. The public was fascinated with Nevin and her glamorous appearance and fashionable outfits were the talk of Ireland during her forty-two-day trial. Catherine Nevin is known to revel in her title as the most notorious prisoner in the women's prison. Reports have suggested that she didn't take kindly to the arrival of Linda and Charlotte Mulhall, who arguably commanded more column inches than she did during her murder trial. Nevin ignores the Mulhalls and tells her friends that their crime was too despicable for her to get involved with them. They bump into each other on an almost daily basis but the Black Widow is said to act as if the sisters don't exist, which many staff and prisoners have put down to jealousy on Nevin's part.

On Monday, 4 December 2006 the Mulhall sisters woke up early and chatted with their fellow prisoners, as they enjoyed a breakfast of eggs, cereal, tea and toast. As they went back to their rooms to get dressed, many of the other women wouldn't even have known that the pair were facing sentencing that day, such were their blasé exteriors.

It was a morning of mixed emotions for the sisters. Charlotte had already had over six weeks to come to terms with the fact that she would spend the rest of her life behind bars. As she dressed in black trousers, with a pinstripe jacket, and applied heavy make-up to her face, she must have been thinking about ending up in prison just six months after becoming a mother for the first time. Her child had been taken into care following her conviction and she would soon apply to look after her son behind bars. This would help to make sure that the long days would be just that little bit shorter, but nevertheless it was not easy to act normal, as she put her silver earrings on and tied the hair-band in her dyed black hair. Staff said she was not as friendly as usual, as she sat nervously awaiting the prison van which would transport her to the Four Courts building in the centre of Dublin, a mere five-minute drive away.

Linda chose to wear a pair of plain black trousers, with a white tightly-fitted shirt, under a black leather jacket. She wore even more make-up than her younger sister and, had circumstances been different, she could easily have been preparing for a night out to celebrate Christmas, which was just weeks away. The mother-of-four had far more reason to be hopeful than Charlotte. She had only been convicted of manslaughter by the jury, which meant that her sentence was at the discretion of Judge Carney. Convictions for manslaughter in the Irish judicial system rarely result in more than an eight-year prison term and the jury had seemed to have had genuine sympathy for a woman who had acted in self-defence to ward off the unwelcome advances of a drunken, violent man.

Four Prison officers met the Mulhalls and placed them in the back of a van at around 10 a.m. They arrived at the Four Courts less than ten minutes later and around eight press photographers were there to greet them as they walked into the court building. The weather was cold and windy and parts of the country were under water from recent sustained heavy rain. Linda pulled the collar of her jacket up to get some extra warmth, as she heard the clicking of the snappers' cameras. As it turned out, the dark clouds in the sky were an omen of what was to come.

The national media had been eagerly awaiting this day and news desks around the country were anticipating big sales with the 'Scissor Sisters' splashed all over the front pages. Court Number 2 was packed to capacity by 10 a.m., nearly a full hour before Mr Justice Carney was due to sit. Dozens of newspaper, radio and television journalists struggled to fit into the tiny courtroom. Anyone who wasn't in attendance by 10.15 a.m. had to make do with standing room only at the back of the room, which was not where the many colour writers, sent to court to file copy on the girls' demeanour and reactions, wanted to be.

Some observers could hardly get their heads around the doors when Judge Carney was finally announced to the court by his registrar. A female prison officer stood guard at the door to the side of the court, from where prisoners and barristers enter from the cells below. Two large gardaí, from the Bridewell Station, stood outside the courtroom, observing everybody who went in and making occasional sweeps to ensure that no jackets or bags were left unattended. It wasn't just the Mulhall sisters, however, who had drawn the press to Court 2 that day. Padraig Nally, a sixty-two-year-old farmer from Co. Mayo, was due to face a retrial for the murder of the traveller John 'Frog' Ward that same day.

On 14 October 2004 the traveller had trespassed on Nally's property, with the alleged intention of stealing from him. The farmer had confronted Ward with a shotgun, opened fire and badly beaten him with a stick. He had then reloaded and shot Ward in the back as he limped away. The original trial, which had taken place in Castlebar, Co.Mayo, in July 2005, had divided the nation. Many people felt that Padraig Nally was more than entitled to defend his property against a well-known criminal, with a string of previous convictions, while others disagreed. At the end of the seven-day trial, Nally had been found not guilty of murder and instead was convicted of manslaughter. On 11 November 2005 he was sentenced to six years in prison. Nally's lawyers, however, subsequently argued in the Court of Criminal Appeal that the trial judge, who just happened to be Paul Carney, hadn't allowed the jury the option of finding the farmer not guilty. The previous conviction had been overturned on 12 October 2006.

Padraig Nally's case was the first of the morning to be called and the nervous looking bachelor pleaded not guilty. He then had to prepare himself for yet another two weeks in court as the twelve men and women of the jury were sworn in. Judge Carney told the jurors that this case had 'engendered a great deal of publicity, perhaps more than any other in the history of this court. It has also engendered extremely strong feelings.' He told the panel that they must hear the case 'strictly on evidence and without discrimination to members of the farming or travelling communities'.

With the Nally case moved to a full hearing in Court Number 3, Counsel for the Director of Public Prosecutions in the Mulhall case informed the judge that the prosecution would be seeking to have the Mulhall sentencing adjourned. This was because they had been unable to arrange for Farah Swaleh Noor's mother to fly to Dublin from Kenya to give a victim impact statement to the court. He also said that a psychiatric report on Linda Mulhall was unavailable.

Judge Carney was clearly displeased and said he wasn't going to deal with any application until the case had been called, but warned that the State had had enough time to arrange for anybody who was needed in court to be there. He stressed that he wanted to see the case finished with that day: 'The matter is in for today and is proceeding today.'

The unexpected application by the prosecution caused panic among the journalists who were faced with the potential of seeing a two-month delay in sentencing. A number of other cases were then called before the Mulhalls were led into the courtroom by two prison guards at 12.25 p.m. The women sat at benches beside the dock, preparing themselves for the next few minutes when the judge would sentence them for their heinous crime. But there was a another delay. Brendan Grehan, Linda's senior counsel, was not in court when the case was called because he was also representing Padraig Nally. His junior was not present either, which led a furious Judge Carney to remark: 'He has been provided by the taxpayer to cover Mr Grehan in his absences. Well we will just have to wait until one of them appears.'

After ten long and tense minutes, the clearly unimpressed Judge adjourned the case for twenty-five minutes until Mr Grehan had finished his official business in the adjoining courtroom. During the delay Linda chatted with a man who came to see her from the public gallery. They whispered in each other's ears and laughed occasionally. She also had a lengthy talk with two of her defence team and seemed relaxed and in good spirits. Charlotte on the other hand, was far quieter and spoke just once to a prison guard, hugged her and smiled weakly. Otherwise she slouched in her seat, putting her left hand on her face and staring at the ground, while sometimes playing with a wristband on her right arm. She'd occasionally look up and stare around her, fidgeting with a yellow lighter and picking at her long nails. Neither of the defendants was handcuffed in the courtroom and just one prison officer watched over them.

Ireland's most respected, experienced – and feared –

criminal judge returned to his courtroom at 12.45 p.m. on the button. He began by saying that the Farah Swaleh Noor murder was 'the most grotesque case of killing' that he had ever experienced in his professional lifetime. He said that this was only the third case in Irish legal history involving the mutilation of the victim in such a horrific manner. The others were the notorious case of South African medical student Shan Mohangi in 1963 and double killer Michael Bambrick, who murdered and mutilated two women after macabre sex sessions, and was sentenced to eighteen years for the double manslaughter in 1996.

Sergeant Liam Hickey gave evidence for An Garda Síochána and told the court that Charlotte and Linda Mulhall had attacked and murdered Farah Swaleh Noor after the Kenyan made advances on Linda and called her a 'creature of the night'. He detailed how the pair had mutilated the body and cut it into eight pieces before dumping it in the Royal Canal and disposing of the head and murder weapons at Sean Walsh Park, in Tallaght. Sgt Hickey accepted that the women had been co-operative with the gardaí once they had owned up to the killings and said that Linda had shown genuine remorse for what she had done.

Linda's counsel, Brendan Grehan, said that she had made a number of attempts to harm herself since the Noor murder and had cut her arms on two occasions. She had spent ten days in a psychiatric hospital just days before the trial started and was taking heroin and drinking up to three bottles of vodka a day. Mr Grehan said that she was a good mother and he pleaded for leniency.

Mr Justice Carney did not agree, however, and immediately sentenced her to fifteen years' imprisonment, to gasps of surprise from the courtroom. He said he had the option of jailing her for life but had to respect the decision of the jury to allow the defence of provocation. He would have sentenced her to eighteen years in jail but for the fact that she had helped point out various scenes to detectives and had assisted the investigation. He said he was not persuaded by arguments put forward by her defence counsel that she was a good mother to her four children, saying, 'As far as you've urged on me that she is a good mother, I don't regard this as particularly persuasive. If she was a good mother she would not have got herself into a situation of this kind.' Judge Carney also pointed out that Linda had attempted to postpone or delay the opening of the trial by going cold turkey in an attempt to get off drink and drugs.

Linda, who had previously stared impassively at the floor while the evidence was heard, sobbed into her hands as the realisation dawned that she would not see her children as a free woman for at least ten more years. Charlotte held Linda's hand as her sister's sentence was handed down.

For the most part Charlotte Mulhall sat motionless during the hour-long hearing, choosing a spot on the wall and staring straight at it. Her cold demeanour and casual attitude had been a trademark of the trial and she was not about to change it now. She had known that she wouldn't see the outside world as a free woman for many years and didn't display any emotion when she was formally sentenced to life imprisonment. 'As far as Charlotte is concerned the sentence is a mandatory one of imprisonment for life,' said the judge.

When Judge Carney left his court, the media ran outside to file early copy while the Scissor Sisters were led to the awaiting van and transported back to their home for the foreseeable future. Linda sobbed and clutched a packet of tissues. The tears running down her face left streaks in her heavy mascara. Charlotte said nothing. Her black eye-make-up remained exactly the same as it had been when she put it on five hours earlier.

Outside the courtroom Detective Superintendent John McKeown said: 'The Garda Síochána are pleased with the outcome and the sentences. I would like to extend my sympathies to the family of Mr Noor, his mother and his wife, and extend our thanks to members of the public who came forward to help us with our investigation.'

In the days following sentencing Linda Mulhall was said by prison sources to be devastated at her fifteen-year term. A decision was made by the prison authorities to monitor her, to make sure she didn't attempt suicide. She spent days lying on her bed sobbing and was heard to mutter 'fifteen years, fifteen years' repeatedly. Her jail friends became very worried for her mental health. Linda really did not expect fifteen years for a murder she truly believed she had carried out to protect herself. It was weeks before she accepted her fate and got on with prison life.

Just two days after Judge Carney handed down what was generally agreed to be a harsh sentence, lawyers for Linda lodged an appeal against the severity of the sentence to the Court of Criminal Appeal. The three-judge court would rule in 2007 and would have the option of decreasing the sentence, although they could also add to it, if they felt that fifteen years was too lenient.

Linda gradually came to terms with her punishment and realised that there was nothing she could do to change it. She started studying behind bars and hoped to complete her Leaving Certificate for the first time, as she dropped out of school at a young age. She also began taking classes in woodwork and jewellery-making and learned how to make handbags and purses in the leatherwork classes. Charlotte also attended these classes and the two were rarely apart and tended to do the same activities. Prison sources said that Linda showed a good aptitude for the classes and was good with her hands. She was also said to be a 'clean freak', who spends hours making sure that her room is spotless. Linda had also expressed an interest in doing a FÁS course in beauty therapy and began the course in late 2007. She became friendlier towards her fellow prisoners and mixed more freely. There were even media reports that she had found God and was wearing rosary beads, reciting decades of the rosary each day. Whether this was true or not, the visits from her four children are said to get Linda through each week and she brags to the other women about how well her children are doing in school.

While Linda was trying to come to terms with the fact that she wouldn't walk free until at least 2017, it was business as usual for Charlotte. Prison officers said there was no change in her demeanour. She still mixed freely with her fellow prisoners and seemed resigned to her fate. Charlotte's behaviour while she was out on bail, however, was still keeping her solicitors in business. A few days after the sentencing, on 7 December, Charlotte was fined €100 in her absence at Dublin District Court for being drunk while caring for a child on the 77 bus, in Tallaght. Her legal representative, Michael Kelleher, pleaded guilty on her behalf to being drunk and a danger to herself on 10 September 2006. The court heard that a fellow passenger became alarmed when they saw Charlotte in a drunken state on the bus while she was minding a young child. The driver called the gardaí and Garda Robert Elliot from Tallaght Station said he arrived on the 77 to find her very drunk. 'She had a small child with her and I believed she was intoxicated to such an extent to be a danger to herself,' Garda Elliot told Judge Bryan Smyth. She was arrested for her own safety and taken to the garda station and released when she sobered up. Her solicitor said there was not much he could say about Charlotte's case except that she was very drunk at the time.

Judge Smyth imposed a seven-day prison sentence in default of her paying the €100 fine and agreed to a request that the fine could be paid immediately, so that the default penalty could be served as part of her life sentence. Like her sister, Charlotte's solicitors also lodged an appeal against her murder conviction, so she would get to argue her case again in the Court of Criminal Appeal.

Charlotte's mind was also occupied with the future of her then eight-month-old son. She made an application to look after him in prison and this is allowed in certain circumstances. Following her conviction, the infant was taken into care by social workers. He was sent temporarily to a foster family but Charlotte was unhappy with this and was said to miss her first-born child. She was interviewed by social workers to assess her suitability for caring for a child in jail. Newborn babies are generally only permitted to be with their mothers in jail when they are being breast-fed. The child then undergoes a medical examination by a doctor when he or she is nine months old to see if this is still necessary. Charlotte was not breast-feeding her son so this didn't apply to her. There was no medical reason why the baby should be taken away from a caring foster family and moved to an environment where he would be surrounded by murderers and drug dealers. It is very unusual to have children in a prison environment after they go beyond a maximum of twelve months and the Prison Service does not encourage the practice. A spokesperson said: 'It is the view of the Irish Prison Service that prison is a completely inappropriate environment for infants.' Despite this a deal was agreed at the Dolphin House Family Court in December 2006 to allow Charlotte to look after her son for a few hours each day. She was transferred to Elm House, the child-care facility within the prison that houses up to eighteen infants at any one time.

Charlotte began seeing her son before Christmas and was said by prison staff to be a very good mother who was devoted to the baby. As a report by a senior prison officer in 2001 had found that the Dóchas Centre was riddled with drugs, she had to undergo regular drugs tests as part of the agreement and passed each one. Charlotte was apparently revelling in looking after her child each day but it lasted only until 28 May 2007, when the baby turned one.

Both women have succumbed to the demon drink while in the Dóchas Centre. On 21 February 2007 prison officers spotted Linda and Charlotte acting suspiciously by the prison boundary walls and kept them under surveillance. Two large plastic bottles were thrown over the wall from outside the jail. Officers confiscated the bottles. It was found that they contained vodka. Both women admitted being in possession of the drink and it is believed that they were subject to internal disciplinary procedures but the results were never made public. Three weeks before the vodka incident a member of the public was caught attempting to pass alcohol to Linda and it was also confiscated by prison officers. No disciplinary action was taken but prison sources said that the officers keep a close eye on both women to make sure that they do not get their hands on either drink or drugs.

An Awkward Family Reunion

THE DETECTIVES WHO spent months investigating the gruesome murder of Farah Swaleh Noor have often wondered what drove two women, from a seemingly normal background, to commit a killing of such horror. It is impossible to say.

Linda and Charlotte Mulhall both attended St Aidan's Community College in Tallaght but dropped out before sitting their Leaving Certificate. They were not involved in crime and only had one or two minor convictions. Kilclare Gardens, in Jobstown, is regarded as quite an upmarket council estate and most of its residents have lived there for decades. It is not blighted by drugs or terrorised by joy riders like some other council estates in Tallaght.

The Mulhalls' neighbours were all shocked when they heard that the girls had managed to get themselves into so much trouble. The family were not whiter than white and had caused a bit of trouble around the estate, but there was nothing to suggest that two killers were growing-up in Number 31. John Mulhall was a hardworking man who worked long hours to look after his family.

Life for the Mulhalls seemed to fall apart, however, when Kathleen met Farah Swaleh Noor and walked out on her husband. It was then that Charlotte started to drift into prostitution and she and Linda turned to drink and drugs to fill the emotional vacuum in their lives – Charlotte because of her mother deserting her, and Linda as a result of her partner physically abusing her children. The Mulhalls were a family that the Celtic Tiger forgot. Farah Swaleh Noor came to Ireland hoping to experience the benefits of Ireland's burgeoning economy but he didn't realise that thousands of Irish people were being bypassed by the economic boom. Linda and Charlotte never had jobs and were brought up claiming social welfare payments. They got extra cash from wherever they could find it, either from robbing or, in Charlotte's case, selling herself for sex. The system let these two women down somewhere along the way.

Out of all the Mulhalls, gardaí had most sympathy for Linda and felt sorry that she had been dragged into a situation that had spiralled out of control. In the book of evidence, forwarded to the DPP by Detective Inspector Christy Mangan, she is described as being 'truthful and sincere' in all her dealings with gardaí after she first admitted her role in the murder: 'She became emotional and upset when she described the details of the killing. At no stage did she retract anything of what she said and Detective Inspector Mangan and Sergeant Hickey could see that despite the abomination of what she had confessed to, she was relieved to have done so and she expressed regret for having done it. I believe that the injuries she inflicted on herself are an indication of Linda Mulhall's state of mind in the aftermath of the killing and of her inability to live with what she did. I believe she is fully prepared to face the consequences of her actions.'

Charlotte Mulhall, although extremely reluctant to admit to her involvement, was also truthful once she finally confessed that she had murdered Farah Swaleh Noor. If she had not given the statement conceding her involvement in the crime, it is very doubtful if gardaí would ever have had enough evidence to charge her with the murder. She would not have been charged on the word of Linda alone and there was no real forensic evidence against her. It was Charlotte's eventual honesty that ensured that she will not walk the streets as a free woman for a very long time.

In June 2007 Linda Mulhall again appeared before Dublin District Court. She left with a further nine-month jail term after evidence was heard that the convicted killer tried to kick in the sitting room door at the home of her former love rival, Mary Behan. 'Don't get smart with me; I'm Linda Mulhall,' Behan was warned.

Linda was charged with criminal damage and trespass after forcing her way into Mary Behan's home. The father of three of Linda's children, Mark Farrelly, had begun an affair with Behan while Linda was eight months pregnant with her youngest child. The ugly incident at Behan's home happened on 13 May 2006 while Mulhall was on bail, charged with the murder of Farah Swaleh Noor. Mary Behan alleged that Mulhall threatened to petrol-bomb her house and kill her children and said she had to leave her home in Drimnagh following the incident. Behan's twelve-year-old is now afraid to go upstairs alone and her ten-year-old still needs counselling.

Linda Mulhall's two sons were celebrating their Confirmation when their mother brought them to Farrelly's home at Benmadigan Road to see their father. Mulhall knocked on the door, looking for her former partner, but Mary Behan answered and told her to go away. Behan claims that Linda became aggressive and forced her way into the house while Behan barricaded herself into the living room to protect her children. Linda Mulhall kicked the door off its hinges and shouted abuse but she eventually left.

The gardaí were called and Linda was later arrested. She told Garda Niall Kenna that she knew Behan because: 'She had an affair with my kids' father,' but claimed, 'I wasn't even inside that bloody house.' Giving evidence in court, Linda said, 'I thought Mark would have been proud to see his sons on their Confirmation day, because he wasn't paying child support or anything.' She denied trespassing at Farrelly and Behan's council house and claimed, 'I certainly didn't kick no door in. It was my kids' special day. I wasn't going to ruin it.' Linda admitted that there was bitterness between her and Behan and said, 'He was my fiancé and Mary Behan went and had an affair with him. When I was pregnant he had an affair, but I'm over that a long time.'

The affair between Behan and Farrelly began in 1999 and Linda and Charlotte Mulhall had previously attacked Mary Behan's home. On 27 March 2003 the sisters went to the house and abused Mary Behan while Charlotte threw cans at the house, breaking a window. Charlotte was subsequently charged with criminal damage and given the benefit of the Probation Act, on 2 October 2005. Linda was interviewed but never charged. She wasn't so lucky the second time around, though. Judge Thomas Fitzpatrick imposed six months for the criminal damage and nine months for trespass. He said Mulhall's evidence was contrived and, after hearing of her appeal against her manslaughter conviction, there was a possibility she could be free before the new sentence expired. The judge agreed to a defence request not to make the sentences consecutive.

Later that year Linda had what sources described as a mini breakdown in prison after the model head she was using for hairdressing training was stolen by another inmate. Linda had been training to be a hairdresser at the Dóchas Centre for the previous year and was assigned her own model head to practise on. She went to class one day in December and discovered the head had been stolen. According to prison staff, when she saw the head was gone she fell to her knees and began crying uncontrollably, saying that the lost head had brought back the image of Farah Noor. She was comforted by staff and other inmates and was offered counselling to help her get over her ordeal. The head eventually turned up but the person who stole it was never identified. It is thought that the theft was a joke that went wrong. One source who witnessed the incident said: 'Linda went to hairdressing class after lunch as usual and when she saw that the head was gone she just lost it and fell to the floor, roaring crying. She wouldn't stop and staff were genuinely concerned for her mental health. Somebody probably took the head as a bit of a laugh, but after what happened, nobody would own up to it. Linda is a tough nut and she didn't find it funny, so you can't really blame the joker for keeping quiet. You do not want to get on the two girls' bad sides.'

While Linda was battling her inner demons, Charlotte was drafted in as a waitress to serve at the official Christmas lunch in the Dóchas Centre. The head of the Irish Prison Service, Brian Purcell, hosted his annual Christmas lunch in the jail for senior staff and guests, and inmates traditionally serve the food. Charlotte was chosen to be part of the waitressing team, which was a sought-after job only given to inmates who were trusted. People who attended the luncheon said she did a very good job and was very polite. You would never have known that she was one of Ireland's most notorious murderers.

There can be little doubt that Farah Swaleh Noor was a nasty piece of work and some would say that he had what happened coming to him because of his own violence towards women. The garda book of evidence describes Noor as 'a highly volatile and aggressive individual and this condition was exacerbated by his excessive drinking'. He certainly carried knives and was prepared to use weapons during violent drunken outbursts. In the months before his murder, Farah Noor was falling further and further into a murky existence of drink and violence. It is quite possible that he could have murdered some poor unfortunate were he not killed himself.

Even though he was an undesirable individual, the fact remains that Farah Noor left a heartbroken family behind him in Kenya. Detective Sergeant Gerry McDonnell was responsible for liaising with Farah's mother, wife and family in Mombasa. He became close to them and contacted Farah's mother, Somoe Bakari Shigoo in January 2006 when the coroner released Farah's body, giving permission for burial. As his family did not have a lot of money they couldn't afford to repatriate his body to Kenya and Det Sgt McDonnell requested permission from Somoe to have Farah laid to rest in Ireland.

On 1 February 2006 the detective received a fax from Mombasa.

It was headed: 'My consent so that my son Sheilila Swaleh/Farah Swaleh is buried' and read:

> Fate is very strong and as human beings we are to succumb to it. This is what befell my late dear son who really cared for me as a mother and his family. I had really cherished the idea of availing myself in Ireland so as to pay my last respect to my beloved son who was brutally murdered. What haunts me and the entire family most is the fact that the remnants of my son's body are yet to be buried. In our holy scripture we are told, "We are from God and to him we shall return." On this note and humbly, with tears of despondency streaming on my face I hearby give the coroner my consent so that his body is laid to rest. On the same note I would like to register my heartfelt appreciation to the government of Ireland for its sincere and genuine concern for human rights, free from favour or discrimination.
>
> Thanking you in advance,
> Somoe Bakari Shigoo.

On 10 March 2006 the body of thirty-nine-year-old Farah Swaleh Noor was taken to Glasnevin Cemetery for burial. About forty people gathered to take part in a traditional Muslim ceremony to remember the dead Kenyan. A prayer service took place in Stafford's funeral home, before a hearse transported his remains to Glasnevin, where he was buried in a plot paid for by the taxpayer. The mourners filled the plot with earth by hand, while branches from yew trees in the cemetery were placed around the grave. The ceremony took nearly two hours and Muslim clerics said prayers as large stones were placed at the foot of the grave. The service ended as the top of the plot was covered with a mound of soil.

In September 2007 this author tracked down Farah Noor's family to their dilapidated home in Mombasa in Kenya, where Noor's wife, Husna Mohamed Said, broke her silence and revealed that Noor's daughter collapsed and died soon after learning that her father had been murdered in Ireland. Husna said her family's life had been torn apart and that she had considered suicide because of what happened to her estranged husband. The thirty-six-year-old was living in severe financial hardship and had not been contacted by the Irish authorities about financial compensation, following Noor's murder.

Husna rejected the allegations that Noor was a violent rapist and said he never once hit her during their marriage. Husna Said married Noor when she was seventeen and the couple lived in Mombasa and had three children together. Noor walked out on his family in 1993, saying he was going to Europe to set up a base and that he would later fly his wife and children over to join him. Said was pregnant at the time. But it appears Noor had no intention of ever seeing his family again. He appears to have lived in London until December 1996, when he managed to board a flight from Rome to Dublin and claim refugee status, making up an elaborate story that he was fleeing from war-torn Somalia. During his years in Ireland, Noor kept in contact with his wife and children and regularly sent his elderly mother money. But Said did not find out her husband had been murdered until six months after he died, when gardaí discovered Noor's identity and tracked his family down.

Said's teenage daughter Somoe was weak and suffered with health problems. She was often confined to a wheelchair and when the seventeen-year-old heard her father was dead, her health deteriorated. 'She got a shock over her father's death and got a fever. She was seventeen years old, the firstborn. When she heard the news, she got a fever and lost her memory. She then fell into a coma for two days and died. She was in high school. She lost consciousness and never woke up. I miss her so much because she was a beautiful person. Sometimes I feel like killing myself,' Husna said.

The couple had two other children: fifteen-year-old Mohamed and thirteen-year-old Zuleh. Husna said her whole family was affected by the trauma of Noor's murder and that they will never get over it. '[Someo] was the most important one and I loved her very much,' she said. 'I have no one to help me and am really going through a hard time. Sometimes I want to commit suicide because I have nothing left in this world.' Farah's mother used to give Husna some of the money her son would send from Ireland but since his death the entire family is living in poverty. She has applied to Ireland's Criminal Injuries Compensation Board for compensation but has heard nothing from them. 'They sent me some forms to fill in and I sent them back last March but I have heard nothing since then. I am supporting my two kids for the last two years without any money,' she said. 'I am a single woman and have no money. Life is very tough with the kids and it is hard bringing them up. I cannot pay their school fees. Farah left us and I have been supporting them by myself ever since. I work long hours as a cook and have to rush home to prepare them dinner. Life is very hard.'

Farah and Husna were from strict Muslim families and Husna had to stay indoors, mourning her husband for at least three months after his death. This meant that she was unable to go out to work to support her children. The Criminal Injuries Compensation Board has the power to give financial compensation to Noor's family but Husna says she is not all about money. 'No matter how much I get, I will never be happy for the rest of my life. I loved Farah a lot. He was my first love and I married him when I was seventeen. It was a marriage of love and not arranged.'

Husna said that Noor's relatives in Kenya were extremely angry Kathleen Mulhall had not yet faced a jury to answer to any alleged role she might have played in the murder of the Kenyan.

'Of course I'd like to see her in jail, and Farah's mum is the same,' she said. 'She complains, asking why is she not arrested or in jail. I want to sue Kathleen. She can't run away just like that. Wherever she is, she will never be comfortable for the rest of her life. Allah will never forgive.'

Husna had asked Noor for a divorce shortly before his murder because 'he didn't care about his family and didn't send money, so we argued. He used to call me about 2005 and I have many letters he used to send me. I told him I wanted a divorce because he was not responsible for the kids. Everything fell on me. He didn't care about the kids. He liked drinking. I didn't trust him; he was an alcoholic.'

Farah Swaleh Noor was portrayed in court as a violent womaniser who used to rape his girlfriends. He got two women pregnant while in Ireland and they both made allegations of violence and rape against him. However, Husna said she did not recognise this description as fitting her husband. 'Farah never beat me or treated me badly. Kathleen was his girlfriend. I don't think Farah raped anybody. He did not ever rape me. She's lying if she says he beat her.'

Noor never attempted to hide the fact he had two children in Ireland and wrote about them in letters to his wife. According to Husna: 'Farah sent me a picture of his son a long time ago. If it was possible I would like to adopt the child and bring him up as a Muslim like Farah would have wanted.'

Farah's family were obviously furious with Kathleen Mulhall and wanted her to answer for what she did.

✂✂✂

Their wish would come sooner than expected because just three months after Husna Said spoke publicly for the first time, this author finally tracked down Kathleen. She had not been seen or heard from since September 2005, but in December 2007, after months of behind-the-scenes investigation and considerable expense, I determined that Kathleen Mulhall was going by the name Cathy Ward. She was living in a free council house in Shepherd's Bush, in London, and was surviving on State handouts. *Sunday Tribune* photographer Mark Condren and I travelled over to London and placed the one-bedroom cottage under surveillance. We had been parked in a blacked-out van, outside her home, for a matter of minutes when the light in Mulhall's porch came on and we saw her passionately kiss a middle-aged black man. The man then jumped on a bicycle and cycled away into the evening darkness.

Kathleen's appearance had changed dramatically since she left Ireland and she had dyed her hair blonde in an effort to disguise her identity. Because it was in the depths of winter and the light was bad we were unable to get a clear photograph of Mulhall, so we returned at first light the following morning. We sat outside the house for three full days but Mulhall did not once leave the house. We suspected that she had left during the first night and had gone to visit relatives in Birmingham. We called to a neighbour's house and asked after Kathleen. The neighbour told us that she didn't venture out of the house much during the day but that she came alive at night and often had male visitors who spent considerable amounts of time in her cottage. She told her neighbours that she had left Ireland years before and had come to London from Birmingham. They said she was very pleasant and friendly and would offer to go to the shops for elderly folk who couldn't leave the house in bad weather.

We showed a photograph of Kathleen around the dozens of pubs around the main drag in Shepherd's Bush, which is home to many Irish immigrants, and several bar workers recognised the woman as Cathy Ward. They said that she regularly drank heavily with a large group of African men and we were told that the man we had seen her kissing was a convicted rapist. Mulhall was still fond of dangerous sex offenders, it seemed. The bar workers said that Cathy was a friendly and jovial woman who drank too much and would often disappear for weeks on end only to come back in and start to chat to punters as if she had never left.

The following week we returned to London and after seven hours in the van we saw Mulhall come out of her cottage and talk to an elderly neighbour. We snapped a photograph of her after spinning the van around and driving into the complex, towards the house. Mulhall was shocked that her hiding place had been compromised and ran indoors and slammed the door. We knocked but she refused to answer and turned out the lights.

The previous April the Director of Public Prosecutions had decided that Kathleen should face charges in relation to the murder of Farah Noor. So when the story appeared in the *Sunday Tribune* gardaí were eager to make the trip to London and extradite her to Dublin to face a jury of her peers. Detectives applied for an extradition warrant and waited the six weeks for it to come through, all the while hoping that she didn't do one of her legendary disappearing acts now that she knew her cover had been blown.

On 12 February 2008 Detective Sergeant Liam Hickey and Detective Garda Mike Smyth flew to London and met up with their counterparts in the London Metropolitan Police. They then travelled to Kathleen Mulhall/Cathy Ward's house and knocked on the door. The fifty-three-year-old opened the door and warmly greeted the two Irish detectives. She knew the game was up and had been expecting a visit since the *Sunday Tribune* had found her over two months previously. She made the officers a cup of tea and listened to them say that the DPP had decided that she had a case to answer about the murder of her former lover. She calmly said that she would voluntarily return to Dublin. Had she refused she would have been arrested by Met officers on foot of the European Arrest Warrant, but that process could have taken weeks or even months, so her unexpected cooperation was warmly welcomed by gardaí.

The following day Kathleen arrived back in Dublin. As soon as she got off the plane and touched Irish soil she was formally arrested and was transported straight to Mountjoy Garda Station. At 7.55 p.m. DS Liam Hickey formally charged her with aiding and abetting in the concealment of a crime. Kathleen made no reply. The next day she appeared at Dublin District Court amid a media circus. Wearing heavy make-up and sporting a peaked cap, white runners, black jeans, black polo-neck jumper and a leather jacket with gold zips, Mulhall stood quietly with her hands behind her back as proceedings got under way. DS Liam Hickey told Judge Patricia Ryan about meeting Kathleen in London and explained that she had agreed to return to Ireland. He also gave evidence about charging her the night before. No bail application was made and she was remanded into custody to the Dóchas Centre, where her two daughters were serving their sentences.

Sources say that the atmosphere inside the Dóchas Centre was extremely tense when Kathleen Mulhall arrived, accompanied by two prison officers. She was immediately taken into the office of the prison governor and told that she would be looked after by staff and treated like every other woman but that any bad blood between her and her daughters that could result in disputes or violence would not be tolerated. Kathleen said that she had no problem with Linda and Charlotte and hoped that they felt the same way. She said that she would serve her time quietly and would not cause any hassle or bother. With that she was taken to her room, where within minutes she was visited by Charlotte.

Charlotte had always been very understanding about her mother's somewhat unusual private life and if she bore a grudge about Kathleen skipping the country and leaving her and Linda to face the rap for Farah, she didn't show it. She ran up and hugged her mother and soon it was like they had never been separated.

Linda was a harder nut to crack, and while she did

acknowledge her mother, she was very quiet and cold towards her for the first few weeks. She was less forgiving than Charlotte and was angry that while she was serving time for killing Farah at her mother's behest, Kathleen had been swanning around in London, drinking heavily and having sex with a string of men. Kathleen worked hard to repair the fractious relationship and was forever apologising for what happened and generally trying to make it up to her daughters for being a lousy parent. Over time Linda relented and they gradually became close again and even moved into the same room together.

Although Kathleen had never been in trouble with the law or seen the inside of a cell – not that you could really describe the rooms at the Dóchas Centre as cells – she assimilated easily into prison life. She was popular with the other women and was regarded as a mother figure to come to for advice, which was ironic considering her shoddy history as an actual mother.

Charlotte had weekly visits with her son and Kathleen really relished spending time with her grandson and doted on the young lad. It was almost as if prison life had freed her and given her a second chance. Every week she would wheel the youngster around on a little tricycle and the prison officers noticed how happy she looked. It was almost like the Mulhalls were a proper family for the first time in years, and Kathleen was certainly enjoying making up with her daughters.

In March 2008 Kathleen Mulhall again appeared before Dublin District Court to face new charges in relation to her partner's gruesome murder three years previously. She was charged with attempting to obstruct the arrest and prosecution of her two daughters by helping to clean up her apartment after Noor's murder. More charges were brought against her for giving gardaí false information about Noor's whereabouts and she was also charged with two counts of withholding information that could have helped in the arrest and prosecution of her two daughters for the murder of Farah Noor. She was remanded in custody.

Later that same month Charlotte Mulhall's day of reckoning came when she was brought to the Court of Criminal Appeal (CCA) to find out whether she would be allowed a full appeal against her conviction for Farah Noor's murder. Her legal team had claimed that comments made by trial judge Mr Justice Paul Carney while the jury was deliberating put them under pressure to reach a verdict in the case. The judge made the comments when the jury came out on the second day of their deliberations to ask the judge for guidance because it had become deadlocked. The foreman asked if the court would accept a majority vote and the judge told them there were five children who had a 'vital interest' in their decision, and then asked them to 'make a final push to reach agreement'. Mulhall's senior counsel, Brendan Grehan, said the only explanation one could make of this remark was that the jury had been put under pressure to reach a verdict. He then claimed that pressure must have led someone who, up until then had been in the minority, to go over to the majority. The jury eventually gave a verdict of 10–2, finding Charlotte guilty.

Counsel for the DPP argued the judge's request that the jury make a final push to reach a conclusion was not an ultimatum or a threat. They said the jury, who had already been over-nighted in a hotel for two days, took another night before reaching a verdict. But leave to appeal was rejected by the CCA with the judges' ruling that they did not find with the submission that the jury's decision was perverse. On the basis of the evidence before them and the statements made by Mulhall, the jury was 'perfectly entitled' to come to the verdict of murder in relation to her, the ruling said. In relation to the remarks made by Mr Justice Carney, the appeal court said there had been no objection raised to them by the defence at the time of the trial, although the prosecution had done so. Common sense would have said the defence would have benefited from the remarks, the ruling continued. It was 'perfectly clear' that the jury had very carefully considered the verdict and it was hard to see that they came under any kind of pressure. The application for leave to appeal was therefore refused.

During the same month Linda had her own appeal D-Day and received a severe blow when she lost her appeal against the severity of her fifteen-year jail sentence for Farah Swaleh Noor's manslaughter. The Court of Criminal Appeal found the trial judge, Mr Justice Paul Carney, had imposed the appropriate sentence in light of the facts of the case. The appeal court had adjourned the case in February 2008 to consider reports by probation officer Scarlett Taylor and a consultant forensic psychiatrist at the Central Mental Hospital, Dr Helen O'Neill. Dr O'Neill's report had been prepared just before the sentencing hearing in December 2006, while Ms Taylor's March 2007 report was based on the detailed notes of her predecessor, who had interviewed Mulhall several times. Linda Mulhall's senior counsel, Brendan Grehan, said the psychiatric report showed that his client felt great remorse to such a degree that she had difficulty touching her own children. It showed she had suffered a brutalised existence from a very early age and that she had taken to drink and self-harm as a means of dealing with her difficult upbringing. He added that the probation report showed she was tearful and distressed and had great difficulty understanding what she had done. Because of this one event in her life, Linda 'should not be written off'. While she could not explain what she did and why she did it, she had never tried to deflect blame for the brutal killing of Farah Noor. The three-judge court said that after considering the two reports it was satisfied that the original fifteen-year sentence was appropriate and should stand. The appeal court said it had considered the submissions by Mulhall's legal counsel and it noted the psychiatrist recommended that she required a structured programme of counselling and rehabilitation to deal with the risk of re-offending. The three judges said there was no doubt that the sentence imposed was lengthy and the trial judge had decided, because of the gruesome nature of the offence, that the sentence should be at the 'very, very serious end of the scale'. The maximum sentence for manslaughter was life imprisonment and Mr Justice Carney considered the appropriate sentence was in the 'late teens or perhaps twenty or twenty-one years'. In settling on fifteen years (eighteen years with the last three suspended), he took into account that Linda Mulhall had co-operated with gardaí after the initial investigation; had assisted in recovering parts of the body; and her lack of previous convictions.

On whether a further part of Linda's sentence should be suspended, the appeal court said it was clear from early on that Mulhall had to engage with counselling and rehabilitation services, but she had not done so by the time of sentencing. They added that long after her arrest and incarceration she had not joined any programme, despite the probation services saying that she was at risk of re-offending. In those circumstances, the trial judge had not erred in failing to suspend part of the sentence, the judgement said. Linda Mulhall was in court for the verdict and sat emotionless with her head down when the decision was read out. She was quickly brought out of court after the ruling.

James Mulhall, the Scissor Sisters' eldest brother, impressed observers during the murder trial because he attended court every day to lend support to his siblings. However, in April 2008 he was jailed for stealing from prostitutes, crimes that he committed during lunch breaks in his sisters' trial. The thirty-five-year-old took advantage of the breaks in Linda and Charlotte's trial to go to the International Financial Services Centre (IFSC) in Dublin's Docklands and steal from prostitutes. He was ultimately identified after detectives recognised him in court from descriptions the prostitutes supplied, which had been circulated around Dublin garda stations. Mulhall pleaded guilty to stealing over €1,000 in cash and fourteen mobile phones from two prostitutes, in September and October 2006. The father-of-two claimed that he committed the crimes because he was desperate for money. He was looking after Linda's four children while she completed her fifteen-year sentence.

On 26 September 2006 detectives from Store Street were called in to investigate an incident in the IFSC. A Brazilian woman who had advertised her services on a website had received fifteen phone calls from a man looking for her apartment. When she let him in, a second man appeared and the pair stole nine mobile phones and €800 in cash, before escaping.

On 5 October a South African prostitute was attacked at

her apartment in Ringsend and robbed of €250, five mobile phones and an iPod. The woman picked up a knife from the kitchen to defend herself, but was threatened with a bottle and assaulted.

Gardaí initially had no suspects. They distributed images of the robbers, taken from CCTV footage. Again, a detective recognised Mulhall from the image because he had seen him in court each day for over a month. Gardaí from Store Street went to the Central Criminal Court and identified Mulhall and detained him. He admitted carrying out the robberies and his accomplice was identified as thirty-year-old Paul Draper, from Tallaght. Both victims were traumatised by their experience and left the country.

The same judge who presided over the Mulhall murder case sentenced James Mulhall. Judge Paul Carney said that he was aware of the family background and of the fact that their father had committed suicide. He said that James would have been under pressure at the time because of the media scrutiny his sisters' case received and also noted his explanation that he needed cash because he was looking after Linda's children. He added that he wouldn't be human if he didn't take these factors into account. Carney jailed both men for five years.

Just weeks later, James Mulhall was back in court and was convicted for robbing two shops at knifepoint. He had been caught on a store's CCTV system after he was briefly trapped inside the store. He admitted the robbery of €1,450 and €620 during separate robberies from shops at Fortunestown Lane and Belgard Square, in Tallaght on 14 and 18 February 2007. He told gardaí he was desperate for money and could not afford to feed his own two children and Linda's four.

Garda Pauline Glennon told the court that Mulhall held a knife to a cashier in the second robbery. He threatened he would 'fucking kill' her if she moved, and he ran towards the door after grabbing the cash. When the employee pressed the panic alarm and trapped him inside the shop, Mulhall kicked the door and shouted that he would kill somebody if they didn't let him out. He eventually managed to force the door open and escape.

Judge Katherine Delahunt said the crimes were committed 'in rapid succession over a couple of days' and that the use of the knife had left staff very traumatised. She accepted that James was in financial difficulties but said that it could not be accepted as an excuse. 'Any person with very significant social problems does not just go out and rob stores,' Judge Delahunt added. He was jailed for four years which would be on top of the five-year term he received just weeks before.

✂✂✂

In August 2008 Charlotte Mulhall burst back into the national consciousness in spectacular fashion when a photograph was published of her holding a twelve-inch kitchen knife to the throat of a male inmate while behind bars. The photograph was taken with a camera phone and given to the *Evening Herald* newspaper. When the *Herald* splashed it on the front page, there was a predictable outcry. The murderous prostitute was snapped holding a long blade to the neck of Mountjoy inmate Denis Gibney, who was celebrating his birthday with a cake. The pair of pals had been joking around in the kitchen of the Dóchas Centre, where they had been working, in July 2008, and looked like they didn't have a care in the world. They were laughing and joking and happily posed for the controversial picture. Prison sources were surprised that the photo materialised, because there was always a high level of supervision when male and female inmates were allowed to mix behind bars.

The Irish Prison Service launched an investigation into the circumstances surrounding the picture. The incident was made more embarrassing by the fact that the Prison Service had only recently launched a high-profile clampdown on mobile phones, and having a notorious murderer making a mockery of the system left the Prison Service chief, Brian Purcell, with a red face. In a statement he said that initial investigations concluded that the photo had been taken twelve months before it was published. 'Evidence we have to date indicates that the photograph was taken over a year ago in the prison kitchen, where the prisoner worked, and the knife itself was a kitchen knife. Security issues are of paramount importance to the Prison Service. We already have a rolling programme of security reviews within the prison system, and in this context we will shortly be conducting a full security audit of the Dóchas Centre. As part of the new package of security measures currently being rolled out across the prisons system, new airport-style security measures, which include walk-through detectors and X-ray scanners are scheduled to go live in the Dóchas Centre, commencing on 4 September. Everyone coming into the prison – prisoners, visitors and staff – will have to pass through the new measures, and all handbags, briefcases, clothing etc. will be subject to screening.'

If Brian Purcell was embarrassed, then politicians were furious about the regime that allowed prisoners to mix and photographs to be taken with such seeming ease. Labour's justice spokesman, Pat Rabbitte, said, 'It's bizarre that someone convicted of a particularly gruesome murder ought to be seen in possession of a potentially lethal weapon. People looking at this photograph in their newspapers will be shaking their heads in disbelief and wondering how such a shocking lack of security could be allowed to happen.'

Rabbitte added that the incident made a joke of Justice Minister Dermot Ahern's credibility in terms of his 'extravagant claims' about tackling the use of mobile phones in prisons. He said the minister needed to explain how such an incident could be allowed to happen. 'There are obvious questions from the point of view of prison security. The minister is responsible for prisons but he seems to want to duck the issue and say it is a matter for the Prison Service. I sincerely hope that this bizarre incident doesn't undermine the regime at Mountjoy for women ... because it has a very good reputation as a progressive women's environment,' he added. Fine Gael was equally critical with its spokesman on justice, Charlie Flanagan, saying: 'Prisoners are holding up two fingers to the criminal justice system and these pictures show that prison security is a shambles. It beggars belief that a convicted knife murderer would be allowed access to a potentially lethal kitchen knife.'

Charlotte Mulhall was immediately transferred to Limerick Prison as punishment, while gardaí were called in to see if there was enough evidence to charge her with possession of a mobile phone, an offence that can result in an extra five years being added to a jail term. It was eventually determined that because there was no proof that the handset belonged to her, a criminal charge could not be filed against her. She was transferred back to the Dóchas Centre after a week or so and lost a number of privileges, but that was the extent of Charlotte's punishment.

Gibney was serving a five-year sentence for the possession of 9,000 E tablets worth €135,000. The drugs were in a shopping bag in his car when he was stopped by gardaí for a routine search. He pleaded guilty to possession and said he was moving the drugs for someone else. He was regarded as a responsible prisoner and was given a trustee job in the kitchen of the female jail. This was obviously a highly sought after position because of the number of females around, which naturally appealed to men spending long periods of time locked up. He was released from Mountjoy shortly after the photo was taken and when he was tracked down to his home in Crumlin, the forty-year-old told reporters, 'I've taken a lot of crap over this photo; I really don't need this shit. I won't be giving any information about that photo. If I want to talk, I'll call you and let you know.'

Perhaps the most bizarre story to emerge about the Scissor Sisters appeared in the *Star Sunday* newspaper, also in August 2008. The reporter claimed that Linda Mulhall had become pregnant behind bars by one of the inmates from the Mountjoy men's prison, who worked with her in the kitchen. She allegedly told family members that a scan had confirmed that she was expecting her fifth child. A Prison Service spokesman immediately came out and dismissed the report as inaccurate and nine months passed without the baby ever appearing.

In February 2009 Charlotte Mulhall broke her years of

silence to give a telephone interview to the *Sunday World* newspaper from her plush room at the Dóchas Centre. In the same week that her mother, Kathleen, pleaded guilty to the part she played in the brutal death of Farah Noor, Charlotte described how she would never tell gardaí where Noor's head was and how she was still haunted by the murder and often cried about it.

When asked by reporter Niamh O'Connor what Noor was like, she said, 'He was an evil bastard … He broke my ma's ribs with a hurley, her hand with a hammer … The things he done.' Describing the day of the murder in March 2005 she said, 'We were very high ... I think I was that out of my head, really, I didn't really realise what I was after doing until the next day. I still can't believe it, that it's true. He was trying to strangle me ma … dragging out of Linda and pulling out of her and saying mad shit to her. He was a weirdo … The most I remember about it is that Linda and my ma panicked and were afraid. They were just screaming, basically, what are we going to do with this [the body]?'

Charlotte then described cutting up Noor's body and how she felt she had to be strong for Linda. 'The two of them were just really losing it altogether. I dunno; it was just a spur of the moment, like, and me ma said we're going to have to cut him, cut him up, like.' She then started to cry and said, 'I dunno; I think it was just panic trying to get rid of it and cut him up, basically. I don't sleep. You always see it in front of you, just like flashbacks all the time. It is really hard to deal with. I try to tell myself that it's not real, kind of, but it's very hard, though, really.'

Charlotte also said that she felt that she and Linda had been wrongly convicted of Farah's killing and that she was unhappy that evidence about Noor's abuse was not heard.

'We were convicted before the trial even started. The jury didn't hear his two ex-partners give evidence. They were sent out for that. The jury were sent out for that in case they, what was the word, prejudiced the jurors. I mean that girl told of how he was molesting his own child and everything. He broke her arm, raping her for years when she was only sixteen. The judge said that would prejudice the jury. He couldn't listen to it, basically.'

Charlotte said she had no hard feelings about her mother fleeing to London, where she spent her time bedding sex offenders. 'Me ma was a great ma. So was me da; that's one thing I will say to them. In later years that [her parents' break-up] was between them, but it never affected any of us in any way.'

She also described the trauma that her mother had gone through after Noor's tragic death, but maintained that Kathleen did not still love the dead African. 'She does not [still claim to love him]. She doesn't even talk about it. It's too hard for her. Even if I try and mention something to her about it, she'll just break down in tears. She is taking it very bad now. I don't think she can really cope with it. She's been drinking and all. She's lost an awful lot of weight. She used to be very happy-go-lucky.'

Even though Kathleen Mulhall admitted to detectives that she sold her body as a prostitute and that Charlotte had coached her, Charlotte denied that this was the case. 'That's a lie. I was out working, me mother never did … I only actually started going out working on the streets after all that hassle [her parents' break-up over Farah Noor]. That's when I started on heroin and heavy drugs, and it was just to pay for my habit really.'

Despite being jailed for life because she'd carried out

the murder on her mother's say-so, Charlotte had a remarkable lack of bitterness towards Kathleen. When asked if she blamed her at all for her predicament, she said, 'I don't know if she actually knew what she was saying, because she was, we were all really out of our heads … To me, me ma, she's an older woman and she didn't even actually see anything that we done that night.'

Charlotte even defended her deadbeat mother when talking about the way Kathleen kicked John Mulhall out of his home so that Noor could take his place. 'Me da was having an affair with someone she knew, so there was always trouble in the family … But to me that was a long time ago,' she said.

Charlotte still wasn't prepared to come clean and confess to what really happened to Farah's head. A lot of detectives had major doubts about Linda's version of events, in which she claimed to have smashed the skull with a hammer, in a field in Tallaght. 'I don't think it would actually make a difference at this stage, not after being sentenced,' was Charlotte's answer when she was asked why she wouldn't come clean about the where the head was. 'They won't even let me appeal against it [the sentence], so I really don't think it would make a difference. I think it's just gone too far. It'd only just start another whole load of publicity again. I think it's just best to leave it be really.' When asked if a full and frank confession would show that she feels remorse for what happened on the night of the Noor murder she replied, 'I don't know. I just can't really say. I swore I wouldn't.' She said she made this promise to her mother and Linda and that, 'I'm the kind of person, if I give someone my word, I just can't go back on it.' she concluded, before hanging up the phone.

✂✂✂

In May 2009 Kathleen Mulhall appeared before the Central Criminal Court to answer for her role in Farah Noor's death. Coincidentally it was Mr Justice Paul Carney who presided over the case. Carney had been the judge in Kathleen's daughters' trial and had famously said of it: 'It was the most grotesque case of killing that has occurred in my professional lifetime.'

Kathleen admitted to cleaning up the murder scene at her flat in Ballybough and was facing a possible ten-year sentence for the cover-up. The strain was clearly evident on her face as she broke down in court and wept as details of Farah Noor's killing were read into the record. Her senior counsel, Hugh Hartnett SC, said Mulhall had been abused by her parents, her husband and later by Mr Noor, but she had never been in trouble with the law and had no previous criminal convictions. He pleaded to Mr Justice Carney that, 'Not to take it [the abuse] into account would be an outrage against justice.' He said that Mulhall had suffered bouts of depression and had turned to religion in the Dóchas Centre. 'She was abused as a child by her father and, indeed, her mother. Despite that, she never got into trouble and got married at a very, very young age.'

Evidence was heard that Mulhall had initially denied any knowledge of the murder but had eventually admitted that she had stayed silent to protect her children. She also offered to take the blame for the killing to protect her daughters, it was heard. Hugh Hartnett said his client had tried to do her 'level best' for her family.

Mr Justice Carney adjourned the sentencing hearing for a number of days and requested a transcript of the short hearing.

When the case went back before the court, Mulhall was more composed, and, dressed in a brown pinstriped jacket and pink shirt, stared ahead and showed little emotion or fear of what she was facing. Mr Justice Carney said he would take into account the fact that Mulhall had returned from the UK voluntarily. He also noted that she was trying to protect her children and had suffered abuse and violence at the hands of Noor, her late husband and other members of her family. The judge imposed a sentence of just five years and backdated it to February 2008, when she first came back to the country and was remanded in custody. This meant that she would be freed at the end of 2011. It was a very good result for Mulhall, who many detectives believe had got off very lightly indeed.

There was some controversy over whether life in the Dóchas Centre was too easy, when the long-serving governor Kathleen McMahon controversially retired early, in May 2010. After she resigned she gave media interviews in which she severely criticised the Irish Prison Service, saying that the Dóchas Centre had become severely overcrowded and that the progressive, non-judgemental regime that she encouraged during her time as governor was being 'cannibalised'. She also claimed that the overcrowding was leading to a major increase in lesbianism among the women.

In response, the director general of the Irish Prison Service, Brian Purcell, highlighted the fact that the prison service was obliged to take every inmate that the courts decided to jail and could not put a 'full up' sign in the jail. He said that overcrowding was undesirable but inevitable and that the new jail planned for Thornton Hall would ease the overcrowding situation. He told the *Sunday Tribune*: 'The Dóchas Centre is our flagship model. The new facility will continue with that regime and improve on it. We will have a lot more space. The bunk-bed situation is not ideal. The regime we have for women at the Dóchas Centre works very well. It wouldn't necessarily work the same for male prisoners. Men and women are different. Men are from Mars, women are from Venus.'

The women in the Dóchas Centre certainly seem to enjoy life there, and there have been dozens of occasions where woman have pleaded to stay there after completing their sentences. The relaxed regime belies the fact that many of the inmates are serious criminals with long and chequered histories. Some 25 per cent of inmates are serving sentences for murder, manslaughter or conspiracy to murder, while 21 per cent have been sentenced for possession of drugs for sale or supply. A further 28 per cent are doing time for offences such as robbery, theft and criminal damage.

Despite the serious nature of the crimes, there are relatively few security incidents at the prison. A spokesman for the Irish Prison Service said of the Dóchas Centre: 'Most of our long-term prisoners we don't have any problems with at all. They know they are in for the long haul. They just put their heads down and get on with their lives. They generally get involved in a lot of the training and education programmes too. They need to do things to fill their days. It's the remand prisoners who are usually the most volatile. We get to know our long-term prisoners very well; we know their personalities. For the women who are here long-term, the worst thing you can do is nothing.'

✂✂✂

Linda finally exhausted all legal avenues in July 2010 when the Court of Criminal Appeal delivered its verdict on her appeal against her conviction and sentence. Linda's legal team had gone back to court to argue that Mr Justice Paul Carney should not have sentenced her without reading the full psychological report on her, which had not been completed when she was first convicted. The three-judge appeal court said in its judgement:

> In light of the severity of the crime, its nature, and the evidence tendered by gardaí at the sentencing hearing as to the particular circumstances of the applicant, this court concludes that it would not be possible in this case to have full regard for the established principles of sentencing, without the reports sought to be procured on behalf of the applicant. In that sense, and in that sense only, the learned sentencing judge erred in law. The court refrains at this time from passing any comment on whether the sentence actually imposed is or is not unduly severe, or on the question as to whether any part of the custodial sentence should or should not have been suspended. It is both inappropriate and impossible to reach a conclusion on these matters without having the benefit of the above referred to reports.

While this was somewhat critical of Judge Carney, the court determined that the eighteen-year sentence handed to Mulhall, with the final three suspended, was appropriate given the nature of her crime. As to whether she had been provoked by Noor's behaviour on the night, it was ruled that this had been accepted by the jury in the original trial, hence her being convicted of manslaughter and not murder, like

Charlotte. This ruling meant that once and for all Linda had to accept that she would serve at least ten years behind bars. Prison sources said she was not overly surprised at the outcome and took it quite well.

In October 2010 the brutal case of the Scissor Sisters and Farah Noor was brought to the small screen by TV3 reporter Dyane Connor, who presented the *24 hours to Kill* series. Professor of criminology at Birmingham City University, David Wilson, gave Connor an interview in which he said he believes the drink- and drug-fuelled crime would have given the sisters terrible nightmares. 'It's a journey into a dark side of the human psyche. I've no doubt that both Linda and Charlotte still think about what happened on that night and probably still have nightmares about it. This is clearly a murder that takes place after the sisters have been using drink and especially drugs for a long and sustained period of time. Without doubt the alcohol and drug abuse distorts the way they think about events. It's that context … that gives the power to this particular murder,' Professor Wilson said.

Wilson was especially struck by how Linda Mulhall had struggled to come to terms with the horrible crime she had committed. 'The most successful murderers I've dealt with have been able to compartmentalise their feelings after the death. They can commit horrific crimes and do horrific things to their victims but then put that into a box, metaphorically, and park it. They leave it somewhere and return to their normal lives. Linda seems to have been unable to do that. What was in that box leaked out constantly.'

There was a sea-change in conditions at Mountjoy Prison after the long-serving governor John Lonergan retired in July 2010. He was replaced by the tough, no-nonsense Ned Whelan. Whelan had been the governor of the country's highest-security jail – Midlands Prison, in Portlaoise – and was used to dealing with tough criminals. He would not be intimidated, despite threats to his life soon after he arrived in Mountjoy. Whereas Lonergan refused to install nets in the exercise yards to make it more difficult for people to throw in drugs to the prisoners, Whelan immediately adopted a zero-tolerance approach to illegal drugs and sanctioned sophisticated anti-drugs nets. This led to several violent confrontations, with large groups of prisoners unhappy that they could no longer get easy access to narcotics as they had been doing for years. As well as targeting prisoners, Whelan also introduced mandatory searches for staff to prevent rogue officers from acting as drug dealers while being paid a good wage by the Prison Service.

In March 2011 it was reported that Linda Mulhall had become a grandmother at the tender age of thirty-four. The report claimed that Linda's son had become a dad two years previously when he was just sixteen years old. The report was never confirmed, but if it is true, it would mean that Kathleen Mulhall would have become great-grandmother at just fifty-four years of age, which may be some sort of record, although not one that most people would brag about.

In March 2011, on the sixth anniversary of the murder, this author again spoke to Farah Noor's family in Kenya. The dead man's son Mohamed Said was now nineteen years old. In the years since the brutal killing of his father, Mohamed had developed into a very promising swimmer and had represented his district. His mother, Husna, revealed how her son wanted to confront the Mulhall girls and beg them to reveal where Farah's head was. She said she blamed Kathleen Mulhall for what happened and that she hopes she rots in hell. 'My son would like to go to Ireland to talk to Kathleen. He wants her to look him in the eye and tell him she is sorry for his father and want to ask why was he killed. When Kathleen sees Mohamed, she will think it is Farah. They look very alike. I hate Kathleen; she is sick. She ruined her life and her family's life and also the life of my family. I hope she is never happy for the rest of her life and pays for what she did.'

Husna revealed how she cannot find peace knowing some of her husband's mutilated body parts have never been found. 'I want Kathleen to say where Farah's belongings are. He stayed in Ireland for ten years but there was nothing left of him, not even a T-shirt. I want to know where they went. I wish I could have Farah back to be buried in Kenya, but he is in pieces now and is in a grave in Ireland. Of course I would like Farah's head and all of Farah's body back, but I wouldn't like to see him like that because he was my husband and I would feel bad.'

Husna also said she felt let down by the Irish State because the Criminal Injuries Compensation Tribunal had still not paid her any compensation. She said it had been fifteen months since she's last heard from them and it was four years since she had made her initial application. The forty-year-old mother said, 'I don't understand why it has taken so long. Farah was killed nearly six years ago and we filled out all the papers and the last ones were done fifteen months ago. We have heard nothing since.

'I have a son and daughter in high school here and have no money since Farah died. I work as a waitress in a restaurant but the salary is low. I was told by the authorities that my family would be compensated, but nothing has happened and we have been left abandoned. I rang a detective who worked on the case but he said he was retired and could do nothing to help. I feel abandoned and cannot survive without this money I was told I was going to receive. Farah sent his family money every month and our lives are very hard since this stopped.'

Husna also revealed how the kindness of ordinary Muslims in Mombasa. 'Farah's mother gives us money and the local Muslim community also supports us because the children are orphans. When Farah died I had to stay indoors for over three months under Sharia law and could not leave the house while I was mourning my husband. I could not work or earn any money, so local people gave us money to help us live and [they] still do.'

Husna's frustration was obvious and it was clear that she and her family were struggling to make ends meet. 'I don't understand why it has taken so long. The gardaí have told me I am entitled to this money but still I hear nothing. All the paperwork is done, so I pray that I get it soon,' she added.

✂✂✂

In May 2011 RTÉ finally broadcast its programme on the Scissor Sisters, which was part of a series entitled *Killers*. It had been filmed over three years previously but hadn't been broadcast because RTÉ was concerned that it might influence Linda Mulhall's appeal.

In the programme Detectvie Garda Dan Kenna, who had by then retired from the force, gave an interview and spoke of how he believed that John Mulhall played a far bigger part in the killing of Noor than has been admitted. He said, 'I always believed that John Mulhall had a more active role at some stage. We're not sure what his role was, but we know there was contact between the father, his wife, and two children. The taking of his own life would not be in keeping with the character of John Mulhall, and we're unsure why that man took his own life. We have accounts of him beating his wife, Kathleen, and his children during their early years. Perhaps the burden of it was too much for him to bear, and the only way for him to deal with it was to take his own life.'

Kenna admitted that the truth of exactly what happen at Richmond Cottages on the night of Farah's brutal death will probably never be fully ascertained. 'We will never establish for certain what went on in Richmond Cottages the day Farah was killed. We are happy we have established the murder scene: we had ample evidence to support the fact he was murdered in that flat. We only have the accounts of Linda Muhall and Charlotte Mulhall to tell us what happened. We have a separate account from Kathleen Mulhall that distances her from the killing. We will never know how they could dismember a body in that area and leave so little evidence. You have to remember this was a living human being who had just been killed, whose body was still warm. For him to be cut up in the manner he was, into so many separate pieces in such a small area, and to leave no trace of that part of the crime poses the question of whether he was actually dismembered at the same location.'

As this book goes to print, in October 2011, Katheen Mulhall is due to be released from the Dóchas Centre, after serving her sentence for covering up Farah Noor's killing. It is unclear what the future will hold for her. Sources say that she will most likely move back to the UK and try to rebuild her life and put her bloody past behind her. She had expressed an interest in trying to adopt Charlotte's son but this never got off the ground because of the circumstances surrounding what happened on the fateful night in March 2005. No health authority would let Kathleen adopt a young child after the lengths she went to to cover-up what happened in her flat.

The Mulhalls notoriety endures, their grim story forever etched on the nation's consciousness. Linda and Charlotte still have many more years to serve in prison but there is no way they will do their time in private; they will always be in the media spotlight, for the public still has a huge interest in the Irish Scissor Sisters. We have certainly not heard the last of them.